Samuel Mendelsohn

The Criminal Jurisprudence of the Ancient Hebrews

Compiled From the Talmud and Other Rabbinical Writings, and Compared

Samuel Mendelsohn

The Criminal Jurisprudence of the Ancient Hebrews
Compiled From the Talmud and Other Rabbinical Writings, and Compared

ISBN/EAN: 9783337008536

Printed in Europe, USA, Canada, Australia, Japan

Cover: Foto ©Suzi / pixelio.de

More available books at **www.hansebooks.com**

THE CRIMINAL JURISPRUDENCE

OF THE

ANCIENT HEBREWS.

Compiled from the Talmud and other Rabbinical Writings, and Compared with Roman and English Penal Jurisprudence.

BY

S. MENDELSOHN, LL. D.

Rabbi Congr. "Temple of Israel," Wilmington, N. C.

BALTIMORE:
M. CURLANDER,
LAW BOOKSELLER AND PUBLISHER.
1891.

COPYRIGHT, 1890,

BY

S. MENDELSOHN.

ALL RIGHTS RESERVED.

TO THE READER.

As these paragraphs, now ready for the printer, lie before me, I imagine them in your hands, and hear you enquire after their author's object in penning and publishing them. To satisfy your natural curiosity, I beg leave to point to the motto and to the conclusion of this work, and to assure you that I had in view no other than the two-fold object of acquainting those to whom the Talmud is "as a sealed book" with an important part of its contents—its system of criminal jurisprudence; and of thus contributing my mite towards the vindication of the Israelitish people's ancient literature from the aspersions cast upon it by inimical and, not unfrequently, ignorant writers. Which of these motives first prompted this labor, I am unable to determine even for myself; but I trust that you will appreciate the importance of both together. Mr. Arnold has truly said: "Every thing of the nature of law has a peculiar interest and value, because it is the expression of the deliberate mind of the supreme government of society; and as history, as commonly written, records so much of the passionate and unreflecting part of human nature, we are bound in fairness to acquaint ourselves with its calm and better part also."

Of the many excellent German works on the particular branch of Rabbinic lore treated of in these pages, I have consulted none, because I wished to let the ancient Hebrew sages speak for themselves, and not through the mouths of modern commentators. English works on this subject I have not seen, except a few articles here and there, and Vargha's chapter on the "Defense in Criminal Cases with the Ancient Hebrews." Wines's valuable work treats of the Mosaic system only.

Only works of generally recognized authority have been referred to for data of historical matters as well as of Greek, Roman, or English Law. Those most frequently cited are the following:

Arnold. Introductory Lectures on Modern History, by Thomas Arnold, D. D. Edited by Henry Reed, M. A. Philadelphia, 1857.

Beccaria. Of Crimes and Punishments, by Caesar Bonesana, Mqs. di Beccaria. Quoted after the German of M. Waldeck. Berlin, 1870.

Blackstone. Commentaries on the Laws of England, by Sir William Blackstone. Edited and annotated by Christian Chitty and others.

Fiske. Manual of Classical Literature, from the German of J. J. Eschenburg, with Additions and Notes, by W. W. Fiske. Fourth Edition. Philadelphia, 1844.

Gibbon. History of the Decline and Fall of the Roman Empire, by Edward Gibbon. With Notes, by the Rev. H. H. Milman.

Graetz. History of the Jews from the Earliest Times to the Present, by Prof. Dr. H. Graetz. Second (German) Edition. Leipzig

Hallam. Views of the State of Europe during the Middle Ages, by Henry Hallam.

Montesquieu. The Spirit of Laws. Translated from the French of M. De Secondat, Baron de Montesquieu. First American Edition. Philadelphia, 1802.

Plutarch. Lives. Translated and annotated by John Langhorne, D. D., and William Langhorne, A. M. Baltimore, 1830.

Roscoe. A Digest of the Law of Evidence in Criminal Cases, by Henry Roscoe. With Notes, &c., by George Sharswood. Philadelphia, 1836.

Smith. A Dictionary of Greek and Roman Antiquities, by William Smith, Ph. D. Third American Edition. New York, 1850.

Wines. Commentaries on the Laws of the Ancient Hebrews, by E. C. Wines. New York, 1853.

The paragraphs or sections, as well as the notes, are numbered consecutively, in order to facilitate reference from place to place, thereby avoiding frequent repetitions of rules, and saving space.

With great pleasure do I hereby express my gratitude to those gentlemen, both of the pulpit and the bar,—whose good opinion might well be an object of pride to writers of literary pretensions far higher than mine,—who have examined the Manuscript of this compendium and encouraged me with their warm approbation. Especially do I thank the friend who helped me to make the phraseology as smooth, and the diction as little involved, as is possible in a work of this nature.

In conclusion, let me assure you that, in presenting the Rabbinic Laws, it was my constant and earnest endeavor to be correct to the letter and to the spirit of the Talmud. How far I have succeeded in this, the learned critic will be able to tell more readily than

THE AUTHOR.

WILMINGTON, N. C., *November*, 1890.

CONTENTS.

Introduction, §§ 1-10 9

I. Crimes and Punishments.

1. As to number, §§ 11-12 25
2. Provisos, §§ 13-19 28
3. Misdemeanors, Crimes and Penalties, §§ 20-24 37
4. Capital Crimes, §§ 25-32 44
5. Homicide, §§ 33-37 58
6. Murder, §§ 38-44 67
7. Persons Indictable, §§ 45-50 78

II. The Synhedrion.

1. Organization and Jurisdiction, §§ 51-56 87
2. Qualifications, §§ 57-58 92
3. Sessions and Recruitments, §§ 59-64 96
4. Honorarium, §§ 65-67 102

III. The Trial.

1. The Participators, §§ 68-71 108
2. Time of Trial, §§ 72-74 112
3. Witnesses, §§ 75-77 115
4. Cautioning Witnesses, §§ 78-79 120

CONTENTS.

5. Examination, §§ 80–91. 123
6. The Defendant, §§ 92–94. 132
7. Disproval and Confutation, §§ 95–99 135
8. The Deliberations, §§ 100–104. 140
9. The Verdict. §§ 105–113. 143
10. Reversal of Judgment, §§ 114–115 150

IV. THE EXECUTION.

1. Between Life and Death, §§ 116–120 153
2. The Executioners, § 121. 156
3. The Consummation. §§ 122–127 157
4. Posthumous Ignominies, §§ 128–133 161
5. Minor Punishments, §§ 134–139 166
6. Rehabilitation, §§ 140–141. 173

MAXIMS AND RULES. § 142... 175
CONCLUSION, §§ 143–144. 185
APPENDIX. 187
INDEX. 255

THE
CRIMINAL JURISPRUDENCE
OF THE
ANCIENT HEBREWS
BY
S. MENDELSOHN, LL. D.

"In the department of law, whatever God allotted to other ages and nations, as contributing to their mental development, must not remain strange to our people, but must be dressed up and offered to them for the enhancement of their own powers and advancement of their moral faculties." SAVIGNY.

INTRODUCTION.

§ 1. Whatever differences of belief people may entertain regarding the "Total Depravity" dogma, all admit the high antiquity of crime. Every observant reader of history, sacred or profane, becomes impressed with the idea that crime is almost coeval with the appearance of man on earth; that no age, no nation, no country, no province, ever was nor ever will be exempt from evildoers: from individuals committing acts offensive to both God and man. And were every human being allowed free scope in the indulgence of his passions and propensities; were there no restrictive laws enacted against the disturbing of the peace of society, or against aggression on individual rights: "one might swallow the other alive."[1] From time to time, therefore, laws are adopted, embodying certain "rules of civil conduct," of right or wrong, of what may or may not be done,[2] and at the same time, as a matter of course, providing modes of punishment for the violation of those laws[3] which constitute the covenant of social life.

§ 2. Accordingly, the earliest penal laws were enacted for emergencies, after the commission of the crime; and since they were framed with special refer-

---

[1] Aboth III. 2. Epicurus says: "The worst of laws are so necessary for us that, without them, men would devour one another."—Plutarch.

[2] The immortal Plato says: "Without laws we should be like beasts." (Laws IX).—Chitty wisely remarks: "The *libertas quillibet faciendi*, or the liberty of doing everything which a man's passions urge him to attempt, or his strength enables him to effect, is savage ferocity; it is the liberty of the tiger, and not the liberty of a man." (Blackstone I, 126).—Laws are, therefore, more or less the expression of man's reason, as opposed to his interest and his passion: they are, "the conditions under which men, leading independent and isolated lives, united themselves into societies, in order to avoid living in a state of constant warfare, although, at the same time, they curtailed the enjoyment of a freedom which the uncertainty of its tenure could not preserve. Of that freedom they voluntarily renounced a part, in order to enjoy the remainder in peace and security" (Beccaria, § 1).

[3] "Law, without sanctions or penalties annexed, is no law, but only counsel, or more or less plausible advice. It becomes law only when, in addition to the precept, there is affixed a penalty for transgression." (Haven. Moral Philosophy, p. 289. Cf. Blackstone I, 57; infra, n. 202).

ence to immediate occasions, they were dictated rather by blind popular impulse, than by the logical conclusions reached by the calm deliberations of legislative wisdom. And although it is in the interest of the people, themselves subject to the laws, to make them as mild as possible, yet inasmuch as the fear of being injured is always more prevalent than the intention of injuring, people are usually influenced by first impressions, and enact cruel laws.—We must not, however, be understood to imply that the early laws were dictated by the free will of the people. On the contrary, in the first stages of the social development of mankind, individuals were the law-makers.[4] But these law-makers were themselves controlled by the influences which prejudiced the popular mind. The natural consequence was that excessive severity prevailed, which, in the progress of time, was meliorated principally by the evasion of those very laws which originally were enacted for the conservation of the safety and peace of society. The opposite extreme, undue laxity, succeeded, and destroyed the principles of justice. Thus we are told that, "as the manners of Rome were insensibly polished,

---

[4] Cf. Beccaria, § 34.—If we cast a glance at history, we shall see that laws which, properly speaking, are or ought to be compacts between free people, have generally been nothing but the instrument of the passions of some few men, or the result of some accidental and transitory necessity. They have never been dictated by the unimpassioned judge of human nature who is able to concentrate the actions of a multitude of men into a single point of view, and to consider them from that point only:— *The greatest happiness for the greatest number* (ib. Introduction).

the criminal code of Decemvirs was abolished by the humanity of the accusers, witnesses and judges, and impunity became the consequence of immoderate rigor."[5] The same was the result of the bloody enactments of Draco,[6] who affixed the penalty of death to almost all crimes alike—to petty thefts, for instance, as well as to sacrilege and murder,—and being asked, why he made death the punishment of most offenses, answered, "Small ones deserve it, and I can find no greater for the most heinous."[7]

§ 3. But we need not climb so very high on the ladder of time in search of harsh and severe laws. The old codes of most civilized nations of the modern epoch are almost as liberal in dispensing capital punishment.

---

[5] Gibbon c. XLIV.—Excessive severity of laws hinders their execution. Where the punishment surpasses all measure, people are obliged to prefer impunity to the laws (cf. Montesquieu, B. VI. c. XIII).

[6] "The laws of Draco, written—says Demades—not with ink, but with blood, had the same fate as usually attends all violent things. Sentiments of humanity in the judges, compassion for the accused, whom they were wont to look upon rather as unfortunate than criminal, and the apprehensions the accusers and witnesses were under of rendering themselves odious to the people, all concurred to produce a remissness in the execution of the laws which, by that means, in the process of time, became as it were abrogated through disuse: and thus an excessive rigor paved the way for impunity."—Rollin, Ancient History, B. V, Art. VIII.

[7] Plutarch, Life of Solon. Conf. Smith's *History of Greece*, c. X. 6.—Schiller (*Legislation of Lycurgus and Solon*) would account for this severity by the fact that "Draco's laws are the attempt of a beginner in the art of governing men;" but harsh legislation was not a peculiarity of the earliest legislators.

Nor may we hold up as examples deserving universal condemnation, those codes which have for their chief elements the decrees of the Civil Law of Rome—the tablets of the decemvirs,[8] the Pandects and the Institutes, where sanguinary despotism wielded undisputed sway. The code of England, where public legislation has, for centuries back, been deeply influenced by popular opinion, was down to a comparatively recent date, extremely cruel and blood-thirsty. Blackstone states that in his time, "among the variety of actions *which men are daily liable to commit,* no less than *one hundred and sixty* were held, by act of parliament, to be felonies without benefit of clergy; or, in other words, to be worthy of instant death."[9]—It is

---

[8] Montesquieu (B. VI, c. XV) says of them, "The law of the twelve tables is full of very cruel punishment," and the reader of these pages will find abundant proof to convince him not only of the truth of Montesquieu's statement, but also that subsequent Roman legislation was almost equally as cruel.

[9] Commentaries IV, 8.—This was written about the year 1760, and in 1809—says the American annotator to Arnold's Lectures on Modern History (n. 9 ad L. V)—when Sir Samuel Romilly devoted himself to the arduous and admirable labor of bringing about a reformation of the criminal law of England, it is stated by Mr. Alison, in his History of Europe (chap. 60), that the punishment of death was by statute affixed to the fearful and almost incredible number of *above six hundred* different crimes, "while the increasing humanity of the age had induced so wide a departure from the strict letter of the law, that out of 1782 persons capitally convicted at the Old Bailey in seven years, from 1803 to 1810, only *one* had been executed."
* * * Well has Landor, in one of his 'Imaginary Conversations,' put these words into the mouth of Romilly: "I am ready to believe that Draco himself did not punish so many

true that the criminal laws of the United States are incomparably more lenient and humane, visiting with death nine crimes only, and that the penal code of this country is, compared with the enactments of other nations, justly held up as an example of moderation, of the wise accommodation of the spirit of justice to the philanthropic views resulting from an advance of civilization. But we must not forget that the laws of this country are comparatively new, that they carry within them the practical wisdom of tens of centuries, that they are the very latest out-growths of civilization.

§ 4. In view of these facts, how greatly must our curiosity become excited when we are assured that "it would not be easy to find a more humane, almost refined, penal legislation, from the days of the old world to our own,"[10] than that of the ancient Hebrews.

---

offenses with blood as we do, although he punished with blood every one. We punish with death certain offenses which Draco did not even note as crimes, and many others had not yet sprung up in society." It is only lately [this was written in 1845,] that the reform begun by Romilly, which the sad catastrophe of his life prevented his witnessing, has been completed so far as to limit capital punishment very much to crimes affecting directly or indirectly the security of life, instead of property. In 1837, Parliament (by the acts of 7th Will. IV. and 1st Victoria) removed the punishment of death from about 200 offenses, and it is now left applicable to treason, murder and attempts at murder, arson with danger to life, and to piracies, burglaries, and robberies, when aggravated by cruelty and violence.

[10] Deutsch on "The Talmud" in the *London Quarterly Review* for Oct. 1867.—"In no other nation were ever current such simple forms of criminal investigation, such ample safeguards for the accused; nowhere, so much as here, has conscientious practice so far surpassed a highly liberal theory, above all, in

From the following paragraphs it will be seen that the system of criminal jurisprudence of the Ancient Hebrews, as recorded in the Talmud and in contemporaneous Rabbinic literature, was one which enforced civil order and secured the safety and peace of society by mildness and consideration, tempering justice with a love of humanity, and all this in an age of savagery and violence, of wars and uncertainty; in an age when among surrounding nations "the life and death of a citizen was determined with less caution and delay than the most ordinary question of covenant and inheritance."[11] In our opinion, even though the judiciary system of the ancient Hebrews, preserved in the Talmud and other Rabbinic writings, be not acknowledged the exemplar of polity among modern governments, or as the universal fountain for general legislation, it certainly deserves better treatment at the hands of the critic than the generality of even modern writers are willing to accord to it. The Christian world stigmatizes the Talmudic system as "cruel, vindictive, sanguinary;" but it does so without good reason,—aye, without attempting to find a reason![12] But we shall let the Talmud speak for itself.[13]

---

point of humanity."—Vargha, Defense in Criminal Cases, c. I, § 1.

[11] Gibbon, Rome, c. XLIV.

[12] It is refreshing to the candid student to meet with an unbiased opinion of Ancient Jewish laws and criminal procedure, and we therefore transcribe a few more lines from Vargha (l. c). "No one of the old systems of procedure for the punishment of crime was more humane than the Jewish; and yet none has been more grievously calumniated, for now nearly twenty cen-

§ 5. Only in the last half of last century, and in the face of constitutional government, we hear the great institutional writer and commentator crying out, in disgust and horror, against the inequality and cruelty of the penal code of his country. He observes: "A multitude of sanguinary laws (besides the doubt that may be entertained concerning the right of making them) do likewise prove a manifest defect either in the wisdom of the legislative, or the strength of the executive power. It is a kind of quackery in government, and argues a want of solid skill, to apply the same universal remedy, the *ultimum supplicium*, to every case of difficulty. It is, it must be owned, much easier to extirpate than to amend mankind; yet that magistrate must be esteemed both a weak

---

turies, because of its cruelty as exposed in the alleged trial of Jesus. The Christian nations, persecutors of the Jews as they were, must needs even in this department, distort and slander the institutions of the dispersed people, unwilling, as they were, to acknowledge that its laws far surpassed their own in wisdom and in moderation."

[13] The name of the gigantic work whose compilation extends over a thousand years, from which mainly the following syllabus is compiled, is derived from the Hebrew radix *Lamad*—to learn (*i. e. study*, in contra-distinction to the Pentateuch generally styled *Torah*—Law), and is the collective name of the *Mishnah* (a kind of second law, *Deuterosis*) and *Guemara* (discussion, complement, doctrines, its radix *Gamar* answering to either).—The Talmud is, in the full sense of the word, the literature of the ancient Jews. It treats of religious, civil and criminal law; of history, mathematics, astronomy, medicine, metaphysics, theosophy.—For a comprehensive view of this repository of ancient Jewish art and science the reader is respectfully referred to the appended *excursus*.

and cruel surgeon, who cuts off every limb which through ignorance or indolence he will not attempt to cure."[14]

§ 6. These were Blackstone's cries as late as one hundred years ago; while the Talmud, some eighteen hundred years ago, stigmatized the Synhedrion (Synod, Court) that condemned to death one human being in the course of every seven years, as a murderous tribunal; and R. Elazar ben Azaria considers it so, if it passes a sentence of death once in seventy years![15] Moreover, Blackstone merely advocates the adoption of a scale of crimes and of a corresponding scale of penalties,[16] but does not deprecate the infliction of capital punishment "when the offender appears incorrigible;"[17] while such leaders among the Jews as R. Tryphon and R. Akiba declare that, had they been members of the Synhedrion during the period of its full judicial power, a sentence of death should never have been passed![18] These, however, are views of individuals only; let us compare laws.

---

[14] Commentaries IV, 17. One might fancy he hears the plaints of Epicurus: "As we formerly suffered from wickedness, so we now suffer from the laws."—Tacitus, Annal. III, 25.

[15] Maccoth 7ª; Maimonides, H. Sanhedrin XIV, 10.

[16] L. c. p. 18.

[17] L. c. p. 12. Incorrigibility "may be collected either from the perpetration of some one crime of deep malignity, or from a repetition of minuter offenses."

[18] Maccoth l. c.—*i. e.* by a searching and perplexing examination of the accusing witnesses, they would have rendered a legal conviction next to impossible. (Cf. infra. § 91, n. 304).

While the Rabbis were quite unacquainted with the modern refined sentiment which represents the reformation of the crim-

§ 7. We have just seen that in England, only one hundred years ago, the different offenses, which men

---

inal as the only legitimate end of punishment; while they had no sympathy with that mawkish philanthropy which pours forth floods of tears over the fate of the hardened perpetrator of crime, so that it has scarcely one left to mingle with those of the unhappy victims of his villainies,—they shrunk from inflicting the death penalty, and endeavored to secure the safety and peace of society and the vindication of law and justice by other means. (Cf. infra, § 24).

There are many jurists and moralists to-day who would gladly see capital punishment abolished, and that not because they doubt the right of the law to impose it, but because they conscientiously believe that it is not an adequate retribution for certain heinous crimes. On the contrary, owing to the circumstances usually consequent upon conviction, death seems to be a blessing to many a culprit. Out of the numbers of criminals that are annually despatched by warrant of law, how many do not ascend the scaffold shouting with joy that they are "going to heaven?" How many are not made to believe that, with the suspension of their bodies, their spirits hie to the realms of eternal bliss? In fact, death on the gallows is to some a passport to heaven! Imagine a man thoroughly depraved and "fallen from grace." His days he spends in devising evil; his evenings, in the practice of the grossest immoralities; his midnights, in despoiling his neighbors. He is apprehended, legally tried, duly convicted and judicially sentenced to the gallows; but also given ample time for "repentance and regeneration." Justice dons the cloak of mercy. Instead of being executed soon after conviction for the purpose of example, the culprit is placed in a cell accessible to every pious minister of the Gospel, who does not delay offering to "the victim of the law" the consolation of religion. Almost day and night he is attended by godly men who cram his mind with metaphysical dissertations on the efficacy of prayer and repentance, and on the eternal mercy of God whose arms are ever open to receive the

are daily liable to commit, and for the commission of each of which the highest penalty was inflicted, numbered not less than *one hundred and sixty*. Among the ancient Hebrews—where idolatry, witchcraft, human immolation, blasphemy, false prophecy, and other transgressions of a purely religious character, which in our age men are not liable to commit daily, were considered capital crimes—the entire number of capital offenses amounted to *thirty-six* only,[19] or to *less than one-fourth* of the number of offenses for which death was the punishment, by the law of a constitutional government, in which the people had voice and influence, and which did not have to take into consideration idolatry, human sacrifices and the like.

---

repentant sinner, especially such an one as the prisoner himself. Thus continually, and for weeks, worked upon, he is gradually made to fancy that a gracious reception awaits him beyond the grave. Indeed he even asserts that he would not now exchange his lot for that of any man who, however honest and good a life he may have led, is not as well prepared to die as himself,—is death a punishment to such a man? Is it not rather a deliverance from a prospective life of gloomy thoughts and frightful dreams, and of remorse for a life of villainy and shame? And the worst of it is that this picture is not drawn from fancy, but from careful observation.—May the advocates of the *jus gladii* earnestly think about this.

[19] Maimon, H. Sanh. XV, 12. Cf. infra § 25.—We say that the number of capital offenses, according to Talmudic law, inclusive of the several deadly sins of a purely religious character, amounted to thirty-six; but on proper classification of the various offenses under their respective general headings, we find *twelve* only, and even less than that (v. infra § 30 and note 101); and leaving out of consideration the crimes of idolatry, witchcraft, blasphemy, violation of the Sabbath and false pro-

§ 8. As a still greater proof of the great humanity of Talmudic jurisprudence, we mention the early abrogation of the *lex talionis*, with which one frequently meets in the legislations of most ancient nations, and traces of which are discernible on the pages of the codes even of some modern countries. The forfeit of an eye for an eye, a tooth for a tooth, a limb for a limb, was rigorously exacted by the Romans.[20] Also "by the ancient law of England, he that maimed any man, whereby he [the latter] lost any part of his body, was sentenced to lose the like part: *membrum pro membro.*"[21] This unequal and inhuman principle, though literally prescribed by Moses,[22] was early abolished by a Rabbinic law substituting a pecuniary equivalent.[23] In the same manner the Talmud abol-

---

phecy—all sins against God,—we find the number of crimes punishable with death by Talmudic jurisprudence, dwindle down to *eight*, or one less than that on the code of the United States!

[20] Gibbon l. c.

[21] Blackstone IV. 206.

[22] Exodus XXI, 23 sq.

[23] Sifra Emor § 20; B. Kama 83ᵇ sq.; Maimon. II. Hobel I, 3-5.—And even this commutation the Talmudists did not authorize individuals to determine for themselves, and thus they prevented every man from becoming at once client, judge and avenger in his own cause. In every instance of the application of this principle it was the duty of the regularly constituted judiciary to adjudge and enforce compliance (Mekhilta Nezikin § 8; B. Kama 91ᵃ, et al. Cf. infra n. 148, 355).

Even Kant, the most zealous advocate of the theory of retaliation as the only principle of penal law affording a measure for punishment, is forced to admit its inadequacy in certain cases of crime, and its inapplicability to others; and finally advises us

ished the Mosaic law ordaining, that the hand of a woman committing a certain immodest act,[24] should be cut off, by substituting a pecuniary forfeiture.[25]

§ 9. Above all and most vividly is the clemency, pervading the ancient Hebrew code, manifested in the rules by which the judges were to direct all proceedings against the accused. Imbued with the humane maxim: "Whosoever occasions the destruction of a single life, is as great a sinner as if he had destroyed the whole world; and, on the other hand, whoso brings about the preservation of a single life, is as meritorious as if he had preserved the whole world,"[26] the Rabbis, sitting in judgment over a human being, laid every possible, but legitimate obstacle in the way of conviction. Almost every page of the Talmud, treating of criminal law, testifies that the Hebrew sages truly and conscientiously believed in, and practised according to their doctrine: "Whosoever compassionates a human being obtains compassion from Heaven."[27] Accordingly they employed every legal means to arrive at an acquittal of the prisoner, to save the life of the accused. It is true, occasionally great rigor was exercised under the Talmudic dispensation.[28]

---

to seek for a generic notion only of the offense, and to apply that to the criminal. (Rechtslehre, Part I, App. 5). Thus also Blackstone (cf. B. IV, p. 12, sq.)

[24] Deut. XXV, 11–12.
[25] Sifre II, § 293; B. Kama 28ª.
[26] B. Kama 11ª; Sanh. 37ª. Cf. infra § 79.
[27] Sabbath 151ª.
[28] "There is no positive law, how equitable soever, that may not be sometimes capable of injustice * * * And indeed the

For instance, it is reported that, for the simple sin of riding a mule on the Sabbath, the convict was sentenced to suffer death by stoning;[29] and another, for a gross violation of the laws of modesty, to be flagellated.[30] But such instances are very rare in the Talmud, and it is doubtful whether their equals are to be found in the acts of the Synhedrion. These, indeed, are said to have occurred at a time when Grecian invasion had demoralized the populace, when the authority of the Rabbis seemed to be unable to check the rapid progress of wickedness,—in short, when extreme rigor alone could hope to effect a wholesome reformation in the manners of the masses.[31] In general, however, the spirit pervading the criminal jurisprudence of the ancient Hebrews—if not tending toward the total abolition of capital punishment—is

---

experience of every age may serve to vindicate the assertion: no law could be more just than that called '*laesae majestis*.' when Rome was governed by emperors. It was but reasonable that every conspiracy against the administration should be detected and punished; yet what terrible slaughter succeeded in consequence of its enacting; proscriptions, stranglings, poisonings, in almost every family of distinction, yet all done in a legal way; every criminal had his trial, and lost his life by a majority of witnesses."—Goldsmith, Letters of a Ch. Philos. LXXX.

[29] Cf. infra § 26.

[30] Yebamoth 90b; Sanh. 46a.

[31] Ibid. Cnf. infra §§ 37. 73.—Sir Matthew Hale writes: "When offenses grow numerous, frequent and dangerous to a Kingdom or State, destructive and highly pernicious to civil societies, and to the great insecurity and danger of the Kingdom or its inhabitants, severe punishment and even death itself is necessary to be annexed to laws in many cases by the prudence of lawgivers."—Blackstone IV, 9.

certainly humane and considerate. While seeking to do justice and punish crime, in order to insure the safety and peace of society, the Rabbis endeavored to save life and limb whenever it was in any way possible.[32]

§ 10. Our favorable opinion regarding the humane tendency of the system of Talmudic criminal jurisprudence will be confirmed and strengthened in the course of our enquiry concerning the rules and usages by which, according to the Rabbis, were to be directed the trial and execution of the criminal under that dispensation—a dispensation the dissertations on which "have exhausted so many learned lives, and clothed the walls of such spacious libraries."

In the following pages we purpose to furnish a comprehensive, though succinct syllabus of the principal penal statutes as established by the ancient Jewish teachers, and preserved in the Talmud and in contemporaneous Rabbinic literature. Eschewing all platitudes and logomachies with which the laws are strangely mixed up, we shall furnish a clear insight into a system of jurisprudence which has occupied thousands of great minds in ages past, and which is almost a sealed Book to the present, though it contains abundant food for thought even for the future.

The whole mass of laws we propose to classify under the following four captions:

---

[32] By *justice* I understand nothing but the bond which is necessary for the conservation of individual interests, and for preventing them from relapsing into their original state of dissociation. All penalties overstepping the bounds necessary for the preservation of this bond, are naturally unjust. (Beccaria § 2).

I. Crimes and Punishments.
II. The Synhedrion.
III. The Trial.
IV. The Execution.

Each of these general divisions will, of course, have to be subdivided under special heads or sections, inasmuch as there are different crimes and different penalties, different cases and different courts. But while our aim shall always be to lay before our readers a clear and correct portraiture of our intricate subject, we shall endeavor to be brief, and not tax their patience too much.

I. CRIMES AND PUNISHMENTS.

1. As to Number.

§ 11. A person acquainted with the hermeneutic rules, by the application of which the ancient Hebrew exegetists and jurists plausibly established, on Scriptural dicta, decisions and decrees concerning each and all of the varied situations in life,[33] a person familiar

---

[33] Cf. Appendix—The Talmud is avowedly based on the firm belief in the permanence and immutability of the Scriptural laws (cf. infra n. 100). But it must be remembered that there can be but little relation between human actions that are constantly changing, and laws that are fixed and immobile. We see almost daily that, however large the number of our laws is, it still holds no manner of proportion to the diversity of cases, and it is safe to prophesy that the multiplication of our inventions will never equal the variety of questions. Therefore have the Rabbis established exegetical rules, comprehensive and elastic, by which occurrences of the future might be coupled and compared with those already decided and recorded, and judgment passed in accordance with the circumstances. According to those rules, a great many laws and decisions (*Halakhoth*), especially a number of those treating of capital punishment, were established long after the *jus gladii* had been taken from the Jews by the Romans (cf. infra n. 224 sq.), and were, therefore, never applied practically. Hebrew jurisprudence was deprived of the power of enforcing its enactments decades before the beginning of the Christian era, but, *as a science*, it continued to be studied and elaborated for centuries thereafter, the Rabbinic maxim being: "Study, philosophize, and thou shalt be rewarded" (cf. infra n. 87, 109).

with Rabbinic readiness to multiply "guard-laws,"[34] might easily suppose that, in the Talmud, there is no end to the number of penal offenses. And, indeed, our impression receives apparent confirmation, when we learn that the Talmud finds in the Pentateuch *six hundred and thirteen* ordinances,—"of these, three hundred and sixty-five (corresponding to the number of days in the solar year) are prohibitive, and the remaining two hundred and forty-eight (corresponding to the number of bones in the human body), are positive commands,"[35] each of which the Israelite must strictly observe, or be accounted a transgressor, and subjected to punishment!

§ 12. Nevertheless, without fear of tenable contradiction, we declare such an idea to be altogether unwarranted by the spirit of Talmudic jurisprudence. Talmudic jurisprudence inflicts punishment for such transgressions only as are accompanied by bodily action.[36] Now, as violations of laws may be committed

---

[34] *Sepes legis.* The Rabbinic term thus rendered, is *S'iag*—fence, *i.e.* outworks, barriers to protect and maintain inviolable the ordinances, both Biblical and Talmudical.

[35] Maccoth 23ᵇ.

[36] Sanh. 63ᵃ, et al.—Among ancient nations we find instances, where mere *thoughts* were punished capitally. Thus, because Marsyas dreamed that he had cut Dionysius's throat, the tyrant put him to death, arguing that he would never have dreamt of such a thing by night, had he not thought of it by day (Montesquieu, B. XII. c. XI). By Talmudic law, only *actions* are subject to punishment. Exceptions are: taking vain oaths, substituting an inferior offering for something dedicated, and cursing by the ineffable name of God, which, though not accompanied by bodily action, subject the offender to the penalty of flagellation

in two ways, either by omission or commission: by
not doing that which ought to be done, or by doing
that which ought not to be done—it is clearly seen
that, according to this principle, no punishment can
be inflicted for the violation of any or all of the two
hundred and forty-eight positive commands, and of a
large number of the prohibitive, where the transgression is not accomplished by means of bodily action.[37]

(Shebuoth 21ª, Temurah 3ª). The same is the rule in some
cases of false testimony and slander (cf. infra § 31, n. 62, 323).

[37] Thus, with reference to the instigator to apostasy, the Rabbis
find in the Scriptural dictum (Deut. XIII, 9) the following five
prohibitive precepts: 1. Not to love him (*Abah*—to long for);
2. Not to cease hating him (*Shama*—to listen to complacently);
3. Not to have mercy on him; 4. Not to defend him; 5. Not
to withhold condemning testimony against him (Sifre II, § 89;
Sanh. 29ª, 33ᵇ, 67ª, 85ᵇ). Of these, only a transgression of the
third may become subject to punishment, for only that one may
be attended by bodily action, as when the culprit is in danger
and one saves him.—Nor is any punishment attached to the
transgression of a general prohibition, not followed by specifications (*Lav shebikhlaloth*). E. g. on the Biblical prohibition:
"Ye shall not eat with the blood" (Lev. XIX, 26), the Talmud
bases a number of prohibitions; to wit: 1. Not to eat of an animal until after all its blood has passed out; 2. Not to eat of the
sacrifice, before the blood has been duly sprinkled upon the
altar (cf. Lev. I, 5, 11, et al.); 3. Not to treat the mourners,
for legally executed criminals, to the breakfast customary in
other cases of death (cf. infra § 132); 4. That the judges eat
nothing on the day they order the shedding of a man's blood,
i. e. a capital execution (cf. infra § 113). Now, as all these prohibitions are based on one general prohibitive precept, wihle
none is specifically mentioned in the Bible, the transgressor
may not be punished, though the transgression of each of them
can be accomplished by means of physical action only (Sanhedrin 63ª, Pesahim 24ª).

Thus, more than one-half of the entire number of all possible transgressions, is at once cut off from liability to punishment; and, in those remaining, there is again a considerable falling off, owing to the enactment exempting from corporal punishment the violation—though it be accompanied by physical action—of such prohibitions, like stealing and robbing, as may be adjusted or counteracted by restitution,[38] or by a subsequent compliance with the positive command concerning the same case.[39]

2. Provisos.

§ 13. The Talmud adopts all the conditions and provisos under which the Mosaic law punishes crime. Unless the culprit was fully conscious of the culpability of his action, knowing while committing the deed, that it was against the spirit and the letter of the law, and unless his guilt was subsequently proved, beyond the least doubt, by at least *two* trustworthy wit-

---

[38] Maccoth 16ª; Maimon. II. Sanh. XVIII. 2.

[39] Ibid; Hullin 141ª.—Thus, concerning the removal of the mother-bird together with her young ones from their nest, the Bible (Deut. XXII. 6, 7), contains a prohibitive, followed by a positive ordinance; viz: "Thou shalt not take the mother with her young ones," and then, "Thou shalt surely let the mother go." Now, if a man happens to violate the prohibition by capturing the mother together with her young ones, he ought to be punished as for the violation of any other negative precept, when accompanied by a bodily act; yet in this case he is not punished, but made to comply with the positive command—to "let the mother go." If, however, after being duly cautioned of his guilt and its consequent penalty (cf. infra § 15), he still refuses to obey the law, due punishment is awarded to him.

nesses,[40] and before a *competent tribunal*,[41] he could not be capitally, or even corporally punished. And even where there appeared a legal number of duly qualified witnesses, their testimony was insufficient to convict,[42] unless they agreed not only with regard to the prisoner's offense, but also with regard to the mode of committing it.[43] Rabbinic law does not subject a person to capital, nor even to corporal punishment, unless all witnesses charge him with one and the same criminal act, their statements fully agreeing in the main circumstances, and declaring that they saw one another, while seeing him engaged in the crime.[44]

[40] Cf. infra § 75 sq.

[41] Cf. infra § 69.—The courts of a feudal barony or manor required neither the knowledge of positive law, nor the dictates of natural sagacity. In all doubtful cases, and especially where a crime not capable of notorious proof was charged, the combat was awarded; and God, they deemed, was the judge. * * * In criminal cases, the appellant suffered, in the event of defeat, the same punishment which the law awarded to the offense of which he accused his adversary (Hallam, Middle Ages c. II, P. 2).

[42] By the law of England, an accusation of treason, the only one which required two witnesses for the prosecution, was considered duly authenticated when one witness testified to one overt act, and the other to another overt act of the same species of treason (Blackstone, IV, 357).

[43] Mekhilta Mishp. § 20; Sanh. 30b; Maimon. H. Sanh. IV. 1; ibid II. Eduth II, 2.—E. g. when two witnesses accuse a person of having committed idolatry, but one of them denounces him for having paid homage to the sun, and the other for having worshipped the moon; or when two witnesses charge him with murder, but one testifies that the killing was done with a sword, while the other avers that it was with a dagger,—their testimony in either case is invalid.

[44] Maccoth 6b; Sahn. 30a. Cf. infra § 83. n. 291.

§ 14. Nor does Talmudic jurisprudence inflict punishment on a person acting under constraint (*duress per minas*). A person committing an unlawful act while his will is not free, cannot be condemned to die for his misdeed. The fear of death, threatened in the event of non-compliance with an order to commit a crime, is an excuse for the commission. The main object of law—the Rabbinic jurists argue—is the promotion of the good of society, not its detriment. Scripture[45] teaches: "Ye shall observe my statutes and my ordinances, which if a man practise, he shall *live* through them," from which we are to infer that no one is bound to *die through them*, *i. e.* to imperil his existence for the sake of their observance.[46]

§ 15. This argument, however, the Rabbis do not adduce to exempt one from due punishment for homicide. In cases of shedding innocent blood, they do not consider duress a valid excuse.[47] Neither is that

---

[45] Lev. XVIII, 5.

[46] Sanh. 74ª; Maimon. II. Yesode Torah V, 1 sq. The modern legal maxim says, *Hominum causa jus constitutum est:* Law is established for the benefit of man.

[47] The Talmudic rules of conduct, in cases of threatened danger, are based on the natural law of self-preservation, and say: "Thy life should be dearer to thee than that of thy neighbor" (B. Metz. 62ª); "Thy property thou mayest prefer to that of another." (ibid 30ᵇ). Accordingly, when two men are in danger of losing their lives, and one can save himself by increasing the danger of the other, he may do so with impunity; or when the property of two men is endangered, each of them is at liberty to save his own, though he thereby increases the danger of his neighbor's. But when an individual's life is endangered, and can be saved only by imperilling the innocent life of another,

argument applied to exempt the male from the penalty of the sexual sins, when he commits the crime under duress.[48]

---

person the case is different. He must sacrifice his life rather than commit the crime. Accordingly, the Talmud (Sanh. 74a) relates that a heathen once ordered his Jewish subject, on pain of death, to assassinate a certain person. The terrified Jew applied to a Rabbi for legal advice in his dilemma, and the Rabbi readily decided that, in such cases, one must suffer himself to be slain, rather than commit so heinous a crime; for no mortal, argued he, can assert with any degree of certainty which of the two—the threatened or the intended victim—is possessed of the more aristocratic blood: which of the two is the worthier life.—In common law a like distinction is made between "positive crimes, so created by the laws of society," and "natural offenses, so declared by the law of God." (Blackstone IV, 30). The Talmudic law, however, extends the divine precept: "Thou shalt love thy neighbor as thyself" (Lev. XIX, 18) even beyond rejecting the idea of paying so dear a ransom for one's own life as to kill an innocent person. The Rabbis teach that when people are required to deliver one of their number to be murdered, they must refuse compliance at the risk of their lives (Tosefta Terum. VII, end; Yerush. ib. VIII, § 10, p. 46b; Maimon. H. Yesode Torah V, 5); and some recommend the same course even when the people themselves are not required to have any hand in the matter; as when a tyrant requires of them simply to disclose the whereabouts of the intended victim of his injustice (cf. Magen Abraham ad O. Hayim c. 156, based on Sabbath 33b).

[48] Yebamoth 53b. Cf. Exodus R. c. XIV.—Its application to cases of idolatry depends on circumstances. Where religious persecutions prevail, or when spectators are present, one must resist all constraint, even at the risk of his life; but in private, and simply to gratify the whim of a tyrant, he may conform to the iniquitous behest, rather than forfeit his earthly existence (Sanh. 74a; Ab. Zarah 27b; Maimon. H. Yes. Torah V. 2).

§ 16. But Rabbinic humanity was not satisfied even with all the provisos thus far enumerated. The anxious desire of the ancient Hebrew sages to save life and limb, invented an additional proviso which certainly precluded every possibility of convicting of crimes which, through ignorance of the law, men are liable to commit.[49] This proviso is the ANTECEDENT WARNING which Talmudic jurisprudence requires not alone in cases involving life and death,[50] but even in minor cases, where only corporal punishment is the consequence.[51]—The warning has to be administered immediately before the commission of the misdeed.[52] If any time elapses between the warning and the execution of the crime, the culprit cannot be sentenced to death, if the crime is capital; he cannot be whipped, if the offense is subject to corporal punishment.— Moreover, the warning must expressly state the penalty to which the would-be offender might be liable, whether corporal or capital; and if capital, the particular mode of death must be mentioned.[53] Furthermore, the would-be offender must acknowledge the warning, or it is of no force. He must signify his readiness, as the case may be, to die for the execution of his intention, or to suffer corporal punishment; he

---

[49] Among the Romans, the degrees of guilt, and the modes of punishment, were too often determined by the discretion of the rulers; and the subject was left in ignorance of the legal danger which he might incur by every action of his life (Gibbon XLIV); and in other countries it was the same (cf. infra n. 355).

[50] Sanh. 8^b, et al.

[51] Maccoth 16^a; Maimon. II. Sanh. XIV, 4.

[52] Sanh. 42^a; Maimon. ib. XII, 2.

[53] Sanh. 8^b; Maimon. ib.

must say to his monitor: I am fully cognizant of the law and of the inevitable consequences of its infraction, or something similar,⁵⁴ else the court cannot consider the condition complied with. — In making this proviso, the Talmud assumes an unique position. This requirement has no equal in ancient or modern law. By the laws of the modern civilized world, only ignorance or mistake of fact excuses the crime, but not error in point of law;⁵⁵ while Talmudic jurisprudence allows conviction only when the criminal is not ignorant of even the slightest point of law and, knowing the law, and being forewarned of the necessary consequences of his intended violation, still sins with a high hand,⁵⁶ thus clearly manifesting his presumptuousness or malice prepense, without proving which there can be no legal conviction.⁵⁷

---

⁵⁴ Sanh. 40ᵇ; Maimon. ibid.

⁵⁵ If a man, intending to kill a thief or a housebreaker in his own house, by mistake kills one of his own family, this is no criminal action; but if a man thinks he has a right to kill a person excommunicated or outlawed, wherever he meets him, and does so; this is willful murder. For a mistake in point of law, which every person of discretion not only may know, but is bound and presumed to know, is in criminal cases no sort of defense. *Ignorantia juris, quod quisque tenetur scire, neminem excusat*, is as well a maxim of our own law, as it was of the Roman (Blackstone IV, 27). By Rabbinic law *presumption* of acquaintance with the law could not convict, wherefore even the scholar rendered himself liable to punishment only after being duly warned (Sanh. 8ᵇ, et al.)

⁵⁶ Sanh. 8ᵇ; Maimon. H. Is. Biah. I, 3; H. Sanh. XII, 2.

⁵⁷ In this respect, the Rabbis agree with the Romans that an act is not guilty, unless the intention is guilty (*Actus non facit reum, nisi mens sit rea.*)—Common law is more severe in this partic-

§ 17. This proviso operates also in another direction: it serves the judiciary as a guide in passing judgment on aggravated transgressions. The court is not unfrequently embarrassed, when called upon to decide cases of uninterrupted and repeated violations of any one law, whether the culprit is guilty of one continued offense (*delictum continuatum*), or of several offenses of the same kind (*delictum reiteratum*). Of course, in capital crimes, the problem meets with a very easy solution: the criminal can not be killed more than once, even for different crimes,—only when he has been duly convicted of two or more offenses, all subject to capital punishment, but to different modes of death, the Talmud ordains that he shall suffer the hardest death,[58] or the one mentioned in the warning.[59] But in cases subject to corporal punishment only, the question is very important, and the answer depends on the number of warnings.[60]

---

ular. Thus while it requires, that "the killing should be committed with malice aforethought, to make it the crime of murder," it declares it sufficient if the malice was implied only (Blackstone IV, 199 sq. Cf. infra § 43).

[58] Sanh. 81ª; Maimon. II. Sanh. XIV, 4. Cf. infra n. 378.

[59] Cf. Sanh. 81ª; Maimon. II. Sanh. XIV, 4.

[60] Thus: The Nazarite, who drinks a certain measure of wine in violation of his vow of abstinence, is, by Talmudic law, subject to flagellation (Nazir 34ᵇ, Maimon. II. Nezirath V, 2). The question now arises whether, if he imbibes this quantity several times in succession, he is to be punished for so many separate and distinct transgressions, or only once for all. The warning decides it. If before each drink he is duly warned not to indulge, he is legally liable to the prescribed punishment for each drink separately; but when no warning is administered

§ 18. Also another and more important decision depends on the due administration of the warning, namely that concerning transgressions rendering the perpetrator liable at once to corporal and to capital punishment. In such cases, when the warning mentioned the corporal penalty, only this penalty is awarded; but when it mentioned the death penalty, the culprit is put to death, without being flagellated.[61] The latter, however, is the case also when the warning mentions both punishments; for Rabbinic law does not impose corporal and capital punishments, to which one makes himself liable by the commission of one and the same crime;[62] it inflicts the greater only.[63]

---

between drinks, he is punished once only (Maccoth 21ª, Nazir 42b).

[61] Hullin 81b; Maimon. H. Sanh. XVI, 5.—Thus, for the violation of the Biblical precept regarding the slaughtering of an animal and its offspring within one day (Lev. XXII, 28), the legal punishment is flagellation (Hullin 78ª; Maimon. H. Shehitta XII, 1). Now, when one violates this prohibition, and adds thereto the deadly sin of sacrificing the victims to a pagan deity, he is liable to suffer also the death of the idolater (see § 26); but as only one punishment can legally be awarded, the warning decides which it shall be.

[62] Sanh. 74ª, et al.—Nor does the Talmud impose pecuniary fine and corporal punishment for one and the same offense (Tosefta ib. IV; Maccoth 13b). However, in an action for slandering a newly married woman, the convict is both fined and flagellated (Tosefta ib. I, § 5; Kethub. 45b; Maimon. H. Naara III, 1). But slander is exceptional in another direction also. For, while no violation of a negative precept, unaccompanied by physical action, is punishable corporally (supra § 12), the slanderer is flagellated: he is considered to have traduced not only the woman against whom his tongue is directly levelled, but all

§ 19. From the benefit of the proviso under consideration, the Talmud expressly excludes the crimes of bearing false witness[64] and inciting to idolatry,[65]—the first, because the nature of the crime admits of no forewarning, no person knowing beforehand that the witness will testify to a falsehood; and the second, on account of the heinousness of the crime in a theocratic government.[66] Also the burglar is excluded from its operation;[67] and so are all the perpetrators of those misdeeds, for the commission of which the Bible predicts the penalty of excision.[68]

---

the maidens in Israel (Sifre II, § 238 ; Yer. Terumoth VII, § 1, p. 44).

[63] Kethuboth 33b sq.; Maimon. II. Geneba III, 1.—The legal maxim being: "The less punishment is discharged in the greater" (Hullin 81b; et al.). Among the Romans, too, it was a rule of law that a fine should not be imposed with another punishment in the same *rogatio*, decree or bill (Smith 522b).

[64] Maccoth 4b; Maimon. II. Eduth XVIII, 4. Cf. infra §31.

[65] Sanh. 67a; Maimon. II. Ab. Zara V, 3; ib. II. Sanh. XI, 5. Cf. supra n. 37.

[66] Cf. infra n. 89.

[67] Kethuboth 34b; Sanh. 72b. "The act of breaking in is in itself sufficient warning."

[68] Maccoth 13b; Kerith. 2a sq. Cf. infra n. 71.—On close examination into the spirit of Talmudic jurisprudence, one cannot help perceiving that the Rabbis aimed at the ultimate abolition of capital punishment. Some expressed themselves plainly to this effect (supra § 6) ; and nothing could accomplish that end better than the proviso of the antecedent warning. To abolish capital punishment suddenly and altogether, they did not deem practicable, as the princely contemporary of the abolitionists referred to remarked with reference to them: "They would increase bloodshed in the world" (Maccoth 7a), for they would remove the greatest deterrent from crime; they, therefore,

3. Misdemeanors, Crimes and Penalties.

§ 20. The philosophic maxim, that it is absurd and impolitic to apply the same punishment to crimes of

---

instituted a condition that would render a judicial execution highly improbable, and yet not altogether impossible. Still it must not be assumed that, barring the exceptions enumerated, all legal convictions were conditioned by strict compliance with this proviso. It is true that, from the oft-repeated dicta of the Talmud (cf. Tosefta Sanh. XI, § 1; Sanh. 80ᵇ), such would appear to be the case; but this would be subversive of all principles of law and order. Was the murderer acquitted, because he had not been duly forewarned? The Talmud, in strict accord with the laws of our own days, not only justifies the killing of the would-be murderer, but makes it everybody's duty to do so, if possible (cf. infra § 34), in order to prevent him from carrying out his criminal purpose; and if there are people near enough to administer a warning, would they not rather interfere and prevent the crime, than merely forewarn the criminal and stand by while the crime is being committed? The probability, therefore, is that only such crimes and trespasses are conditioned by the warning, as are liable to be committed in ignorance of their criminal nature; e. g. a profanation of the Sabbath, or eating on Atonement Day, whose holy character had possibly been forgotten: the Sabbath might be mistaken for a week day, and the day of Atonement for an ordinary day. In such cases one must be duly warned of the sanctity of the day and of the consequences of presumptuously violating it (supra n. 55); and if, in spite of the warning, the trespasser persists, he becomes the subject of punishment (cf. Finneles, Darcah shel Torah, §115).

Such, we conceive, is the rationale of the requirement; but since all Rabbinic jurisprudence, Talmudic and contemporaneous as well as that of later date, yields the benefit of the warning to all cases, except those explicitly mentioned, we are bound to follow it in these pages, and we suggest the following as the principle underlying the curious proviso.—Society is founded

different malignity, which the great commentator[69]
on a compact guaranteeing mutual protection: "that the whole should protect all its parts, and that every part should pay obedience to the will of the whole; or, in other words, that the community should guard the rights of each individual member, and that, in return for this protection, each individual should submit to the laws of the community" (Blackstone I, 48. Cmp. Grotius, Right of War and Peace, B. III c. XXIII; Beccaria, § 21). This compact is generally understood or implied, though seldom written. Israel's compact is the Pentateuch, "the Book of the Covenant." Now, as long as one acts up to society's compact or constitution, so long is he a member of society, and entitled to all the rights and privileges it confers upon its adherents; but when he flagrantly and presumptuously violates the requirements of the fundamental principles of the constitution, he ceases to be a member of society: the compact between him and the fraternity is broken by his own volition, and he has no more claim to the protection which its expressed, or implied, provisions formerly conferred on him. Still this would not authorize society to do him harm. But when the warning is duly administered and he acknowledges it, he delivers himself up to punishment (Sanh. 40ᵇ; supra § 16), virtually offering to suffer corporal or capital punishment in exchange for the gratification of his passion. Or, when, by his determination to break the compact, and thus to throw up his membership and become a stranger to society, he is duly warned by members of society that, in case he should defy the provisions of their compact, they would look upon him as upon a dangerous foreign invader, whose just reward is provided for; and when, in spite of the warning, he defies the law and offends the provisions of the compact, the government considers him a traitor, and justly treats him as such. When, however, the condition is not strictly complied with, the Rabbis do not consider themselves justified in inflicting bodily pain, and much less death, but provide other punishments (cf. infra, § 24).

[69] Blackstone IV. 17. Cf. Luzzatto ad Exodus XXI. 37.— Montaigne says: "Vices are all alike as they are vices, and 'tis

so ably and justly advocated only one century ago, was early recognized and acted upon in Talmudic jurisprudence. Not only is there in the Rabbinic law a well drawn scale of crimes and punishments—the latter ranging between flagellation and death,—but in the mode of capital punishment itself, as will appear hereafter,[70] there is a gradation commensurate with the magnitude of the crime. At this juncture we will take a general view of the various misdemeanors and crimes, and of their consequent penalties, beginning with the lightest.

§ 21. *Flagellation* is the penalty of three classes of offenses: 1. The violation of any one of the prohibitive ordinances punishable, according to the Mosaic law, with *excision*,[71] to which, however, no capital

---

thus, perhaps, the Stoics understood it; but though they are equally vices, yet they are not equal vices; and that he who has transgressed the bounds by a hundred paces, whence we cannot deviate without going wrong, should not be in a worse condition than he who has transgressed them but ten, is not to be believed; or that sacrilege is not worse than stealing a cabbage" (Essays, B. II, c. II). And since it is naturally essential that a great crime should be prevented rather than a lesser one, and that which is more pernicious to society, rather than that which is less so: it is also essential that there should be a certain correspondence in the punishments, the means employed to prevent the occurrence of crime (cf. Montesquieu, B. VI, c. XVI; Beccaria, § 6).

[70] Cf. infra §§ 122–139.

[71] What one is to understand by this term does not clearly appear. In the Mosaic law we frequently meet with the expression: "* * * and that being shall be cut off from the midst of its people," without being accompanied by any directions as to how this is to come about. Some modern exegetists assert

punishment at the instance of a human tribunal is attached.⁷² 2. The violation of a negative precept, deadly in the sight of heaven.⁷³ 3. The violation of any negative precept, when accomplished by means of a positive act.⁷⁴

---

that the law-giver thereby implied capital punishment (cf. Gesenius, Thesaurus, p. 718); but one is loath to admit that Moses awarded the death penalty for transgressions affecting ceremonial rites only (e. g. Ex. XII, 15; XXX, 38. Lev. VII, 20. Num. IX, 13. Where the death penalty was intended, he unequivocally expressed it; as with reference to the Sabbath—Ex. XXXI, 14). Jewish commentators generally understood by it something not depending on human instrumentality. Basing their opinion on tradition, they assert that excision is only a heavenly visitation of early death (cf. Iben Ezra ad Gen. XVII, 14; Abravanel ad Num. XV; Luzzatto ad Gen. XVII, 14); and this opinion seems to have scriptural authority for its foundation (cf. Lev. XX, 5-6; Ezek. XIV, 8). If so, then there is no difference between this penalty and that of the next class (cf. Munk, Palestine 438).

⁷² Maccoth 13ᵇ; Maimon. II. Sanh. XVIII, 1.
⁷³ Sanh. 83ᵃ; Maimon. ib. XIX, 2.
⁷⁴ Maimon. ib. XIX, 2 and sources. Cf. infra n. 323.—The enumeration of the different offenses comprised under this section would be too tedious, and useless to both the reader and the compiler. Suffice it therefore to state, that Maimonides who has, in l. c., carefully arranged and numbered them, furnishes a grand total of two hundred and seven. The first class includes twenty-one offenses, seven of which are of the nature of sexual correspondence, not coming under the head of capital crimes (cf. § 26 sq.), and the rest are mostly violations of Levitical laws. The second class comprises abuses of Levitical functions and privileges to the number of eighteen. The third and last class, comprising the remaining one hundred and forty-eight, are offenses of various kinds: such as against the temple, against agrarian laws, against the dietary laws. The greater part of each class

§ 22. *Penal servitude* is the punishment of the person duly convicted of theft, and unable to make the prescribed restitution.[75]

§ 23. *Exile*[76] is the penalty of accidental homicide.[77]

---

was applicable to the period during which the sacrificial rites obtained in Israel.—Less formal than flagellation (cf. infra § 138 sq.). but akin to it, is the punishment known as *whipping for insubordination* (*Mackath Marduth*). This was administered to all refractory persons as well as to the immodest (Kiddushin 12ᵇ; Maimon. H. Sanh. XVIII, 5).

[75] Exodus XXII, 3; Mekhilta Nezikin § 1; ib. § 13; Kidd, 18ᵇ. This is the only case where the Mosaic-Talmudic law imposes servitude on a Hebrew, and it is a kind of retaliation on the culprit who attempted to enrich himself and to establish his independence by means of the property of others (cf. Maimon. II. Geneba I, 4; More Neb. III, 41; Beccaria § 22).—Herod ordered all thieves to be exposed and sold to *foreigners;* but this was against the express law of Moses (Josephus, Antiqu. XVI, I, 1; infra n. 412). Among the early Romans a conviction of theft affected the civil status of the thief. When the stolen thing was found in his possession (*furtum manifestum*). a freeman duly convicted was flogged and consigned to the injured party. This punishment was subsequently changed to a quadruple fine, both in the case of a slave and a freeman. The penalty for theft when the stolen thing was not found in the thief's possession, was a twofold fine (Smith 463ᵇ). Among the Athenians, Draco made theft capital, but Solon changed the penalty to a pecuniary mulct. The ancient Saxon law nominally punished theft with death, if the stolen thing was valued above twelve-pence, which theft was denominated grand larceny; but the criminal was permitted to redeem his life by a pecuniary ransom. In the reign of Henry I, the power of redemption was taken away, and all persons guilty of grand larceny were directed to be hanged (Blackstone IV, 237 sq.).

[76] Although this is the correct rendition of the term *Golah*, under which the penalty is known, in Talmudic jurisprudence

This punishment, however, is not imposed on the unfortunate culprit, unless the victim of the acci-

we are to understand thereby *emigration, flight, sanctuary, asylum (Miklat)*.—The punishment of exile or banishment (*deportatio, exilium, aquae et ignis interdictio*), so universal among ancient nations, was never practised among the Jews. Indeed, in Palestine emigration was deprecated, if not strictly forbidden, the Rabbis seeing in it a tendency to irreligion, if not a direct step towards idolatry (cf. Keth. 111a; Guittin 6a; B. Bathra 91a; Ab. Zara 8a). Nor must our term be understood in the sense of *sanctuary* in the old English law, which was accompanied by confession of guilt and abjuration of the realm forever (Blackstone IV, 322). A confession of guilt was never required before a Hebrew trial court, and when voluntarily made, was not considered in judgment (cf. infra § 93), except in cases involving pecuniary mulct, when it led to the remittance of the legal fine (B. Kama 14b, et al.). Besides, pleading guilty to an overt act would, by the Talmudic law, not entitle the culprit to sanctuary, this privilege being accorded to the unintentional slayer only (Exodus XXI, 12-13; Maccoth 7a; Maimon. H. Rozeah V. 1), and not, as among other nations, to all sorts of dangerous criminals (cf. Smith 117a, 135a). The Jewish *Golah* was a "city of refuge" from the "avenger of the blood" (cf. Num. XXXV, 9, 35; Deut. XIX, 1-10; Maccoth 9b), and not from the power and authority of the court. Every homicide had a right to flee to this sanctuary, and to demand protection there, until he was taken out by the proper authorities for preliminary trial. If the charge of intentional murder was proved against him, he was proceeded with according to law; but if found innocent of guilty intentions, he was restored to the city of refuge, and there left under the protection of the priests and Levites (Sifre I, § 160, et al.; Tosefta Maccoth III. Cf. infra § 134).

[77] Maccoth 7a; Maimon. H. Rozeah V. Cf. infra § 35.—Among the early Greeks, too, the privilege of asylum was accorded to the author of accidental, unintentional homicide (Fiske III, § 37).

dent dies immediately after the infliction of the injury.[78]

§ 24. *Imprisonment*[79] is the punishment of five different classes of offenders: 1, Of homicides whose crime cannot be legally punished with death, because some condition or other, necessary to produce a legal conviction, has not been complied with.[80] 2, Of instigators to, or procurers of murder, such, for instance, as have the deed committed by the hands of a hireling.[81] 3, Of accessories to loss of life; as, for instance, when several persons club one to death, and the court cannot determine the one who gave the death blow.[82] 4, Of persons who, having twice been

---

[78] Guittin 70ᵇ; Maimon. II. Rozeah V. 2.

[79] Among the Greeks, imprisonment was seldom applied as a legal punishment. They preferred banishment to the expense of keeping prisoners in confinement. Plato, however, proposed to erect some prisons, one of which was to be a penitentiary, and another, a penal settlement away from the city (Smith 213ᵃ). Among the Jews punishment by imprisonment was not practised under the Mosaic dispensation, and the cases mentioned in the Pentateuch (Lev. XXIV, 12; Num. XV, 24), refer to the simple detention of the transgressor until sentence could be passed on him. During the reign of the later Kings of Israel's first commonwealth, imprisonment does appear as a mode of punishment (cf. I Kings XXII, 27; II Chron. XVI, 10; Jerem. XXXVII); but even then it was not as the result of a legal decision, but as an order of arbitrary despotism. The Talmud, however, instituted this penalty and legalized its application among the Hebrews.

[80] Sanh. 81ᵇ; Maimon. II. Rozeah IV, 8.

[81] Kidd. 43ᵃ; Maimon. ib. II, 2.

[82] B. Kama 10ᵇ; Sanh. 78ᵃ; Maimon. ib. IV, 6.—All such as were imprisoned for the offenses named thus far, remained in

duly condemned to, and punished with, flagellation for as many transgressions of one and the same negative precept, commit it a third time.[83] 5, Of the incorrigible offender who, on each of three occasions, had failed to acknowledge as many warnings antecedent to the commission of one and the same crime, the original penalty for which was excision. This punishment is superseded by flagellation, only if it appear in evidence that the warning had been heard by the culprit.[84]

4. Capital Crimes.

§ 25. Talmudic jurisprudence provides four modes of capital punishment. These are: 1. Stoning; 2. Burning; 3. Decapitation; 4. Strangling.[85] The first of these is, in the opinion of the Rabbis, the se-

---

confinement for the balance of their natural lives, shortened in some cases, by keeping the prisoner on a barley diet. (Sanh. 81b; Maimon. II. Sanh. XIV, 4).—The substitution of barley for wheat, as an article of food, was practised among the Romans as a common punishment, especially for military insubordination (Plutarch, Life of Marcellus).

[83] Sanh. 81b; Maimon. II. Sanh. XVIII, 5.—According to others, he must have received the punishment of flagellation three times, and have been convicted of the same crime a fourth time.

[84] Ibid. Cf. supra § 21.—Of course, the Talmud authorizes temporary imprisonment or detention during the interval between the indictment and the close of the trial (Mekhilta Nez. § 6; Sanh. 78b).

[85] Sanh. 49b; Maimon. II. Sanh. XIV, 1.—Maimonides (ib. XV, 10—13) groups all capital crimes together under the headings of their respective penalties, and we follow his arrangement.

verest, the last, the mildest;[86] and the number of crimes to which they are applicable, is thirty-six.

§ 26. All crimes for the commission of each of which the offender, after due trial and conviction, was to be sentenced to death by *stoning*, are eighteen in number: 1. Criminal conversation with one's own mother; 2. with his step-mother; 3. with his daughter-in-law; 4. with a betrothed virgin (rape); 5. pederasty;[87]

---

[86] Sanh. 49ʳ; Maimon. H. Sanh. XIV, 4.—The modes of inflicting capital punishment in Athens were as follows: 1. By the *sword:* beheading; 2. by the *rope:* strangling or hanging; 3. by *poison:* usually hemlock; 4. by the *precipice:* casting from a rock or height; 5. by the *katapontismos:* drowning; 6. by *crucifixion:* a mode used by the Greeks less frequently than by the Romans; 7 by the *cudgel:* beating, during which the malefactor was hung to a pole; 8. by throwing into the *pit (barathron)* which was a noisome hole with sharp spikes at top and bottom; 9. by *stoning;* 10. by *burning* (Fiske III, § 115).— Among the Romans death was inflicted as follows: slaves were usually crucified; others it was customary first to hang, afterwards to behead or strangle in prison, or to throw from the Tarpeian rock, or to cast into the sea or the river. Sometimes the criminals were obliged to fight with wild beasts in the amphitheatre, or with each other as gladiators; or they were thrown to wild beasts to be devoured. Another form, still more horrible, perhaps, was to wrap the offender in a garment covered with pitch and set it on fire (Ib. § 264).

[87] That this unnatural crime, as well as bestiality, was prevalent at an early age, appears from the fact that Moses incorporated its penalty in his law (Ex. XXII, 18; Lev. XX, 13); but it reached its maximum in later years among the Greeks and Romans. "However pure might originally have been the relations and habits of intercourse between the boys in Sparta and Crete, and whatever excellent qualities might have belonged to the Theban *sacred band*, it is nevertheless true that the most

6. bestiality, practised by a man; 7. the same practiced by a woman; 8. blasphemy; 9. idolatry;[88] 10. sacrificing one's own children to Moloch; 11. instigating individuals to embrace idolatry; 12. instigating

---

hateful debauchery and most odious forms of licentiousness commonly designated by this term, were extensively practised" (cf. Fiske III, § 182; Smith 503ᵇ). By the Scatinian law, "the rape, perhaps the seduction of an ingenuous youth was compensated as a personal injury, by the poor damages of ten thousand sesterces, or fourscore pounds, among the Etruscans and Greeks"; but among the later Romans the penalty of that crime was most severe. "A painful death was inflicted by the amputation of the sinful instrument, or the insertion of sharp reeds into the pores and tubes of the most exquisite sensibility; and Justinian defended the propriety of the execution, since the criminals would have lost their hands, had they been convicted of sacrilege. In this state of disgrace and agony, two bishops, Isaiah of Rhodes and Alexander of Diospolis, were dragged through the streets of Constantinople, while their brethren were admonished by the voice of a crier, to observe this awful lesson and not to pollute the sanctity of their character" (Gibbon, XLIV). In England both these crimes were punished either by burning or burying the offenders alive (Blackstone IV, 216).— Among the Israelites, however, these crimes were never prevalent, as the Talmud itself testifies (Yerush. Kidd. IV, §11, p. 66ᶜ; Babli ib. 82ᵃ). That a crime is more or less frequently discussed in the Talmud is no proof of its frequent occurrence in Israel (cf. § 32), for it must be borne in mind that the Rabbis considered all literary pursuits as very meritorious in themselves: "Study and be rewarded," was their maxim (Sanh. 51ᵇ; ib. 71ᵃ, et al.), and on that principle they elaborated their system of laws, touching even unusual crimes (cf. supra n. 33).

"The punishment of the idolater and of the blasphemer is rendered more ignominious by the addition of post-mortem hanging (cf. infra § 129).

communities to do the like;[59] 13. pythonism; 14. ne-

---

[59] By the Attic law, an action could be brought against persons who were considered to have misled the people, by misrepresentations or false promises, into acts of injustice, or into measures injurious to the state; and those found guilty were punished with death (Smith 21ᵇ).—The prohibition of idolatry among the Jews was founded upon the principle that God, having delivered them from slavery and constituted them an independent people, was, by their own free choice, made the *civil head* of their politico-religious commonwealth. He was, therefore, to be honored as their King, as well as their God. Hence, even assuming the truth of polytheism, supposing that there actually were other gods, this principle bound every subject of the government to worship none but the God of Israel. Hence, idolatry among the Jews was an offense against the state; and while, by their penal system, punishments were inflicted for criminal actions only (supra § 12), words spoken against their divine King were considered as designing the overthrow of the government, and were accordingly made punishable. Hence, too, blasphemy and inciting to apostasy were considered similar to other overt acts of treason, and punished as such (cf. Maimon. II. Accum. II, 4 sq.; More Neb. III, 29).—Keeping this in mind, and remembering that the only end or intent of human laws is, to regulate the behavior of men as they are members of society, and stand in various relations to each other, and that they consequently have no concern with any other but social or relative duties (cf. Blackstone I, 124),—the reader will readily perceive the essential difference between the right of the ancient Jews to punish the crimes in question, and that of other *civil* governments. The former sought to prevent acts prejudicial to the safety and tranquillity of their social system; the latter pretended to avenge the offended majesty of God! The consequences were equally different. Among the former, only the truly guilty ones had reason to fear the severity of the laws; among the latter, the most unexceptionable conduct, the purest morals and the constant practice of every duty in life, were not sufficient security against the persecutions of fanaticism. The

cromancy; 15. magic;⁹⁰ 16. violating the Sabbath; 17. cursing a parent;⁹¹ 18. violation of filial duty, making the "prodigal son."

former proceeded against the accused on the direct and corroborative testimony of at least two eye-witnesses (supra n. 43; infra § 82); among the latter, the slightest suspicion endangered the life or liberty of the subject (infra n. 286). Among the former, no human being was exempt from due obedience to the general laws (infra § 45); among the latter, "the servants of the Lord" were their own masters, and subject to their own laws only (infra n. 166). Hence it came about that, while the Rabbis could confidently prophesy that no community would ever be punished for apostasy (cf. infra § 28, n. 106), Roman pontiffs excommunicated kings and peoples, and disposed of crowns and kingdoms (Hallam VII; Blackstone IV, 46). Verily, where human laws undertake to avenge the cause of the infinite Being, they are directed by his infinity, and not by the ignorance and caprice of man (cf. Montesquieu XII, 4), and hence there is no limit to the means they employ to detect crime, and no measure to the punishments they inflict on the alleged criminal.

⁹¹ Witchcraft, conjuration, enchantment, sorcery as well as heresy, were formerly penal offenses in England, punishable by burning to death, and Blackstone did not consider the abolition of the death penalty for these offenses an improvement (cf. Com. IV, 60, and ib. 436). The civil law punished with death not only the sorcerers themselves, but also those who consulted them (ib. 60).

⁹¹ This deadly sin, as well as blasphemy, was not visited with capital punishment, unless the culprit employed in connection therewith the ineffable name of God (Sanh. 55ᵃ, 66ᵃ; Maimon. II. Ab. Zara II, 7; H. Mamrim V, 2). By the laws of Athens, those guilty of ill-treating their parents generally lost their civil rights (*atimia*), though they were allowed to retain their property; but when the ill-treatment consisted in *beating* their parents, the culprits lost their hands (Smith 185ᵃ). Among the Romans, he who *killed* a father or mother, grandfather or grand-

§ 27. Those punished by *burning* are ten in number: 1, Criminal commerce of a priest's daughter;[92] 2, criminal commerce with one's own daughter; 3, with one's own daughter's daughter; 4, with one's own son's daughter; 5, with one's own step-daughter; 6, with one's own step-daughter's daughter; 7, with one's own step-son's daughter; 8, with one's own mother-in-law; 9, with her mother; 10, with one's father-in-law's mother.—These nine cases of incest[93]

---

mother was punished (*more majorum*) by being whipped till he bled, sewn up in a sack, with a dog, a cock, a viper and an ape, and thrown into the sea, if the sea was near by, and if not, by a constitution of Hadrian, he was exposed to wild beasts, or, in time of Paulus, he was burnt. Other parricides were simply put to death (Smith 308). In China, it is said, there is a decree "that a child or grandchild, who is guilty of addressing abusive language to his or her father or mother, paternal grandfather or grandmother, shall suffer death by being strangled" (Chambers, Inform. for the People I, 81).

[92] By the Roman law, to have knowledge of a Vestal virgin was considered *incestum*, and both parties were alike punished with death (Smith 533b).

[93] Gibbon (l. c.) thus briefly sums up the different customs in that regard: "An instinct, almost innate and universal, appears to prohibit the incestuous commerce of parents and children in the infinite series of ascending and descending generations. Concerning the oblique and collateral branches, nature is indifferent, reason mute, and custom various and arbitrary. In Egypt, the marriage of brothers and sisters was admitted without scruple or exception: a Spartan might espouse the daughter of his father, an Athenian that of his mother; and the nuptials of an uncle with his niece were applauded at Athens as a happy union of the dearest relations. The profane lawgivers of Rome were never tempted by interest or superstition to multiply the forbidden degrees; but they inflexibly con-

are punishable by burning, only when committed during the life of the criminal's wife; otherwise they are considered as cases of adultery, and punished as such.[94]

§ 28. With *decapitation* only two crimes are punished; viz: murder[95] and communal apostasy from Judaism to idolatry.[96]

---

demned the marriages of sisters and brothers, hesitated whether first cousins should be touched by the same interdict; revered the paternal characters of aunts and uncles, and treated affinity and adoption as a just imitation of the ties of blood."

[94] Sanh. 76^b; Maimon. II. Is. Biah II, 8. Cf. § 29.

[95] In the first instance the duty of bringing a murderer to justice rests on the "avenger of the blood"—the nearest relative or heir of the victim of the crime; where there is no avenger, or he fails to perform his duty, the proper authorities must see it done (Sanh. 45^b; Maccoth 12^a; Maimon. II. Rozeah I, 2, 5).—By the laws of Solon, too, the task of prosecution devolved upon the nearest relatives of the deceased, and in the case of a slave, upon the master. To neglect to prosecute, without good cause, was deemed an offense against religion; that is, in any relative not farther removed than a first cousin's son. Within that degree the law enjoined the relatives to prosecute, under the penalty of impeachment for impiety (*asabeias graphe*) if they failed to do so. They might, however (without incurring any censure), forbear to prosecute, where the murdered man had forgiven the murderer before he died; or in cases of involuntary homicide, where the offender gave the satisfaction which the law required; unless the deceased had given a special injunction to avenge him (Smith 769^b). Among the Arabians, as among the barbarians of every age, a fine or compensation for murder often releases the perpetrator from further prosecution; but the kinsmen of the dead are at liberty to accept the atonement, or to execute with their own hands the law of retaliation. The refined malice of the Arabs generally refuses even the head of the murderer, substitutes an innocent for the guilty person, and transfers the penalty to the best and

§ 29. Finally, six crimes are punished by *strangulation:* 1, Adultery;[97] 2, bruising a parent;[98] 3, kid-

most considerable of the race by whom they have been injured (Gibbon c. L). Among the Franks murder was not a capital, but a finable offense, "since the loss of one citizen cannot be repaired by that of another (cf. infra n, 281)." With them murder was expiated by the payment of *Weregild* (head-money), which was paid partly to the state as a remuneration for the loss of a subject, partly to the bereft family, and partly to the church for the benefit of the departed soul. This head-money was fixed by the Salique law at 600 solidi for an Antrustion of the King; at 300 for a Roman noble; at 200 for a common Frank; at 100 for a Roman possessor of lands; and at 45 for a tributary or cultivator of another's property (cf. Hallam, l. c., c. II, part I).—Talmudic jurisprudence expressly forbids taking blood-money from the murderer, or even from the homicide *per unfortunium*, in strict accordance with the Mosaic prohibition (Num. XXXV, 31 sq.), and that even when the avenger is willing to compromise by the acceptance of a ransom (Sifre I, § 160; Kethuboth 37^b). Nor was blood-money permitted in Athens. The unintentional slayer of a person could, indeed, abridge his year's banishment (cf. infra n. 123), and even after having joined issue before the Areopagus, the person accused of murder could escape capital punishment by voluntary exile, and none could prevent him; yet the party thus evading the extreme punishment, was never allowed to return home; and even when a decree was passed to legalize the return of exiles, the murderer who thus fled the country, was always excepted (Smith 89^b).

[93] Cf. supra n. 89; infra § 32.

[97] By a constitution of Constantine, this offense in the adulterer was capital, but the adulteress, after being whipped, was put into a convent. If her husband did not take her out in two years, she was forced to assume the habit of, and spend the rest of her life in the convent (Smith 23^b). Among the Chaldeans, it seems, mutilation was the penalty, the nose and the ears of the offenders being cut off (cf. Ezek. XXIII. 25). In England

napping;[99] 4, maladministration (the "Rebellious Elder"); 5, false prophecy; 6, prophesying in the name of heathen deities.[100]

---

the temporal courts took no cognizance of the crime of adultery, otherwise than as a private injury (Blackstone IV, 65).— That strangulation, and not stoning, was the penalty of the adulterer among the ancient Hebrews is certain (cf. Sanh. 52b sq., 84b, 89b; Sifra Kedoshim § IX; Maimon. II. Sanh. XV, 13; et al.), notwithstanding that we find it stated (John VIII, 4-5) that "Moses, in the law, commanded us that such should be *stoned.*" If the whole account there given (3-11) is at all true (and many there are who suspect its authenticity, because it does not appear in most Mss.—v. Renan, Vie de Jesus p. 245, n. 2), then we may assume that an illegal penalty was purposely mentioned, "in order to try him, that they might have whereof to accuse him" (ib.), as clearly appears from the purport of the narrative.

[98] As a safeguard, the Talmudists object even to a child's performing venesection or any other operation on its parent, unless there is none else to do it (Sanh. 84b; Maimon. II. Mamrim V, 7).

[99] The offender is not put to death for this offense, unless he carries his victim home, enslaves him and sells him (Sanh. 85b; Maimon. II. Geneba IX, 2).—In Rome the penalty of this crime varied at different times. A lex Fabia made it pecuniary; but this fell into disuse, and persons convicted of *plagium* were generally condemned to the mines (Smith 781ª). Blackstone (IV, 219) tells us that in the civil law it was punished with death, and the common law of England punished it with fine, imprisonment and the pillory.

[100] It is an old established rule in Rabbinic jurisprudence that capital punishment may be inflicted only where the Mosaic law imposes it (Sifre II, § 154. Cmp. Yer. Sanh. XI, § 6, p. 30c top; Babli ib. 87ª), and from the above exhaustive list of capital crimes it clearly appears that, with all the muliplicity of Rabbinic enactments (supra § 11), and notwithstanding the extreme

§ 30. All capital crimes here enumerated, if classified according to their respective natures, will appear as follows : *a.* Adultery 2 ; *b.* bestiality 2 ; *c.* blasphemy 1; *d.* idolatry 7; *e.* incest 12; *f.* kidnapping 1; *g.* maladministration 1; *h.* murder 1; *i.* pederasty 1; *k.* rape 1; *l.* violations of filial duty 3; *m.* violation of the Sabbath 1; *n.* witchcraft 3.—Of these thirteen classes, four (*c, d, m* and *n*), including twelve offenses, comprise such crimes as more immediately offend God, for they are, in the main, transgressions against the letter and the spirit of revealed religion. The remaining nine categories, containing twenty-four crimes, are more immediately repugnant to that universal law of society, which regulates intercourse between man and man, and which is established for the conservation of the safety and peace of individuals and communities.[101]

---

severity attributed to the Pharisees, the Rabbis did not add a single crime to the Mosaic catalogue of capital punishments, while in the course of these pages it will be as clearly demonstrated that, by their despised and often vilified laws, they rendered the execution of a death-sentence all but impossible.

[101] This is certainly a formidable array ; but if the reader has followed us attentively, he will have noticed that the crimes punished with death by these laws, are either of deep moral malignity, or are such as aimed against the very being of the Jewish nationality. He will, moreover, have discovered that, in reality, there are but four classes of capital offenses known to Talmudic jurisprudence—'treason, murder, deliberate and gross abuse of parents, and the more unnatural and horrid crimes arising out of the sexual relations; but no injury simply affecting property could draw down upon the citizen an ignominious death. The Talmudists respected moral purity more than gold. Moral turpitude, and the most atrocious forms of moral turpitude,—these were the objects of their severity.'

§ 31. Our list of atrocious crimes would be incomplete, should we fail to speak of one which, though already mentioned in these pages,[102] could not on account of its peculiar nature, be classed with those of any particular category,—the crime of bearing *false witness*. Scripture ordains: "If the witness be a false witness, and has testified falsely against his brother, then shall ye do unto him, as he had thought to do unto his brother * * * and thine eyes shall not pity him: life shall go for life, eye for eye, &c."[103] Accordingly the Talmud teaches that he, by whose testimony an innocent man has been condemned to death, shall himself suffer the death to which the victim of his falsehood has been sentenced; if the false testimony brought about a sentence of flagellation, its author shall receive it; and if one of pecuniary fine, he shall pay it.[104]—However, the penalty is not im-

---

[102] Supra § 19.

[103] Deut. XIX. 16-21.

[104] Maccoth 5ᵃ; Maimon. II. Eduth XVIII, 1.—In **Athens**, only the witness to a summons was liable to be criminally prosecuted, in case he had been found guilty of *falsum;* while the witness in a cause was liable to a civil action only (Smith 820ᵃ). By the Gothic law, if one was executed in consequence of false testimony, the judge and the prosecutor as well as the witnesses were severely punished; and among the Romans, the *Lex Carnelia* (*De Sicariis*) punished the false witness as being guilty of a species of assassination. In England it was once attempted to introduce the law of retaliation as a punishment for such as preferred malicious accusations against others; that is, they were to incur the same pain that the other would have had, in case the accusations had been found true. But after one year's experience, the punishment of taliation was rejected, and imprisonment adopted in its stead (Blackstone IV. 14). Hence,

posed on the false witness, unless his testimony is confuted by other testimony touching himself, as when other parties testify that, at the very time at which he alleges that he witnessed the perpetration of the crime, he was with them at another place. But when his testimony is disproved by other means, as by an alibi of the accused or of the *corpus delicti*, at the time the crime is said to have been committed, his testimony is rejected; but no punishment is decreed against him, except some stripes, in addition to the infamy resting on him.[105]

§ 32. As a matter of history it deserves to be stated, that the apostasy of a Jewish community, in the sense

---

the modern law (to avoid the danger of deterring witnesses from giving evidence upon capital prosecutions, if it must be at the peril of their own lives) does not punish false testimony as severely, though jurists admit that "the guilt of him who takes away the life of an innocent man by a false oath, is more atrocious than that of an assassin who murders by a dagger or by poison," since he adds to the privation of life public ignominy, the most excruciating of tortures to an honorable mind, and reduces an innocent family to ruin and infamy (ib. 196; Chitty ad l. c.).—The Talmudists did not entertain such fears. The assumption that "few honest witnesses would venture to give evidence against a prisoner tried for his life, if thereby they made themselves liable to be prosecuted as murderers," did not enter the minds of the Rabbis; and if it did, it was soon dissipated by their noble faith in the moral sense of the honest man who would not fail to comply with his obligation, based on two Scriptural precepts (cf. Lev. V. 1; ib. XIX. 16) as well as on his social relations to the state: to bear witness to the truth, when he is thoroughly acquainted with the facts in the case (Sifra Kedoshim § 4; B. Kama 56ᵃ; Maimon. II. Eduth, 1, 1.—Cf. infra n. 281).

of Talmudic jurisprudence, or the execution of a
"prodigal son," the Rabbis assert, never occurred
under the Talmudic dispensation; and R. Jonathan
reports his having met with the graves of persons convicted of these crimes, as an extraordinary and wonder-
ful event.[106]—Executions for witchcraft, too, seem to
have been exceedingly rare. Only one occurrence of
this kind, under the presidency of Simon ben Shettah,
is recorded in the Talmud;[107] and that is considered by
the Nestor of Jewish history[108] anachronistic, and the

---

[105] Maccoth 5ᵃ. Cf. infra § 95.

[106] Speaking of the laws concerning the prodigal son, a Rabbi remarks: "Is it probable or reasonable that, because a young man consumes, outside of his parental house, a certain quantity of meat and Italian wine, his father and his mother (for the law requires the joint accusation by both his parents—Sanh. 71ᵃ; Maimon. H. Mamrim VII, 10) would bring about his being stoned to death? This never did and never will happen!" And the student of Scripture cannot fail to perceive that by prescribing the original law (Deut. XXI, 18-21), Moses intended to restrict the parental authority over the life and death of the child, generally exercised among ancient nations; and the Rabbis abridged it still more.—As regards the razing of a city the majority of the inhabitants of which simultaneously embrace idolatry—this, too, the Rabbi declares to be an unheard of event, and confidently predicts its never occurring (Sanh. 71ᵃ; Cf. supra n. 88).

[107] Yerush. Haggiga II, § 2, p. 77ᵈ sq., where it is related that eighty women were engaged in practising witchcraft; that the sage named, who was at the time chief of the Synhedrion (cf. infra § 55), discovered them and had them executed for this nefarious offense.

[108] Graetz, Geschichte d. Juden III, 163.—That the occurrence was a rarity as well as unaccountable (since idolatry, the mainspring of witchcraft was not rampant in Judea at that time) is certainly true; but it seems equally true that something

whole Talmudic account thereof defective. Only homicide would seem to have been of more frequent occurrence than any other atrocious crime, if the frequency with which the Talmudists, in illustrating judicial proceedings, refer to it be accepted as a criterion.[109] — Following this example, we shall

---

of the kind did happen. It is referred to in both the Palestinean and Babylonian Talmud (l. c. and id. Sanh. VI, § 9, p. 23$_c$; Babli ib. 45^b) and in contemporaneous Rabbinic lore (Sifre II, § 221) as to a well authenticated event, and is not incompatible with the characteristic zeal of its author. The Talmud (Yer. Sanh. ib. § 5, p. 23^b bot.) explicitly states that "the hands of Simon ben Shettah were hot," i. e. he was exceedingly severe in judgment, and relates that he thereby drew upon himself the bitter resentment of the families of those who had experienced the pain of his iron rule. The consequences were terrible to him. Some of his enemies conspired against him, to obtain revenge. They accused his only son of a capital crime, and so skilfully did they plan their charge and frame their evidence, that the innocent youth was convicted and executed (cf. infra n. 239). Rashi (Sanh. 44^b) and some learned and discriminating writers of modern times connect the two stories, and consider the latter as a complement to the former.

[109] E. g., the court enquires of the witnesses, whether they knew the *victim*, and whether the *death-blow* was struck immediately after the administration of the warning (Sanh. 40^a: Maimon. H. Sanh. XII, 1). On opening the proceedings, the court is to encourage the accused, addressing him in such terms as: If thou hast not *killed* the person, thou hast nothing to fear (Sanh. 32^b). Illustrating how witnesses might be convicted of *falsum* (cf. supra § 31), the Talmud instances the supposititious question by the confuting witnesses (infra § 95, n. 317): How do ye testify thus in the face of the fact that, at the time ye allege to have witnessed the commission of the *murder*, ye were with us at another place (Maccoth 5^a). So also the prince's objection to the abolition of capital punishment: "These, too,

pause here to review briefly what, in their opinion, constituted this crime, and how its different grades were treated.

5. HOMICIDE.

§ 33. Like modern law, the Talmud recognizes three species of homicide: *justifiable*, *excusable*, and *felonious;* but it knows also of a fourth species which might be termed *culpable*, and which is a light degree of the felonious. We shall consider them separately, and in the order of their criminality.

§ 34. *Homicide is justifiable:* 1, in the execution of the condemned criminals by the legal executioners.[110] 2, In defense of human life; thus if one attempts the life of another, the crime should be prevented, if necessary, by the killing of the would-be criminal.[111] 3, In defense of chastity. If one attempts to commit rape, or adultery, or incest, or pederasty,[112] his death,

---

would spread *bloodshed* in Israel" (Maccoth 7a; supra n. 68). —Still it must not be concluded from these and similar Talmudic references, that murder was necessarily of very frequent occurrence among the ancient Jews (cf. supra n. 33. 87). In times of peace history can point to but little bloodshed in Israel's state; and what is here quoted comes down to us from the troublous times of the declining years of Israel's independence, when foreign customs had invaded Palestinean homes; when Grecian and Roman characteristics superseded the peaceful and moral habits of the Jews who then became divided among themselves into parties and factions, and internal strife doubtlessly induced an occasional murder as a natural consequence.

[110] Cf. infra § 121.

[111] Cf. infra § 36.

[112] By the Attic law it was justifiable in the husband to slay an adulterer if caught *in ipso delicto;* or in the father or the brother

brought about in the act of preventing the crime, is justified. 4, In self-defense, and that not only when one directly attempts his life, but also when he discovers a burglar on his premises during the night.[113]— In all these cases of prevention, the killing is justifiable if done, with a view to prevention, before the crime has been accomplished, and only when prevention

---

to slay a paramour caught in the same way with his daughter or his sister. Even when thus caught with a concubine, the paramour could lawfully be killed by her master, if the status of her children was that of free men (cf. Smith 770a.) Similar to this was the law of Rome. Modern law, while justifying the woman's killing one who attempts to ravish her, and the husband's or father's killing the one who attempts rape on his wife or his daughter, condemns the killing of an adulterer who is such by the consent of the woman (Blackstone IV, 181).— The Talmud draws no distinction between rape and adultery in this particular, and prescribes it as a duty devolving not only upon immediate relations, but upon every law-abiding citizen, to prevent by all necessary force the commission of the crime (Sanh. 73a; Maimon. H. Rozeah I, 6–12).

[113] The Bible says: "If the thief be found breaking in, and be smitten that he die, there shall be no blood-guiltiness for him" (Exodus XXII, 2), whereupon the Talmud remarks: The burglar certainly intends to murder thee if he meet with resistance at thy hands, and the rule is: "Kill the one attempting unlawfully to kill thee" (Sanh. 72a). But a distinction is made between the criminal's entering the premises by the regular way of ingress—the door, for instance, or by breaking in, *i. e.* entering by an irregular method. In the former case he must not be killed, unless he persists in trespassing after being duly warned off the premises (Sanh. 72b; Rashi ad. l. s. v. Zoo; Maimon. H. Geneba IX, 8 sq).—There is, however, in that case no distinction between his being killed by the party on whose premises he trespasses, or by any other person.

can be effected by no other means, as, for instance, by maiming the culprit; otherwise it is considered culpable.[114]—The commission of no other crime, however heinous in the eyes of the law, and however dangerous to the institutions of the country, may be prevented by such violent measures;[115] and no other species of homicide is so free from guilt and consequent punishment as the justifiable.

§ 35. By *excusable* homicide the Talmud understands two species: the *fortuitous* and the *accidental*.[116] Thus, if a ladder breaks under an ascending man, who falls upon and kills a by-stander, this is fortuitous; but when the man, in descending the ladder, falls down upon and kills a person, the killing is accidental.[117]

---

[114] Sanh. 74ª; Maimon. II. Rozeah I, 13. to which, however, no death penalty at human hands is attached (cf. infra § 36).

[115] "The one uniform, principle that runs through our own and all other laws seems to be this: that where a crime, in itself capital, is endeavored to be committed by force, it is lawful to repel that force by the death of the party attempting" (Blackstone IV, 181).—The Talmud is more tender where human life is concerned. While it authorizes or commands the prevention of the above crimes, if necessary, by the death of the person attempting them, it discriminates between crimes against humanity (which are *mala in se*), and those against religion (which are *mala prohibita*), even where the latter are of the deepest dye, as idolatry (cf. supra n. 89), though, indeed, the penalty of both, after due trial and conviction, is death (cf. Maimon. II. Rozeah I, 11; Sanh. 73ª).

[116] By the first is meant homicide which is the result of the highest degree of chance, without premeditation or negligence; the second, though also the result of chance, is still not in so high a degree as the former.

[117] Maccoth 7ᵇ; Maimon. II. Rozeah VI, 12. 14.—In order that a case of homicide be classed under the accidental, the

So also when a parent or a teacher, while engaged in the discharge of his duty of instructing his child or his pupil in *something useful,* chastises him and occasions his death, this is fortuitous,—provided he uses not too much force nor an instrument calculated to produce death; otherwise the death of the victim will be accounted as accidental.[118] Or when an officer of the court, *servato juris ordine,* in administering the legally prescribed flagellation, causes the death of the convict, it is fortuitous; but when, by mistake, he administers more than the prescribed number of stripes, it is accidental.[119] Or when an authorized and practical

---

Talmud requires that the death-stroke be given while the author thereof is in a downward motion, probably because there is then a better opportunity for observing the surroundings, and taking precautions to avoid accident. Or is this discrimination based on the scientific principle, established centuries after the close of that microcosmic compilation, the Talmud, that the velocity of a body is accelerated as it approaches the earth, and it therefore requires more care and circumspection in its downward course to avoid danger?

[118] Maccoth 8a; Maimon. H. Rozeah V, 5 sq. Cf. Tosefta B. Kama, ed. Zuck., IX, § 11; Sifre I, § 160.—In common law, too, "where a parent is moderately correcting his child, or a master his apprentice or scholar, or an officer punishing a criminal, and happens to occasion his death, it is only misadventure: for the act of correction is lawful; but if he exceeds the bounds of moderation, either in the manner, the instrument, or the quantity of punishment, and death ensues, it is manslaughter at least, and in some cases (according to circumstances) murder" (Blackstone IV, 182).

[119] Maccoth 8a, 22b; Maimon. H. Sanh. XV, 12. Cf. Tosefta Guittin IV, § 6; ib. B. Kama VI, § 17; IX, § 11; ib. Maccoth II, § 5.

physician administers medicine, or performs a surgical operation, which instead of curing, kills the patient, his death is fortuitous;[120] but when the patient's death is the result of the physician's mistake, it is accidental.[121]—Fortuitous homicide being devoid of every semblance of design and negligence on the part of the unfortunate perpetrator, the Talmud attaches no blame or penalty thereto, and even the *vindex* is enjoined not to avenge the blood.[122] Accidental homicide, on the other hand, though also free from mischievous intention, implies negligence, and is therefore not altogether exempt from punishment, which is death at the hands of the avenger, or exile.[123]

---

[120] Sanh. 84b; Mekhilta Nezikin, § 4.

[121] Tosefta l. c.—By the Attic law, too, a physician who caused the death of a patient by a mistake or by professional ignorance, was excused, but although he was excused, he was not considered free from pollution: this had to be expiated by lustrations (Smith 770ª). By common law, the regular physician cannot be held criminally responsible in such cases, but the impostor may be convicted of manslaughter (Blackstone IV, 197).

[122] Maccoth 10b; Maimon. H. Rozeah VII, 3.

[123] Maccoth 11b; et al.—Among the Greeks those who were convicted of unintentional homicide, not perfectly excusable, were condemned to leave the country for a year. They were obliged to depart within a certain time and by a certain route, and to expiate their offense by certain prescribed rites. It was their duty, also, to appease, either by presents or humble entreaty and submission, the relatives of the deceased, or, if he had none within a certain degree, the members of his clan. If the convict could prevail upon the latter to grant him permission, he might return even before the year had expired (Smith 770b). By Talmudic law, based on the Mosaic code

§ 36. Homicide is *culpable:* 1. When it is the result of gross negligence, as, for instance, when one is engaged in razing a wall near a thoroughfare, and unwittingly throws the debris on a passenger and thereby causes his death.[124] 2. When one, in his endeavor to prevent the commission of an atrocious crime, intentionally kills the would-be criminal, without trying

---

(Num. XXXV, 25), this was not permitted (cf. supra n. 76. infra § 134).

[124] B. Kama 33[b]; Maccoth 8[a]; Maimon. II. Rozeah VI, 6.— Among the Romans, a person who throws or pours anything from a place or upper chamber upon a road which is frequented by passengers, or upon a place where people are in the habit of standing, is fined with double the amount of damage he causes by his negligence; if he thereby injures a person, he is obliged to pay the expenses of a medical attendant, remunerate the sufferer for his loss of time and the like; and if the offense results in the death of a person, he must pay a fine of fifty *aurei*, or about $200 (Smith 342[a]). By common law, "where a person does an act, lawful in itself, but in an unlawful manner, and without due caution and circumspection: as when a workman flings down a stone or piece of timber into the street, and kills a man, this may be either misadventure, manslaughter or murder, according to the circumstances under which the original act was done; if it were in a country village, where few passengers are, and he calls out to all people to have a care, it is misadventure only; but if it were in London, or other populous town, where people are continually passing, it is manslaughter, though he gives loud warning; and murder, if he knows of their passing, and gives no warning at all, for then it is malice against all mankind" (Blackstone IV, 192). According to Talmudic jurisprudence, it would be purely fortuitous in the first case; accidental in the second; and culpable in the third, unless the workman had been duly warned, on pain of death, not to throw anything on the streets where people were at the time.

other means of prevention.[125] 3. When committed through ignorance of the law: as when one believes that the law does not forbid the killing of the intended victim.[126]—In all these cases, though the judiciary have no legal authority to punish the offender capitally, the avenger of the blood may kill him with impunity, no sanctuary protecting him.[127]—4. When the criminal is not the immediate cause of the death, as when he is an accessory before the fact: procuring, counselling or commanding another to commit the crime,[128]

---

[125] Sanh. 74a; Maimon. H. Rozeah I, 13. Cf. supra § 34.

[126] Maccoth 7b; Maimon. l. c. VI, 9. Cf. supra § 16.—By common law, only ignorance or mistake of fact excuses a crime, but not an error in point of law; so "if a man thinks he has a right to kill a person excommunicated or outlawed, wherever he meets him, and does so, this is wilful murder" (Blackstone IV, 27). By Talmudic law this is culpable homicide only, the rule in such cases being that, even though the person be duly condemned to death, no one, except the proper executioners (cf. infra § 121), has a right to kill him; still no capital punishment can be imposed on the perpetrator, since his victim had already forfeited his life and had virtually no longer any being (Tosefta B. Kama IX, § 15; Sifre I, § 161; Arakhin 6b).

[127] Maccoth 7b, 9a; Maimon. l. c. VI, 5.—We have already seen that only homicide *per infortunium* is subject to the punishment of exile (supra § 26, n. 76); hence this one is excluded; for while the perpetrator was unfortunate in being ignorant, the act was willful.

[128] Kidd. 43a.—Some authorities consider this a plain case of *murder*, and would see it punished as such. These base their opinion on the case of David and Uriah (II Sam. XI), where though David did not lay hands on the victim (ib. 17), the prophet nevertheless charged him with murder, saying: "Thou hast slain him with the sword of the children of Ammon" (ib. XII, 9). The Halakha, however, is as stated above; and, with

or exposing the victim at a place where wild beasts
may, and eventually do kill him.[129] 5. When the per-

reference to other crimes, even the stricter authorities admit
that where the agent is the sole beneficiary of the crime, the
instigator cannot be punished (Kidd. l. c. Cf. Tosafoth ib. s. v.
Shello).—By Attic law, when one instigated another to commit
a murder, and the deed was accomplished, he was deemed a
murderer (Smith 769ª); but in other Grecian states, the criminality of conspirators against human life, was independent of
the result of the conspiracy, and the penalty upon conviction,
was the same as that incurred by actual murderers (ib. 171ª).
Common law punishes the accessory before the fact as the principal (Blackstone IV, 39); but the advisability of discriminating between the person procuring the commission of a crime,
and him who actually commits it, agreeably to Talmudic jurisprudence, is ably advanced by the great commentator (l. c.).
He argues that, "if a distinction were constantly to be made
between the punishment of principals and accessories, even *before* the fact, the latter to be treated with a little less severity
than the former, it might prevent the perpetration of many
crimes, by increasing the difficulty of finding a person to execute the deed itself, as his danger would be greater than that of
his accomplices, by reason of the difference of his punishment."
—The Talmud makes this distinction because, to render the
criminal liable to capital punishment, the crime must be committed by himself (cf. infra § 43), by his direct and immediate
force (Sanh. 77ᵇ; Maimon. II. Rozeah III, 13), i. e. he must be
what is termed in common law, "a principal in the first degree."
So if A puts B near a waterfall, even where the water is certain
to come eventually, and it does come and drown the victim,
this is culpable homicide only, for at the moment the culprit
placed his intended victim there, the cause of death was not
there; but if A puts B right under the cataract, and B is drowned,
this is murder (Sanh. l. c.).

[129] Sanh. 76ᵇ, sq.; Maimon. II. Rozeah III, 9.—By common
law, "where a man has a beast that is used to do mischief:
and he knowing it, *suffers* it to go abroad, and it kills a man;

petrator is the direct cause of the calamity, but the victim has had a chance of averting it: as when one willfully and maliciously pushes a person into fire or water, whence the victim can easily escape with his life.[130] 6. When the death is the result of miscarried felonious intent; as when one intends to kill a certain person, or even an animal, but the missile, taking a different direction, strikes and kills an unintended party.[131] 7. When the deed is accomplished by more than one party: as when several men together club one to death, or shoot at one, and it cannot be clearly ascertained which of them was the immediate cause of his death.[132] 8. When the missile miscarries and strikes a part not aimed at by the thrower. Thus, A using a missile which is heavy and formidable enough to kill a person when it is struck at his thorax, but presumably not elsewhere, aims at one of the less vital spots upon

---

even this is manslaugter in the owner [by Jewish law, the beast was killed, and its owner fined—Ex. XXI, 28—32; B. Kama 42, et al.]: but if he had purposely *turned it loose*, though barely to frighten people, and make what is called sport, it is as much murder, as if he had incited a bear or a dog to worry them " (Blackstone IV, 197).

[130] Sanh. 76b; Maimon. H. Rozeah III, 9.—But where the criminal prevents his escape, it is murder.

[131] Maccoth 7b, 9a; Maimon. l. c.—Common law transfers in such cases the felonious intent from one victim to the other, and punishes the perpetrator just as if he had carried out his original intention (Blackstone IV, 201).

[132] Sifra Emor §20; Sanh. 78a. Cf. infra §§ 43, 86.—By common law, if two or more come together to do an unlawful act, of which the probable consequences might be bloodshed, as to beat a man, to commit a riot, or to rob a park: and one of them kills a man, it is murder in them all (Blackstone IV, 200).

B's body, and causes death: or, *vice versa*, A aims the same missile at B's thorax, but it strikes a less dangerous spot, and contrary to probabilities, kills B.[133]

§ 37. The penalty of culpable homicide depends partly on the exigencies of the times. If the court finds that circumstances call for examples of rigor, the culpable slayer is executed;[134] otherwise he is scourged and imprisoned.[135]

6. MURDER.

§ 38. Homicide is *felonious* when all conditions required by the Talmud and enumerated above (§ 13, sq.), have been duly complied with, and there is none of the justifiable, excusable, or even of the culpable circumstances mitigating the crime. Thus, if one wilfully and maliciously kills a human being,[136] male or female, old or young,[137] Israelite or non-Israelite, free-

---

[133] Sanh. 78ᵃ; Maimon. H. Rozeah IV, 2.

[134] Sanh. 46ᵃ. Cf. supra § 9.—Coke somewhere says: *Transgressione multiplicata, crescat pœna inflictio.* When transgression is multiplied, let the infliction of punishment be increased.

[135] M. Katan 16ᵃ; Sanh. 81ᵇ. Cf. supra § 24, n. 82.

[136] To kill a child in its mother's womb, is not murder, but a finable offense (Exodus XXI. 22; Mekhilta Nezikin § 8; B. Kama 49ᵃ. Cf. infra n. 355), as in Attica, where a civil, but not a criminal action could be brought against a person procuring an abortion. Among the Romans, this crime (*partus abactio,* or *abortus procuratio*) seems to have originally been unnoticed by the laws; under the emperors, however, a woman who had procured the abortion of her own child was punished with exile, and those who gave the potion were either condemned to the mines or banished to an island (Smith 47ᵃ).

[137] By this is meant even a new born infant, provided it was born at the end of the full natural time. The prematurely born

born or slave,[138] it is murder, and its perpetrator, after due trial and conviction, undergoes the penalty of decapitation.[139] And in this respect Talmudic jurisprudence draws no distinction between a sound and a diseased victim: it is murder, even if the victim was moribund at the time the attack was made on him[140]—provided, however, his disease was not the result of blows or wounds previously received at the hands of

---

was not considered in Talmudic law as a living being, until after the thirtieth day of its life (Nidda 44ᵇ, sq.; Yer. Yebamoth XI. § 9, p. 12ᵇ top; Maimon. II. Rozeah II, 6). In this the Talmud differs from common law, according to which, "if a child be born alive and dieth by reason of the potion or bruises it received in the womb, it seems by the better opinion to be murder in such as administered or gave them" (Blackstone IV, 198).

[138] Mekhilta Nezikin § 7; Maimon. II. Rozeah II. 10.—In the case of the slaying of a slave the Talmud makes the same distinction as in the case of the slaying of a child or pupil (supra § 35, n. 118.—Mekhilta l. c.; Sifre I, § 160; Maimon ib. 14). So by an edict of Constantine, the Roman master was allowed to chastise his slave with rods or imprisonment; and if death accidentally ensued, he was guilty of no crime; but if he struck him with a club or stone, and thereby occasioned his death, he was guilty of murder (Blackstone IV, 183).

[139] Sanh. 76ᵇ; Maimon. II. Rozeah I, 1.

[140] Neither does common law make any distinction between the killing of a sound or a diseased victim. "However feeble the condition of the deceased may have been, or however short his tenure of life, it is equally murder, as if the person killed had been in the prime of youth and vigor" (Roscoe 574); and Blackstone (IV, 197) cites a case of an "unnatural son who exposed his sick father to the air, against his will, by reason whereof he died," and the son was found guilty of murder.

other parties, human or brute.[141] On the other hand, if the criminal is the diseased person, the legal consequences depend on the witnesses of the crime: if the offense is committed in the presence of a competent tribunal,[142] the offender may suffer the penalty of death; but when it is perpetrated in the presence of private individuals, he escapes the ordeal of a trial for his life, and is guilty of culpable homicide only.[143]

---

[141] In this case the offender would be guilty of culpable homicide. But no man is considered diseased in the sense of this proviso, unless physicians declare him to be incurable, and assert that, even if nothing will intervene to accelerate his death, the disease will soon end his life (Maimon. H. Rozeah II, 8. Cmp. Maccoth 7ª).

[142] Cf. infra § 69.

[143] Sanh. 78ª; Maimon. H. Rozeah II, 9.—The distinction here made readily suggests the modern rules governing cases of "contempt of court," which, if committed in the face of the court, may be instantly punished by imprisonment, even without the formality of an examination (cf. Blackstone IV, 286). An assault in court was formerly very rigorously punished. "By ancient common law before the conquest, striking in the king's court of justice or drawing a sword therein, was a capital felony: and our modern law retains so much of the ancient severity, as only to exchange the loss of life for the loss of the offending limb. Therefore a stroke or a blow in such a court of justice, whether blood be drawn or not, or even assaulting a judge sitting in the court, by drawing a weapon, without any blow struck, is punishable with the loss of the right hand, imprisonment for life, and forfeiture of goods, and of the profits of his lands during life" (ib. 125). Now, as it is highly improbable that a full court (twenty-three competent judges—(infra § 53) should be assembled to witness the commission of a murder outside of the court house, it might be presumed that such an event could happen in the court house only, while the court

§ 39. Nor does it matter how and by what means the crime is accomplished. Whether the killing is done with the bare hand or with an instrument of any kind, by blows or by suffocation, by burning or by drowning: it is murder;[144] provided that the victim

is engaged in the administration of justice; wherefore the offender is severely dealt with for both the shedding of the blood and contempt.—The true reason, however, for this discrimination seems to be the following:

Talmudic jurisprudence recognizes such testimony only, as when confuted, would subject the witness to the same penalty which the accused would have suffered, had the testimony not been confuted (cf. supra § 31, infra § 95); wherefore the Rabbis have established the legal maxim: "Testimony to which the law of confutation cannot be fully applied deserves not the name of testimony" (B. Kama 75ᵇ; Sanh. 41ᵃ, et al.). Now, in our case, if the witnesses to the crime be laymen, their testimony would be subject to be confuted by other witnesses, and should they be convicted of *falsum*, they could not undergo the same *degree* of punishment which they *intend* (cf. Deut. XIX, 19) to inflict on the alleged criminal: they having conspired to bring about the premature death of one who is already doomed to death by his malady, while they themselves are in good physical condition, likely to enjoy many years of life. But where the judges themselves are witnesses to the crime, there is no need for other testimony: they may convict him on their personal observation. For although the general rule of Talmudic law is: "The witness to a crime must not turn judge of the criminal"—for having himself witnessed the commission of the deed, he may be too excited to look for extenuating circumstances (cf. Rosh Hash. 26ᵃ; B. Kama 90ᵇ; infra n. 293).—here they need not be particularly anxious to bring about an acquittal of the criminal, he being already a dying man (cf. Sanh. 81ᵇ; Tosafoth ib. s. v. *Wenigmar*).

[144] Sifre I, § 160; Sanh. 76ᵇ.—The Talmud requires that, in order to convict of the crime of murder, violence on the part of

MURDER. 71

had no chance of escape before being physically disabled,[145] and that his death was the natural and immediate consequence of the violence exercised on him by the criminal.[146]

§ 40. The perpetration of a crime having been reported, it devolves upon the court to hold a preliminary examination, an inquest.[147] If the victim be still alive, the court must carefully examine his condition, and pass an opinion as to the probabilities of his recovery. When they opine that he is not fatally injured, the prisoner may be liberated on payment of

---

the accused must first be proved: an *act* touching the body of the victim. But where there is no such act of violence; as when one frightens another to death, there is legally no murder (cf. B. Kama 91ᵃ; Maimon. H. Hobel II, 7).—In short, the criminal must have put his hand to the deed (Kidd. 43ᵇ, Maimon. H. Gezella III, 11).—The same is the rule of common law. While it considers it murder whether the killing was done by poisoning, striking, starving, drowning, or by any other of the thousand ways in which human nature may be overcome (cf. Blackstone IV, 196), "it is not murder to work on the imagination so that death ensues, or to call feelings into so strong an exercise as to produce a fatal malady" (ib. 197, n. 30).

[145] Cf. supra § 36, n. 130.

[146] Cf. B. Kama 85ᵇ; Sanh. 77ᵇ; Maimon. II. Hobel II, 20.— In common law, "If a wound itself be not mortal, but by improper applications become so, and terminates fatally, and it can be clearly shown that the medicine and not the wound was the cause of death, the party who inflicted the wound will not be guilty of murder" (Blackstone IV, 197, n. 30).

[147] Cf. Sanh. 37ᵃ.—Among the Greeks, three months were allowed for the preliminary enquiry in a case of murder, and there were three special hearings, one in each month, before the matter was ready to be regularly tried (Smith 769ᵇ).

legal damages;[148] but when they regard the injuries as necessarily fatal, the criminal is detained under guard to await the results of his crime. If the victim ultimately recovers, the prisoner is required to pay the damages; but when death ensues, even if in the interval the patient improved, and gave promise of recovery, the prisoner is tried for his life.[149]

---

[148] Sanh. 78b; Tosefta ib. IX, § 1.—These damages are quintuple. 1, For deterioration in value: the victim is appraised as if he were to be sold in the slave-market, and the difference between his values with or without the injury is awarded to him. 2. For his pains: an estimate is made how much one would charge and voluntarily undergo like pains. 3. For medical attendance: an estimate is made of the expenses the sufferer necessarily must incur in that direction. 4. For the loss of time: it is estimated how much a hireling, in a like crippled condition, could earn during the probable period of the victim's disability. 5. For the mortification: it is estimated how much a man would take and subject himself to a like insult. The second and fifth assessments are made with due reference to the physical condition and social standing of both the criminal and the victim, and all damages must be paid at once (B. Kama 83b, sq.; Maimon. II. Hobel I. 2; II, 9; II. 14, 15; III, 1). When once liberated, the culprit cannot again be tried for that offense, even when the victim subsequently grows worse, and dies from the effects of his injuries (Sanh. l. c.) By the Attic law, even when the injuries did not prove fatal, if the criminal was found guilty of *intended* murder, his property was confiscated and he was exiled (Smith 135a). By common law, 'if one give another a stroke which, though in itself not mortal, but with good care the injured party might be cured, yet if death results from it within the year and a day, it is homicide or murder, as the case may be, and so it has always been ruled' (Roscoe 573).

[149] Sanh. 78b; Maimon. II. Rozeah IV. 5.

§ 41. As even medical skill cannot, in many instances and without due reference to the peculiar circumstances in the case, decide as to whether death resulted from natural causes, and was only accelerated by the violence, or solely from the acts of the criminal; and as persons of science, in order to form their own opinions, must at least partly rely on external circumstances,—it is incumbent upon the court at the inquest critically to observe and to note all accompanying facts with the greatest possible accuracy. Thus, if the killing was effected by the brute force of the criminal, without any instrument, the court examines the physical build of both the victim and the criminal, and judges whether the former was not too powerful a man to be overcome and killed by the latter;[150] if, by striking with a missile, the weight and bulk of the missile must be considered, and it must be judged whether that missile[151] is at all likely to cause death, and if so, whether it was sufficient to kill by striking at the spot it did.[152]—If the criminal caused the death of

---

[150] Sifre I, § 160; Maimon. II, Rozeah III. 5.

[151] If the missile is lost among others and it cannot be ascertained which one was actually used, the smallest of all is selected and considered as the one (Tosefta Sanh. XII, § 4. Cmp. Mekhilta Nezikin § 6).

[152] Sanh. 78ª; sq.; Maimon. H. Rozeah III, 1.—The object of the examination is to establish the malicious intent of the offender (Sifre I, § 160; Maimon. l. c. 6), and, as in common law, if the missile is found likely to produce the result, the prisoner is presumed to have used it with the intention of killing; if, on the contrary, it is a weapon not likely to produce death, that presumption is wanting (Roscoe 588). For this reason a metal instrument, with a point or edge, need have

his victim by pushing him into fire or water, the court must enquire whether there was no chance of escape; and if by throwing him down a precipice, the depth of the fall must be carefully measured, and it must be judged whether that was likely to bring about the result.[153] In short, the court must critically examine every circumstance, however insignificant, that might directly or indirectly have had some bearing on the result of the crime; and if any reasonable doubt arises as to whether death is indeed the direct effect of violence, and not of a natural cause, the benefit of that doubt is invariably given to the prisoner, as will appear later on.[154]

§ 42. Although in general, to convict a person of murder the law requires positive proof that the crime was prompted by malice, there may be cases in which the criminal will be found guilty even without malicious premeditation. For instance, when one kills another in compliance with the latter's own request or command;[155] or when one is engaged in idle and

---

neither weight nor bulk, for even a needle can cause death (Sifre l. c.; Sanh. 76b; Maimon. l. c. 4).

[153] Sanh. 76b; Maimon. H. Rozeah III, 7, 9. Cf. supra n. 130.

[154] Shebuoth 46b; Hullin 10. Cf. infra § 93.

[155] Cf. B. Kama 92a, 93a.—This follows from the Talmudic maxim: "There is no agency in crime" (Kidd. 42b; B. Kama 59; Yer. Terumoth VII, 44c bot., et al.); and since crime is forbidden by a higher power than the party ordering its commission, the executor of a criminal order cannot be considered an agent, but is the principal, and as such responsible.—So in common law. "he who kills another upon his desire or demand, is in the judgment of the law as much a murderer, as if he had done it merely of his own head; and the person killed is not

dangerous sports, as throwing stones or playing ball, and though warned that he is endangering the lives of passengers, continues to play, and unintentionally strikes a man and kills him.[156]

§ 43. In order that the full penalty attached to the crime should be inflicted upon the criminal, Talmudic jurisprudence requires that the crime shall have been committed as a whole by one person, unless it cannot be executed without assistance.[157] According to this rule, the person who is the immediate cause of the loss of life, is answerable with his own life; and with regard to capital punishment, no cognizance is taken in Talmudic jurisprudence of accomplices or accessories to murder. Therefore when several shoot at a person missiles, the size and weight of neither of which is likely to cause his death, and then one of them hurls at the same person a missile which is likely to produce that result, this last one is responsible with his life for that of the victim, while the others escape capital punishment.[158] When several parties simultaneously,

---

looked upon as a *felo de se*, inasmuch as his assent was merely void, being against the law of God and man" (Blackstone IV, 190, n. 15).

[156] Sanh. 77b.—By the Attic law it was excusable to kill one in gymnastic combat (Smith 770ᵃ), but common law agrees with the Talmudic, laying down the rule: "whenever death is the consequence of idle, dangerous, or unlawful sports, or of heedless, wanton and indiscreet acts, without a felonious intent, the party causing the death is guilty of manslaughter" (Blackstone IV, 184).

[157] Sabbath 92b; Beza 22a; Maimon. II. Sabbath I. 17. Cf. supra § 36, n. 132.

[158] Sanh. 78b. Cf. infra n. 297.

or even closely following each other, beat one, and cause his death, none of them is punished capitally.[159]

§ 44. Still less punishable, though not less of a criminal, is the self-murderer;[160] *i. e.* one who, while in full possession of his senses, declares himself about to commit suicide, and thereupon deliberately kills himself.[161] Being beyond the reach of human justice, the

---

[159] By this we certainly do not mean to imply that, under the Talmudic dispensation, murder in any shape or degree could be perpetrated with impunity. Far from it. All that the Rabbis aimed after was the avoiding of inflicting capital punishment; but they did not fail to protect life. The destroyers of human life, whom the law could not visit with capital punishment—justifiable and excusable homicide excepted,—were imprisoned (supra §§ 24, 36). In all cases of capital crime, when the accused was found guilty, he was duly executed; when not, when the slightest preliminary requirement for conviction had not been duly complied with, he was declared to be not guilty, and thereupon set at liberty,—in some cases, after receiving a flogging (Maimon. II. Sanh. XVIII, 8). In cases of bloodshed, however, the law went further and was more rigorous. Whoever occasioned an illegal loss of life, was prevented from repeating his atrocities by being deprived of his freedom (Sanh. 81ᵇ; Maimon. II. Rozeah IV, 9).

[160] B. Kama 91ᵇ; Gen. R. XXXIV; Semahoth II, § 1.—It is remarkable that the Hebrew language has no regular term expressive of this crime, and Rabbinic lore resorts to circumlocution. Thus: "Consciously destroying one's self" is the name of the crime; "He who consciously destroyed himself" the appellation of the criminal. Most probably this want of a technical term is owing to the rarity of suicides among the ancient Hebrews; for if "the existence of a word bears testimony to the existence of the thing" it denotes, or of the act it expresses, the non-existence of a proper term testifies to the non-existence, or at least to the people's ignorance of the thing or act.

[161] Semahoth II, 2; Maimon. II. Abel I, 11; Yore. Deah. c. 345.—So tender is the Talmud of man's honor, even posthumous,

criminal is left to receive his just desert at the tribunal of God.[162] But as a slight manifestation of the abhorrence with which the crime is looked upon, the Rabbis forbid all marks of mourning for its author, such as wearing sombre apparel, eulogizing him, and like manifestations of grief.[163]

---

that it would not permit one to be called a suicide, unless there was not the least doubt that he was such. When a person was found dead, no verdict of suicide was rendered, even when circumstances very strongly pointed to him as the immediate author of his own death, as when he was seen throwing himself down a precipice. In such cases death was attributed to accident.

[162] B. Kama 91b; Gen. R. XXXIV; Maimon. H. Rozeah II, 2.—In Attica, suicide was not considered a crime in point of law, though it seems to have been deemed an offense against religion; for, by the custom of the country, the hand of the suicide was buried apart from his body. In England, the suicide was ignominiously buried on the highway, with a stake driven through his body, and all his goods and chattels were forfeited to the King: "hoping that his care for either his own reputation, or the welfare of his family, would be some motive to restrain him from so desperate and wicked an act" (Blackstone IV, 189 sq.). The Rabbis took the more philosophic view of the crime, and concluded to "neither honor the criminal nor insult him" (Semahoth II, 1); for, as Beccaria (§ 32) says: "He who deliberately dispenses with the happiness of life, and hates it so strongly as to prefer an unhappy eternity, cannot be moved to restraint by the less effective and more remote consideration of children and parents."

[163] Semahoth II, 1; Maimon. H. Abel I, 11.—As in homicide so in suicide, there are cases which the Talmud considers excusable or justifiable, if not meritorious. Such are: when the chief of a vanquished army is sure of disgrace and death at the hands of the exulting conqueror, as was the case of Saul (1 Sam. XXXI, 4); or when one has reason to fear being forced to renounce his religion (Guittin 57b. Cf. II Macc. XIV, 37-46). Under all

7. Persons Indictable.

§ 45. According to the Talmud, all persons, with the few exceptions to be presently stated, are amenable to the laws of the country, and therefore indictable for crime. As the Hebrew commonwealth was based upon the principle of national unity and equality,[164]

---

other circumstances, the Rabbis consider it criminal to shorten one's own life, even when the person is undergoing tortures which must soon end his earthly career (Ab. Zara 18ª).

[164] The idea of national unity was, in the age of its originator, Moses, as new and startling as the doctrine of the divine unity. The most ancient sages made their ideas of the material universe the type of their political and social institutions. The Egyptian priest regarded the universality of things as composed of two distinct essences: the one intellectual and active, the other physical and passive (Hesiod I, 2). This philosophic dogma had a predominating influence on the civil state. In the political system framed by them, the spiritual essence of the universe was the symbol of the sacerdotal aristocracy; while the baser material essence represented the common people. Thus the higher and lower classes, the nobility and commonalty, were separated by a gulf, as impassable as that which divides the inhabitants of different planets. Moses, endowed with a capacity and animated with a principle higher than any preceding philosopher or statesman, rejecting this doctrine of dualism in the formation of his commonwealth, substituted in its place the principle of national unity. His, however, was not that species of unity, which the world has since so often seen, in which vast multitudes of human beings are delivered up to the arbitrary will of one man. It was a unity, effected by the abolition of caste; a unity, founded on the principle of equal rights; a unity, in which the whole people formed the state, contrary to what happened in Egypt, where the priesthood was the state, and contrary to the celebrated declaration of Louis

the Israelite, the Levite and the priest, the freeborn and the slave, were alike subject to the laws. Even the high priest could be called upon to answer before a competent judiciary for his infraction of the laws, and judgment given against and executed upon him.[165] Talmudic jurisprudence knows of no *privilegium clericale*, which so much troubled other states in earlier and even later ages.[166] The Jewish legislators, from

---

XIV, who avowed himself to be the state (Wines, B. II, c. I). This principle manifests itself, in every ancient Jewish institution, its spirit pervading every page of the Talmud, the professed commentary of the Mosaic system (cf. supra n. 33). Nowhere, however, does this spirit appear more clearly, nor pregnant with more importance, than in the Talmudic enactments respecting life and liberty, although they were elaborated in ages of barbarism and tyranny, when penal laws magnified the offense according to the littleness of the offender, considering that as almost venial in a man of high rank, which brought terrible retribution upon persons of inferior rank (cf. Montesquieu, B. VI, c. XV; Pike, History of Crime I, p. 13).

[165] Sanh. 18ᵃ; Maimon. H. Kle Mikdash I, 8.

[166] One needs to be reminded only of the difficulties under which Europe labored during the supremacy of papal authority, especially from and after the beginning of the twelfth century, when not only every one who had received the tonsure, but "orphans and widows, the stranger and the poor, the pilgrim and the leper, under the appellation of persons in distress (*miserabiles personae*) came within the peculiar cognizance and protection of the church; nor could they be sued before any lay tribunal. And the whole body of crusaders, or such as merely took the vow of engaging in one, enjoyed the same clerical privileges" (Hallam l. c., c. VII). By Talmudic law, based on Scriptural ground (Exodus XXI, 14), the priest, even while engaged in the performance of his sacerdotal offices at the altar, is subject to the civil law, and must be removed thence to suffer the penalty of his crime (Mekhilta Nezikin, § 4; Sanh. 35ᵇ).

Moses down to the completion of the Talmud (in the fifth century C. E.), were too patriotic and discreet to tolerate in their midst a body of men protected by, and at the same time independent of the laws established for all the citizens of the state. Therefore, too, were the members of the royal house of David subject to the authority of the general laws.[167]

§ 46. *Exceptions.*—That "*duress per minas,* or threats and menaces which induce a fear of death or other bodily harm," exempt one from punishment for all crimes, except murder and the sexual sins, we have seen above.[168] The other exemptions are: *Deafness, Idiocy, and Nonage.* In any one of these conditions, a person is not presumed to be possessed of the capability of premeditation or of willing in general, and of malice in particular.[169] Accordingly Talmudic juris-

---

[167] Sanh. 19a: Maimon. H. Sanh. II, 5; id. II. Melakhim III, 7.—With the change of dynasties in the Maccabean epoch, the subjection of royalty to the judiciary was abolished, owing to the overt insubordination of Hyrcan II, to the enactments of the Synhedrion (Sanh. ib. Cf. Graetz III. n. 17).—In Rome we hear Emperors Severus and Antoninus asserting their supremacy to the coercive powers of the laws (Just. Inst. L. II. Tit. XVII. § 8); and Blackstone supposes the King incapable of committing a folly, much less a crime. He thus accounts for the striking omission of the law to make provision to remedy such an impossible grievance (cf. Com. I, 244 sq.; IV, 33).

[168] Cf. supra § 14 sq.—Common law says: *Actus me invito factus, non est meus actus.* An act done by me against my will is not my act (Bouvier Dict. s. v. Maxim).

[169] Makhshirin III, § 8, VI, § 1; Mekhilta Nezikin § 4.—Common law argues: "As a vicious will, without a vicious act, is no civil crime; so on the other hand, an unwarrantable act without a vicious will, is no crime at all" (Blackstone IV, 21);

prudence declares the collision with these parties to be always disadvantageous: when one injures them, he is subject to the legal penalties; but when they inflict injury, they cannot be held responsible.[170] The Talmud almost invariably cites these three classes together; but we must see what is understood by them severally.

§ 47. *Deafness*, to exempt one from punishment for crime, must be accompanied by dumbness,[171] whether congenital or adventitious.[172] When one or the other is wanting, the offender is not exempted.[173]

§ 48. By *idiot* the Talmud understands not only the confirmed lunatic, but also the monomaniac: as the one who habitually and unnecessarily exposes himself to danger; or who betrays general destructive proclivities, as by willfully tearing his clothes; or who manifests any other reprehensible idiosyncrasy.[174] The periodical maniac, however, is amenable to law for

---

wherefore "an idiot, or a person born deaf and dumb, or one who is *non compos* at the time, cannot be approver;" yet "if he who wants discretion commit a trespass against the person or possession of another, he shall be compelled in a civil action to give satisfaction for the damage" (ib. 25, n. 5).

[170] B. Kama 87ª, et al.
[171] Terumoth I. § 4; Hagiga 2ᵇ.
[172] Cf. Sifthe Daath ad Yore Deah I, § 5.—The same is the rule of common law (cf. Blackstone IV, 25).
[173] Tosefta Terumoth I, § 2; Hagiga 2ᵇ.—Roscoe (l. c. 95) says: "A person born deaf and dumb, though *prima facie* in contemplation of law an idiot, yet if it appear that he has the use of his understanding, he is criminally answerable for his acts."
[174] Yer. Terumoth I, § 1, p. 40ᵇ top; Hagiga 3ᵇ; Guittin 68ª.

actions committed during his lucid periods;[175] while temporary aberration of mind produced by the offender himself, as by drunkenness, does not exempt him from the consequences of infringing the laws of justice.[176] But when a person is so intoxicated as to be entirely unconscious of his own movements, he is considered for the time being an idiot, and not accountable for his actions committed while in that state.[177]

§ 49. *Nonage.*—The Talmud divides the age of minors into three periods: *Infancy,* from birth to six years;[178] *Impubescence,* from the beginning of the seventh year to the first day of the twelfth or thirteenth year, according as the person is a female or a male;[179] and *Adulescence,* from that age to twenty years,[180] when every

---

[175] Yer. l. c.; Tosefta Terumoth I, § 3.—So by common law. "If a lunatic has lucid intervals of understanding, he shall answer for what he does in those intervals, as if he had no deficiency" (Blackstone IV, 25).

[176] Tosefta Terumoth III, § 1; Erubin 65ᵃ.—The Roman law made allowances for this vice; but the law of England, considering how easy it is to counterfeit this excuse, and how weak an excuse it is (though real), will not suffer any man thus to privilege one crime by another (Blackstone IV, 26).—The Talmud says: "Drink not, and thou wilt not sin" (Berakhoth 29ᵇ. Cf. Tanhuma ad Gen. IX, 20; Yalkut I, § 61).

[177] Erubin 65ᵃ; Maimon. H. Ishuth IV, 18.

[178] *Ketane Ketanim* (=wee little ones). Kethuboth 65ᵇ. Cf. B. Bathra 155ᵇ.

[179] *Naaruth* (Kethuboth 29ᵃ sq.; Nidda 45ᵇ).—But neither is considered pubescent, even after reaching the prescribed age, unless he or she can show at least two hairs on any part of the body, except the head (Kidd. 16ᵃ; Nidda 45ᵇ, et al.).

[180] *Bagruth* (Kidd. 4ᵃ; B. Bathra 155ᵇ).—That stage, however, does not really begin for either, until six months and

person, except the hermaphrodite, becomes a major.[181] But while it makes these distinctions, Rabbinic law nowhere states at what particular age a person ceases to be a minor, with reference to liability to capital punishment,[182] and the student is left to learn that particular age by induction.

§ 50. That impubescents are exempt from capital punishment, there is no doubt; for the Talmud explicitly states that a child nine years and one day old, which has committed a capital crime, cannot be condemned to death.[183] Moreover, even the prodigal

---

three months respectively after the close of the preceding age (Yer. Yebamoth I, § 2, p. 3ª top; Kethuboth 39ª; Sanh. 69ª).— The division of minority into several different stages was established in Roman law also. Thus: *infancy*, from birth until the end of the seventh year; *impubescence*, from seven to twelve for females, and to fourteen for males; *adulescence*, from twelve and fourteen respectively to twenty-five, after which the persons became *majores* (Smith 537ᵇ).

[181] Kiddushin 4ª, et al.

[182] To corporal punishment a person becomes liable at the age of pubescence. Thus the prodigal son (supra § 32, n. 106) is at that age judicially flagellated or otherwise flogged for his offenses (Sifre II, § 218; Sanh. 71ª).

[183] Sanh. 69ᵇ; et al.—In common law there obtains a maxim: *Malitia supplet aetatem* (Malice supplies the want of age,—Blackstone IV. 23), and an instance is recorded (ib. 24) where a boy of *eight years* was tried for firing two barns; and it appearing that he had malice, revenge and cunning, he was found guilty, condemned and hanged accordingly.—By Talmudic law, no matter how much malice and cunning a child may be possessed of, he cannot be found guilty of a capital crime, for there the legal maxim is, "A child has no discretion" (Makhshirin III. § 8, VI. § 1; Mekhilta Nezikin § 4), and normal cases are accordingly judged, not by the degree of the actor's mental develop-

son who is not convicted for his peccadillos in the past, but with a view to the future, cannot be adjudged as such ere he has reached the stage of puberty.[184]— Accordingly it might seem that with pubescence liability to capital punishment begins. The Talmud does, indeed, speak of that age as the age of responsibility;[185] but that refers to religious obligations and the marital relations.[186] And since, with reference to

---

ment, but by his age. It is only with reference to the validity of certain religious acts on the part of a child, that the Rabbis say: "The object of the child appears from his act" (Hullin 13ª).

[184] Sifra II, § 218; Sanh. 68ᵇ, 71ᵇ sq.—The Rabbis say: "Let the incorrigible die while in a state of comparative innocence, rather than live and go from bad to worse." This agrees with the Roman view of punishments. Seneca (Of Anger B II, c. 31) says: "The end of all correction is either the amendment of wicked men, or to prevent the influence of ill example; for men are punished with a respect to the future: not to expiate offenses committed, but for fear of worse to come."

[185] B. Bathra 156ª; Aboth V, § 21; Nidda 52ª.

[186] The idea that a child becomes responsible for all its own actions at the age of pubescence, is universal among the Jewish casuists, and is plausibly supported by two Rabbinic dicta, to wit: "A man is obliged to take pains with his sons until they are thirteen years old, after which he must bless the Lord who has released him from responsibility for them" (Gen. R. c. 63); and "The lower courts punish persons of thirteen years" (Tanhuma Korah, ed. Buber, § 6). But a careful study of these passages together with their respective contexts does not bear out the inference of the casuists. The first passage obviously refers to a father's duties of supporting his little children (Keth. 49ᵇ; 65ᵇ; Maimon. II. Ishuth XII, 14), and of instructing his sons in the law and a trade (Keth. ib.; Kidd. 30ᵇ. Cf. Matnath Kehuna ad Gen. R. l. c., and Lorje ib.).—The last might, in-

crime, the Talmud does not divide the different stages of minority, but considers the end of the period the

---

deed, be construed to imply that a child, at the age of pubescence, becomes a responsible being, accountable for his actions before a human tribunal; but only in exceptional cases! The passage in question reads as follows: "Dire are the consequences of sedition! The Supreme Judge does not punish an offending person of less than *twenty* years [cf. n. 188]; the courts below punish persons of thirteen years; while of the revolting party of Korah even new-born infants were consumed and swallowed up by the nether world!" (Cf. Num. XVI, 32).—The author speaks of sedition, and, as in that connection he makes the lower courts, human tribunals, punish children of thirteen years, we must suppose that he means seditious children only; otherwise we may justly ask, in the words of the Talmud (Sanh. 82ᵇ) : "Is it thus, that where Heaven sees fit to condone, men condemn to death?!" This is contrary to the spirit of Talmudic jurisprudence, which does not authorize the infliction of capital punishment even for culpable homicide (supra § 37), declaring it to be free from human punishment (*i. e.* as to exacting life for life), though subject to punishment at the instance of the heavenly tribunal (cf. sources quoted n. 135; B. Kama 56ª, et al.)!—Moreover, a person under twenty years was, by Rabbinic law, not competent to dispose of his real estate, or even to be a witness in a case concerning real estate (B. Bathra 155ᵇ sq.; Maimon. II. Mekhira XXIX, 12 sq.); and should the law, declaring a person incompetent to transact a little business, declare the same person to have full capacity for crime?!—Therefore, the dictum that "human courts punish persons of thirteen years," if capitally, must be applied, as the context warrants to the case of the prodigal or "*rebellious* son" only, who may be punished as such, on the sustained accusation of both his parents (supra n. 106), between the beginning of the age of puberty (thirteen years and one day) and three months thereafter (Sifra II, § 218; Sanh. 69ª; Maimon. II. Mamrim VII, 6), to prevent him from committing more heinous crimes (n. 184); or it must be applied to corporal punish-

same as the beginning thereof,[187] we may reasonably conclude that, according to Talmudic law, liability to capital punishment begins with the beginning of the person's majority—*at the age of twenty.*[188]

---

ment, to which a person may legally be condemned after reaching the age of puberty (n. 182), and not before it (Sanh. 68b).

[187] B. Bathra 155b; Nidda 45b.—By the civil law, in the case of a *pubertati proximus* (*i. e.* a person in the last half of the period of impubescence), there was a legal presumption of a capacity to understand the nature of crimes; therefore the act determined the guilt or innocence of the offender, according as it was one which he should have known to be illegal, or one which a young person is not expected to understand (cf. n. 183).

[188] The Talmud repeatedly declares that "Heaven visits no punishment on man for sins committed before the age of twenty" (Yer. Biccurim II. § 1. p. 64c bot.; Sabbath 89b; Yer. Sanh. XI. § 7. p. 30b; Nidda 45a; Num. R. c. 18; Tanhuma l. c.).

II. THE SYNHEDRION.

1. Organization and Jurisdiction.

§ 51. For the administration of justice under the Talmudic dispensation, there were three classes of courts: the Great Synhedrion,[189] the Lesser Synhedrion, and the Court of Three.[190]

§ 52. The Court of Three, as its name implies, consisted of three members. Its jurisdiction was confined to civil affairs, and to such penal cases as in-

---

[189] In these pages the term Synhedrion is generally used, it being appropriate to the courts, whose jurisdiction extended over capital cases, of which we mainly treat. This name was given at Athens to any magisterial or official body, as to the court of Areopagus; or to the place where they transacted business, their board or council room (Smith 935b).

[190] Sanh. 2a; 17b.—The individual members of the several courts are frequently styled *Dayanim* (=judges), and in the aggregate *Beth Din* (=house, court of justice), similar to the Attic appellation *Dicasterion*, which indicated the judicial body (*Dicastes*) that sat in court, as well as the place at which they held their sessions (Smith 356b). In Rome the reverse was the case. There the term *jus* was transferred from the *law* to the *place* where the law was dispensed: an application of the name of what is done to the place where it is done (ib. 562a). But while the "Court of Three" shared this appellation with the highest tribunal, it was a kind of judiciary committee only, with very limited criminal jurisdiction, and must therefore not be confounded with the other courts, which are frequently termed

volved fines or flagellation only.[191]—Such tribunals were established at every place, however small.[162]

§ 53. The Lesser Synhedrion consisted of twenty-three members, and was established, in Palestine, in every city or town having a male population of not less than one hundred and twenty souls, and, in other countries inhabited by Jews, in each district or province[193]; while Jerusalem had two such courts.[194]— Its jurisdiction extended over capital as well as over civil matters.[195]

§ 54. The Great Synhedrion consisted of seventy-one members. This was the highest court in Judea, and was akin to the Senate of the Roman Republic. Its authority was supreme in all matters: civil and politi-

---

Synhedrin, or *Synhedre gedolah,* when reference is had to the *Great Synhedrion.*

[191] Sanh. 2ª; Maimon. H. Sanh. V. 8.

[192] Maimon. H. Sanh. I, 4.—This court is a purely Rabbinic institution, at least in so far as civil cases are concerned, wherefore the casuists are of opinion that a decision of even a single judge, provided he is recognized as an expert in the law, and duly authorized to act in the capacity of judge, is perfectly valid (cf. Sanh. 3ª; Maimon. ib. II, 10). Among the Romans, in many cases a single judex was appointed (Smith 550ᵇ).

[193] Sanh. 2ᵇ; Tosefta ib. III. § 10; Maccoth 7ª.

[194] Sanh. 86ᵇ; 88ᵇ.—Not only because Jerusalem was a very populous city, but also because they exercised, in addition to original jurisdiction, certain appellate functions (cf. infra n. 226).

[195] Sanh. 2ª; Maimon. H. Sanh. V. 2.—But its authority, too, was to a great extent circumscribed, inasmuch as it not only was subject to appeal (cf. infra § 62), but it had no jurisdiction in a number of cases, such as those touching false prophecy, or those in which the person of the king (supra § 45, n. 167) or of the high priest was concerned (Sanh. ib.; Maimon. l. c. 1).

cal, social, religious and criminal. Without the sanction of this august body, no public action could legally be inaugurated.[196] Its opinion was final,[197*] and to its

---

[196] Sanh. 2ᵃ: Maimon. H. Sanh. V. 1.—While all writers on ancient Jewish institutions agree as to the great importance of its prerogatives and functions, great diversity of opinion exists regarding the origin and antiquity of this justly celebrated council. Rabbinic lore (Sifre I, §92; Sanh. 2ᵃ; Maimon. H. Sanh. I, 3) identifies the Great Synhedrion with the council of elders established by Moses (Num. XI, 16, sq.), and consisting of an equal number, including Moses himself; and, accordingly, claims that this august body continuously existed from the days of Moses until the extinction of the Jewish patriarchate (425 C. E.—cf. Graetz, IV, n. 22). On the other hand, some modern scholars ascribe its origin to a comparatively recent date, arguing that, inasmuch as a national council of this kind can be traced back no farther than the Apocryphal books of Maccabees (cf. I Macc. XII, 6, 35), and, inasmuch as the very name of that council, *Synhedrion*, is of Greek origin, and probably did not come in vogue among the Hebrews before the Greeks had invaded Judea,—this council cannot antedate that epoch. We are inclined to accept the traditional opinion on this vexed question, believing that whatever vicissitudes it experienced, the council maintained a continuous existence from the very beginning of Israel's independence. Raphall (Post Bibl. Hist., vol. II, pp. 106-110) who, with great acumen, traces its origin and progress, thus concludes his interesting enquiry: "We have thus traced the existence of a council of *Zekenim* [elders] founded by Moses, existing in the days of Ezekiel [VIII, 11-12], restored under the name of *Sabay Yehudai* [Elders of the Jews—Ezra VI, 8; cmp. ib. X, 8, where the original appellation *Zekenim* is used] under the Persian dominion, known as *Gerousia* [elders—Macc. l. c. et al.], during the supremacy of the Greeks, and as *Sanhedrin* under the Asmonean kings and under the Romans." As to the Greek name of this Jewish council, the same historian argues, that "it affords no proof against the antiquity of its in-

jurisdiction was subject even the high priest, as also the royal house of David.[198]

§ 55. Each Synhedrion organized by selecting from among its foremost members a presiding officer. That officer was styled, in the Lesser Synhedrion, *Rosh* (head, chief, *prætor*); in the Great Synhedrion, *Nasi* (prince, *princeps*).[199] His deputy was called *Ab-beth-*

---

stitution; since, however often the name was altered, the council itself never ceased to exist."

[197] Sanh. 88ᵇ; Maimon. H. Mamrim III. 8.—Original jurisdiction it had in certain celebrated cases only (Sanh. 2ᵃ; Maimon. II. Sanh. V. 1); appellate functions in all (infra § 62. n. 226).

[198] Cf. supra n. 167.—What Gibbon (c. III) says of the prerogatives of the Roman Senate is only the counterpart of those possessed by this great council of the ancient Jews. "With regard to civil objects it was the supreme court of appeal [cf. infra n. 226]; with regard to criminal matters, a tribunal, constituted for the trial of all offenses that were committed by men in any public station, or what affected the peace and majesty of the Roman people. The exercise of the judicial power became the most frequent and serious occupation of the senate; and the important causes that were pleaded before them, afforded a last refuge to the spirit of ancient eloquence. [The Jewish tribunal did not allow forensic art to sway its opinion. Cnf. infra n. 327]. As a council of state, and as a court of justice, the senate possessed very considerable prerogatives; but in its legislative capacity, in which it was supposed virtually to represent the people, the rights of sovereignty were acknowledged to reside in that assembly. Every power was derived from their authority, every law was ratified by their sanction."

[199] Altogether the Talmud names twenty-one such princes who successively presided over the highest tribunal in Judea, during a period of six hundred years (180 B. C. E.—425 C. E.), but whether all bore the official title is rather doubtful. Those who

din (father, chief of the court), and his second deputy, *Hakham* (wise man, sage, *Quaesitor*).²⁰⁰

§ 56. The other officials necessary to complete the organization were two secretaries,²⁰¹ and two messengers or servitors (*Apparitores*).²⁰²

---

occupied that position during the first quarter of this period, are never quoted in Rabbinic lore with the title, though the Talmud (Hagiga 16ᵃ, et al.) explicitly states that they were princes in their respective days. Hillel the Great (30 B. C. E.—10 C. E.) is the first of those whom the Talmud often styles *Nasi;* and he, being a lineal descendant of the house of David, the patriarchate, with but slight interruption, remained hereditary in his family, until the suppression of that office. The Greek appellation of that office was *Ethnarch* (prince of the people), which indicates that the office carried with it princely prerogatives, almost equivalent to royalty itself, even under foreign domination. The usual title, *Patriarch*, also implies supreme functions (Graetz IV, p. 67; ib. n. 22).

²⁰⁰ Tosefta Sanh. VII, § 8; Horayoth 13b.—The functions of the last named officer seem to have been like those of the modern Speaker, "to lay all matters before the house" at the Synhedrial sessions (cf. Sabbath 33ᵇ; Guittin 67ᵃ; glossaries ad l.; Graetz l. c.).

²⁰¹ Sanh. 34ᵃ, 36ᵇ.—Whether one recorded the testimony and arguments of the prosecution, and the other those of the defense; or both recorded all the proceedings on either side, cannot clearly be established. From the language of the Talmud either view might be taken, but Maimonides adopts the first. There is, however, another tradition which speaks of *three* secretaries: one of whom noted down all proceedings on the side of the prosecution, the other those of the defense, while the third transcribed all the proceedings on both sides (Sanh. 36ᵇ).

²⁰² Sanh. 17ᵇ; Maimon. II. Sanh. I. 9.—Their duties were like those of the Roman *viatores* and *lictores* combined: to execute the orders of the court both as to summoning people and administering flagellations or scourgings to the convicts. Rabbi Elazar says: "Where there are officers [to enforce the law],

2. Qualifications.

§ 57. Numerous and varied are the qualifications required to render one eligible to judicial honors. Besides being a worthy man, possessed of true piety and an untarnished character, the candidate must be a Jew and a lineal descendant of Jewish parents;[203] thoroughly versed in the written and unwritten laws, and familiar with many languages[204] and with the sciences of the times.[205] He is required to be affable,[206] of good

---

there may be judges; but where there are no officers, there can be no judges " (Sifre II, § 144. Cf. supra n. 3).

[203] Kidd. 76ª; Sanh. 32ᵇ; Nidda 94ᵇ.—Plutarch (Life of Romulus) states that the members of the Roman Senate were styled *patricians*, because they had fathers to show!—Before the Athenian *Archons* were permitted to enter on the discharge of their offices, they were subjected to a twofold examination: one in the senate, and another in the *Heliastae*. Among the points of examination were: whether their ancestors for three generations had been Athenian citizens; whether they had competent estates; and whether they were free from bodily defects (Fiske III, § 101). Among the Rabbis, while poverty was no particular recommendation to office, it was not a bar thereto (cf. infra n. 235).

[204] The courts were not allowed to avail themselves of the services of an interpreter, lest he mislead them by misinterpretation; wherefore the judges were required to understand the language of the litigants, so that they could personally hold converse with them (Sanh. 17ª; Maccoth 6ᵇ. Cf. infra n. 288). However, when the judges understood the language of the parties before them well, but were not able to converse fluently in that language, they could employ an interpreter to assist them and thus facilitate matters (Maccoth ib.; Maimon. II. Sanh. XXI. 8).

[205] Sanh. 17ª; Menahoth 65ª.—"The Mosaic code has injunctions about the Sabbatical journey; the distance had to be meas-

appearance, and not haughty.[207] He is to be advanced
in years, i. e. a man of experience, but not too old, for

ured and calculated, and mathematics were called into play.
Seeds, plants and animals had to be studied in connection with
the many precepts regarding them, and natural history had to
be appealed to. Then there were the purely hygienic paragraphs, which necessitated for their precision a knowledge
of all the medical science of the time. The 'seasons' and the
feasts were regulated by the phases of the moon, and astronomy
—if only in its elements—had to be studied. And—as the commonwealth successively came into contact, however much against
its will at first, with Greece and Rome—their history, geography
and language came to be added as a matter of instruction to
those of Persia and Babylon" (Deutsch, "The Talmud").—
The Roman *judex* was not necessarily a man of profound learning, for although he alone was empowered to give judgment, he
was generally aided by counsellors (*jurisconsulti*) learned in the
law (Smith 550ᵇ). Outside of the Roman state, disputes were
decided according to the usage of each place, and pursuant to a
few simple customs received by tradition (cf. supra n. 41). In
Beaumanoir's time there were two different ways of administering justice: in some places they tried by peers, in others by
bailiffs. In following the first way, the peers gave judgment
according to the usage of their court; in the second, it was *prodes
homines*, or old men, who pointed out this same usage to the
bailiffs. This whole proceeding required neither learning, capacity, nor study (Montesquieu B. XXVIII. c. XLII).

[20] The affability required of the judge must, however, not be
confounded with what is nowadays understood by "popularity."
The Rabbis severely censure the sage who appears to be too
popular among his followers; for—say they—the scholar's popularity with the masses of his fellow-citizens is not always owing
to his exalted position and righteous bearing, but frequently to
his catering to their depraved tastes, and to his failing to notice
their vices and to rebuke them (Keth. 105ᵇ).

[27] Sanh. 17ᵃ; Menahoth 65ᵃ.

high age is frequently accompanied by high temper ;[208] and he must be the father of a family, that he may always be animated by paternal feelings.[209] In short, only true merit entitles one to the hope of ever gaining a seat on the judicial bench. No personal fear or favor should influence the Synhedrion to elevate to the dignity of a judge one, whose qualifications for that office are not of the highest order.[210] Nor do we meet in

---

[208] According to the Rabbis, a person does not deserve the title of *Man*, before reaching the age of twenty-five years (Yalkut Exodus § 167); but he is not eligible to a seat in the Synhedrion before he is forty years old (Sotah 22ᵇ; Tosaphoth ib. s. v. *Beshawin;* Ab. Zarah 19ᵇ), for then only can he be said to have arrived at the age of understanding (Aboth V, § 21: Exodus R. c. I).—Aristotle finds fault with the circumstance in the institution of the Spartan senate, that the senators were to continue in office for life; for as the mind grows old with the body, he thought it unreasonable to put the fortunes of the citizens into the power of men who, through age, may have become incapable of judging (Government, B. II, c. VIII). The Talmudists believe, on the contrary, that wisdom increases with age (Sabbath 152ᵃ).

[209] Sanh. 36ᵇ; Maimon. H. Sanh. II, 3.—While the Rabbis teach that no mercy may be shown when that be contrary to justice (cf. Keth. 84ᵃ), and fully agree with the Roman maxim: *Fiat justitia pereat mundus* (cf. Sanh. 6ᵇ), they would not have the judge be hasty in condemning people (cf. infra n. 255).

[210] Sanh. 7ᵇ.—After enumerating the qualifications, it is scarcely necessary to catalogue the disqualifications. We shall therefore simply mention that royalty disqualified from holding the office, because of the high station that forbids opposition, and a king's participation in the deliberations might hamper justice (Sanh. 18ᵇ). The following are excluded: the person whose secular vocation is not an honorable one, admitting of suspicion of irregularities, because of his low character (Sanh. 24ᵇ); the man whose

the Talmud with examples of modern electioneering. Office-hunting is thoroughly repugnant to the spirit of Talmudic law.²¹¹ If ever any one obtains his seat by unfair means, no respect is shown for his learning. His judicial robe is looked upon with scorn,²¹² and no respectable judge will associate with him.²¹³

§ 58. The disciple endowed with all these mental and personal qualifications was termed *Haber*

---

body is not perfect (Sanh. 36ᵇ); and in general, all those who are not competent to appear as witnesses in criminal cases (infra § 78), are ineligible to a seat in the Synhedrion. The relatives of a member of a court, connected with him either by the ties of consanguinity or of affinity, were disqualified from membership in the same court (Sanh. 27ᵇ).

²¹¹ Yer. Biccurim III, § 3, p. 65ᶜ.—Commenting on the Scriptural saying: "* * * to love the Lord thy God, to obey his voice and to cleave unto him" (Deut. XXX, 20), the Rabbis remark: No one may say, "I shall devote myself to the study of the law, that people may call me a *sage;* I shall thoroughly familiarize myself with the Mishnah, that I may be called *Rabbi;* I shall acquire a knowledge of the whole traditional law, that I may be entitled to a seat on the teacher's or judge's bench. It is, on the contrary, the duty of every man to acquire knowledge for its own sake, out of love for it: honors will come spontaneously (Nedarim 62ᵃ. Cf. Sifre II, § 41).

²¹² Yer. Biccurim III, § 3, p. 65ᵈ top.

²¹³ Sanh. 23ᵃ; Maimon. II. Sanh. II, 14.—In Rome, in spite of the many penal enactments against the practice, solicitation of votes, and open or secret influence and bribery (*ambitus* and *largitiones*) were the universal means by which a candidate secured his election to the offices of state. Even while the choice of candidates was in the hands of the senate, bribery and corruption influenced the elections (Smith 46). Rumor says that similar practices might be disclosed even under modern governments!

(associate, fellow),[214] but was ineligible to a seat in either Synhedrion until he was solemnly ordained, when he received the honorary title of *Zaken* (elder) or *Rabbi*.[215]

3. Sessions and Recruitment.

§ 59. Originally there were no regular court days. Whenever occasion required it, the Synhedrion was convoked, and disposed of the cases laid before it.[216] But, as this not unfrequently occasioned disappointment and hardships to litigants from the country, who came to the towns and found no courts in ses-

---

[214] Sanh. 8b, 41a, et al.

[215] Sanh. 13b.—This ceremony was called *Semikhah* or *Minnuy* (= ordination, promotion, authorization), and was originally attended by the master's imposing his hands on the head of his chosen disciple. Thus Moses laid his hands upon his successor, and administered the charge (Num. XXVII, 18, 23). Under the Talmudic dispensation, though the term *Semikhah* (= leaning) was retained, the imposition of hands was not an indispensable prerequisite of the ceremony. The master of the academy, assisted by at least two colleagues, named the candidate whose competency had been carefully ascertained, and awarded him the title of *Zaken* (Elder, Archon, Senator), by virtue of which the invested party was authorized to conduct schools, and became eligible to membership in the Synhedrion (Sanh. ib.). Subsequently the title Rabbi (Master, Teacher, Doctor) came in vogue (Tosefta Eduyoth III end; Arukh s. v. *Abaye*; Graetz IV. n. 9), and the right of ordination was transferred to the *Nasi* (supra § 55), at least his confirmation was required to render the act legal and valid (Horayoth 10a); but a still later law provided, that even the Nasi shall not have the right to ordain Rabbis, unless he obtain the consent of the Great Synhedrion (Yer. Sanh. I, § 3, p. 19d).

[216] Keth. 3a. Cf. Tosafoth ib. s. v. *Shebatay*.

sion,—Ezra and his coadjutors enacted that Mondays and Thursdays should be regular court-days.[217]

§ 60. The official hours for holding court were between the morning service and noon;[218] but a suit entered upon during the legal hours could be carried on till evening, and civil cases could be continued even after nighfall.[219]

---

[217] B. Kama 82a; Maimon. II. Ishuth X, 15.—This enactment. however, did not prohibit the holding of court on any or every day of the week at places where such was deemed necessary. It only established the compulsory and uniform holding of court every where on those days (cf. Keth. 3a; Yer. ib. I, § 1. p. 24d.) The reason assigned for the selection of these days is that on these days the people from the country generally congregated in the more populous places, possessed of houses of worship, there to hear the public reading and interpretatation of the law, and, once being in the city. they could attend to their business at court (B. Kama l. c.).—The reader may here be reminded of a similar institution in Rome—the *nundinae*. These were originally market days for the country folk, on which they came to Rome to sell the produce of their labor, and at the same time attended to their law suits before the King, thus rendering the "ninth day" a partial business day; and as the patricians gradually accustomed themselves to do likewise, the nundinae finally became regular *dies fasti* (Smith 667. Cf. infra n. 250).

[218] Sabbath 10a.—By the laws of the Decemvirs (Table I. Laws VIII-X), it was provided that the prætor shall "hear causes from sun-rising till noon," and give judgment in the afternoon. No judgment could be given after sunset (Cooper's *Justinian,* p. 590). In England, the *horæ judiciæ,* or the hours during which the courts were open for the transaction of legal business, were, in Fortescue's time, from 8 to 11 A. M. (Bouvier, Dict.).

[219] Sanh. 32a.—The Courts of Greece usually held their sessions at night and in the dark. Thus the *Areopagus,* though it several

§ 61. In all cities and towns the Court held its sessions in the most public place, the city gate;[220] but the two Synhedrions of Jerusalem held their sessions at the entrance to the Temple-mound and to the women's department respectively.[221]

§ 62. The Great Synhedrion held daily sessions, from morning to evening.[222] For a long time this national council had for its meeting place an apartment in the national temple at Jerusalem, known as the *Lishkhath haggazith* (hall of hewn stones),[223] whence it removed, in consequence of Roman interference, about the beginning of this era to Bethany,[224] and thence to various other places.[225] From

---

times changed the number of its meetings—at first it met on the last three days of the month only, then more frequently, and finally every day,—it never changed the time of its meeting (Fiske III, § 108; Smith 89ª).

[220] Cf. Deut. XVI, 18; Sifre II, § 149, et al.—The Romans and Greeks generally administered justice in the open air. Viewing crimes, especially murder, more as ceremonial pollutions than as political offenses, to avoid the contamination which the judges might incur by being under the same roof with the criminal, their places of trial were open to the sky (Fiske III, § 108; Smith 89ª).

[221] Sanh. 86b; Maimon. H. Sanh. I, 3.

[222] Tosefta Sanh. VII, § 1; Sanh. 88b.—This Court was not obliged to have all its members present at the sessions. Twenty-three members thereof, i. e. as many as constituted a Lesser Synhedrion, were considered a legal quorum for the transaction of its business (Tosefta ib.; Sanh. 37ª).

[223] Tosefta Sanh. VII, § 1; Sanh. 88b, et al.

[224] Sanh. 41ª; Yer. ib. VII, § 2. p. 24b; Ab. Zara 8b; et al.—In rigid adherence to the Scriptural dictum: "Thou shalt do according to the tenor of the sentence, which they may point out to

these places it asserted its authority over all the Israelites, and to those places all appeals from the lower courts were directed. The judgment emanating from it was irrevocable.[226]

---

thee *from the place which the Lord shall choose*" (Deut. XVII, 10), the Rabbis argued that only as long as the great national council occupies the spot chosen by God,—a locality connected with the great temple,—and thence watches over the administration of the laws, the courts not only have a right, but are bound to try capital cases and inflict capital punishment; but when this august tribunal is not domiciled at the sacred place, and cannot send forth its verdicts from there, no capital cases can be tried by the Jewish law (Ab. Zara l. c.). Accordingly, when Rome began seriously to interfere with the administration of justice in Palestine, and Coponius, the Roman procurator was invested with the powre to decide over life and death (John XVIII, 31; Josephus II Wars, VII, 1; Graetz III, n. 25), the Jewish supreme tribunal found itself unable to continue to administer justice, in accordance with the laws of Moses and its own interpretation; it therefore removed from the consecrated spot, thereby divesting itself and the subordinate courts of the duty of acting on capital cases. During the revolutionary period, however (67-70 C. E.), the Great Synhedrion returned to its original place, and, as far as possible, administered its offices (Graetz l. c.).

[225] Rosh Hashanah 31ª sq.; Maimon. II. Sanh. XIV, 12.—It is only the *jus gladii* that the Talmud considers inseparable from the temple, for other purposes the place is immaterial; and the Great Synhedrion, though moving from place to place, continued to be the legislative body of the Jews for several centuries after the total destruction of the temple (Sifre II, § 153; Berakhoth 58ª; Sanh. 14ª; Yer. ib. XI, § 4, p. 30ª), and to ordain teachers and judges. Even when the Romans prohibited the ordination of disciples, proclaiming death and destruction to the persons by whom, and the congregation and city where, the solemn act was carried out, the religious leaders in Israel did not neglect to confer the authorization in due form on their

§ 63. The seats of the Synhedrion were ranged in a semi-circle,—the president occupying the middle

worthy disciples, so as to preserve an unbroken chain of regularly ordained Rabbis. Thus it is related of R. Judah ben Baba (137 C. E.). Fearing that, through the slaughter of Rabbis by Rufus, there might be left no ordained sages to teach and guide future generations, unless the surviving disciples be at once ordained, he performed the ceremony on several of the foremost disciples of R. Akiba, in spite of the dire punishment threatened by Roman tyranny. However, he involved no city or congregation in his violation of the Roman edict; for he conducted the ceremony outside of city limits. He himself lost his life for his act of piety. He was surprised by some Romans in the very act, and three hundred Roman lances perforated his body! The just ordained Rabbis escaped (Sanh. l. c.).

[226] Tosefta Sanh. VII, § 1; Sifre II, § 152; Sanh. 88[b].—Appeals were carried in the following manner: A deputy of the Court of Three, when that court had jurisdiction in the matter (cf. supra § 52), applied for a decision on the mooted question to the nearest local Synhedrion. When the decision of that Synhedrion proved satisfactory, the matter ended there; otherwise, or when the question originated in a local Synhedrion, a deputy from that body presented it to the Synhedrion sitting at the foot of the Temple-mound (§ 53); if no satisfactory conclusion was reached there, the question was in the same manner laid before the Synhedrion sitting at the women's department (ib.); and if there was still no satisfactory decision, the question was carried to the court of last resort, the Great Synhedrion. A deviation from the decision thus obtained from that august body, subjected the recalcitrant judge or teacher to criminal prosecution and death (Sifre l. c. sq.; Sanh. 86[b]. Cf. infra n. 255).—Among the Greeks, owing to the heterogenous characters of their different courts, "there was little opportunity for bringing appeals, properly so-called" (Smith 72[b] sq.). Among the Romans, appeals were common, "on account of the injustice or ignorance of those who had to decide" (ib. 74[a]. Cf.

seat,—so that all the members could see each other at a glance. Facing them were three rows of seats occupied by probationers.[227]

§ 64. All ordained disciples were eligible to membership in the different courts; but that no inexperienced sage might ever occupy a seat on the highest bench, the Great Synhedrion appointed the newly ordained disciple to a seat in the Court of Three; after a time, he was promoted to the local Synhedrion; thence to the first, and later on to the second Synhedrion at Jerusalem, and finally to the Great Synhedrion itself.[228] And as there always were more candidates than vacancies, supernumeraries, to three times the number of members in the regular Synhedrions, were enlisted as probationers (*apprenticii ad legem*). Whenever occasion required it, the probationer occupying the seat nearest the last of the judges, was promoted to a seat on the bench. The vacancy thus created by his re-

---

supra n. 205).—Under the feudal system, an appeal from the judgment of the court below could be carried to the suzerain, and had to be decided by combat. The appellant was obliged to fight successively every one of the members of the court, and, unless he vanquished them all within the day, his life, if he preserved it against so many hazards, was forfeited to the law. If fortune or miracle made him conqueror in every contest, the judges were equally subject to death, and their court forfeited its existence (Hallam c. II, P. II).

[227] Sanh. 36b; Maimon. H. Sanh. I, 3.—Ancient courts generally presented the form of a circle (Fiske III, § 36).

[228] Tosefta Shekalin, end; Tosefta Sanh. VII, § 1; Sanh. 88b.— In Rome, the *Lex Calpurina* (149 B. C. E.) established an *Album Judicum*. The list contained, it is said, 350 names gathered from among the tribes, and out of that body the *judices* were chosen (Smith 252b).

moval, was filled by his immediate neighbor, who again was succeeded by his nearest neighbor, and so on till the last one made room for the admission of a new probationer.[229]

4. Honorarium.

§ 65. The secretaries and servitors of the several courts were paid for their services, but the judge who adjourned causes from day to day, or from place to place, thereby increasing the labors of these officers and raising their emoluments, was himself considered mercenary.[230]

§ 66. The judges themselves, on the other hand, were originally not paid at all. The offices of teacher and judge in Israel were offices of trust, not of emolument: they were truly offices of honor, not of lucre and gain.[231] The regular court days the judge spent

---

[229] Sanh. 36b.—Under certain circumstances, as when the probationer showed himself particularly apt, saving the life of an accused by his sagacious and profound argument at the trial (cf. infra § 102, n. 331), he was promoted to the bench even before the arrival of his turn.

[230] Sabbath 56a; Maimon. H. Sanh. XVII, 3.

[231] Nedarim 37a; Bekhoroth 29a.—Referring to Deut. IV, 5, where Moses says: "Behold, I have taught you statutes and judgments as the Lord my God commanded me," the Talmud argues that, as Moses taught his followers gratuitously, so must every Israelite teach gratuitously; as he sat in judgment without the expectation of material reward, but for the sake of duty, so must every judge act for the sake of justice only (Nedarim and Bekhoroth ib.). The duty of imparting instruction in the law was considered by the Rabbis so sacred, that

on the bench, without expectation of any reward for his services; the rest of the week he employed in earning a livelihood.[232] If his services were required on the days when he was engaged in his private pursuits, he had the right either to claim a substitute to attend to his work during the time to be occupied by the suit, or to demand adequate remuneration for the loss of time. But even this right was not fancied by the Rabbis, except when the party devoted all his time to the bench. Then he was either supported from the communal treasury,[233] or permitted to accept

---

they said: Whosoever refrains from communicating a knowledge thereof to a disciple, is cursed even by the embryo in the mother's body (Sanh. 91ᵇ), and their anxiety to teach, they compared to the eagerness of the mother to suckle her young ones, which is even greater than that of the latter to drink (Pesahim 112ᵃ).—In Carthage, the Council of Five which was the Superior court of that country, received no salary, "the single motive of the public good being thought a tie sufficient to engage honest men to a conscientious and faithful discharge of their duties" (Rollin l. c., B. II. P. I. § 3). The same seems originally to have been the case with the Roman judges, for among the salaried offices (cf. Fiske III, § 267, 5; Smith 849) that of the judge is not mentioned; but the Athenian *Dicastai* were usually paid three *oboli* (=about ten cents) a day (Fiske III, § 110, 2).

[232] Some of the leading Rabbis were dependent on their respective handicrafts for a living. There were among them carpenters and smiths, millers and bakers, tailors and sandalmakers, wood-cutters and stone-masons, physicians, surgeons, perfumers, and all other kinds of craftsmen.

[233] Kethuboth 105ᵃ.—While it is not the aim of these pages to expose the abuses of our magistracy, we cannot refrain from suggesting that it were indeed a blessing had we magistrates discharging their functions, if not altogether for the sake of

fees from the litigants.[234] In general, however, the

duty, at least not solely for the sake of the "legal fees." As matters stand, the magistrate is paid according to the number of cases he "sends up," or of the persons he convicts; the law thus offers him an incentive to seek convictions. It is true. "the law does not suppose a possibility of bias or favor in one who is sworn to administer impartial justice" (Blackstone III. 361); but the law-makers ought to remember the fact, so well described by the "Chinese Philosopher," that "a mercenary magistrate who is rewarded in proportion, not to his integrity, but to the number of convicts, must be a person of unblemished character, or he will lean on the side of cruelty; and when once the work of injustice is begun, it is impossible to tell how far it will proceed. It is said of the hyena that naturally it is in no way ravenous, but when once it has tasted human flesh, it becomes the most voracious animal of the forest, and continues to persecute mankind ever after. A corrupt magistrate may be called a human hyena" (Goldsmith, Cit. of the World LXXX). Were the incentive removed, not only would the public be relieved of the annoyance of constantly being followed by the ever-watchful eye of the inevitable detective or "runner" who, under the guise of law, pries into everybody's private affairs, but actual justice would gain in respect. Sycophancy, in all its hideous forms, would be banished from the land, and no "case" would be made out "for costs" against innocent parties, simply because they are better able to pay than the guilty ones—at least, the real incentive to extortion and to injustice being removed, there would be no reason for suspecting a *Justice* of the Peace of any sordid motives in indicting and convicting people whom the public considers guiltless.—Talmudic jurisprudence is exceedingly careful in such matters. It disqualifies the judge from acting on a cause in which he is ever so remotely interested (cf. B. Bathra 43ª; Maimon. II. Eduth XV, 1 sq).

[234] Keth. 105ª; Maimon. II. Sanh. XXIII. 5.—While the Talmud does not specify the amount of these fees, it forbids taking more from one than from another. All parties to a cause had

Rabbis discountenanced the appointment of judges who were not fully competent to support themselves.[235]

§ 67. As for giving or receiving bribes,—this was so strictly forbidden and thoroughly detested, that even the manifestation of unusual kindness or respect on the part of a client towards the judge was looked upon as a kind of bribery, and the recipient of the attentions was disqualified from participating in a suit to which he who bestowed them was a party.[236]

---

to contribute equal sums towards the maintenance of the judiciary (ib.). But when it was discovered that the judge had been compensated, not for his time, but *for his opinion*, though that opinion was fully borne out by law and equity, it was invalidated by that act, for this was considered tantamount to bribery (Bekhoroth 29ª; Maimon. l. c.).

[235] Mekhilta Amalek § 2; Kethub, 105ᵇ; Sanh. 7ᵇ.—They interpret the Salomonic aphorism: "The King by judgment establishes the land, but the man that receiveth gifts overthroweth it" (Prov. XXIX, 4), as meaning: when the person sitting in judgment is, like a King, well provided for, he will establish the land [on justice. Cf. Aboth I, 18.]; but when, like the priests, he relies for his subsistence on gifts, he will overthrow it; for the standard of justice will be degraded in the eyes of the people. For the same reason the Talmud would have judges who are not compelled to expose their privations to the eyes of the masses, but who live comfortably and respectably (cf. Keth. ib.; Yer. Sanh. II, § 8, p. 20ᶜ bot.).

[236] Keth. 105ᵇ; Sanh. 7ᵇ.—Evidently it was the aim of the Talmudists to maintain the judicial courts pure and healthy, wherefore they erected almost insuperable barriers around them, so that not a single foul breath might reach them. The Talmud records many instances showing how far removed its votaries kept themselves from any and every act that bore even the least semblance to, and therefore might provoke suspicion of bribery. E. g., a Rabbi was crossing a river, and, as his boat

neared the shore, a stranger very considerately assisted him to a safe landing. Soon thereafter the same stranger appeared before the Rabbi's tribunal as a litigant, whereupon the Rabbi declined to sit in judgment on the case, remarking: Friend, I must not be your judge, for I am under some obligations to you.—Another merely had his garment brushed by a would-be client before his tribunal; and he likewise declared himself disqualified from acting on the case. In short, it is a principle of Talmudic jurisprudence to sit in judgment neither on friends nor on enemies: not on the former, lest the judge be blinded by friendship, and fail to perceive guilt; not on the latter, lest he be carried away by antipathy, and fail to perceive extenuating circumstances (Keth. ib.). And when one considers the frailties of human nature, he can scarcely find it strange that truly conscientious people of every age are inclined to erect such barriers around justice. How much perversion of justice has contributed towards the fall of the mightiest of ancient empires, no reader of history needs be told. Nor need it be stated how old England groaned under similar circumstances. The fact that a long-suffering people rises in arms and compels its sovereign to sign a document binding himself to "sell to no man, not to deny or delay to any man justice or right," shows to what straits the people must have been brought, no less than it "stamps with infamy that government under which it had become necessary" (Hallam c. VIII, P. II). And when we come down several centuries, we find that even so great a man as Bacon could not rise superior to temptations. "Under his own signature, owned by himself to be 'his act, his hand, his heart,' he pleads guilty to three-and-twenty instances of bribery and official corruption" (Potter, Introd. to Bacon and Locke, p. XII); while Montaigne represents the condition of the French judiciary of his days as no better. "What can be more outrageous"—cries he—"than to see a nation, where, by law and custom, the office of judge is to be bought and sold, where judgments are paid for with ready money, and where justice may legally be denied to him that has not the wherewithal to pay!" (Essays B. I, c. XXII). And, since "history repeats itself," even at this day in our own country, though we entertain the highest respect for our judiciary, we cannot but consider the Talmudic "hedge-laws" to be as necessary of enforcement, as they have ever and everywhere been. Nor can one help considering the Talmudic laws which guarded justice so carefully, and the civil and canon laws which did not discriminate between judge and juror, as more just, because more in accord with human nature and experience, than modern law which holds "that judges and justices cannot be challenged, for the law will not suppose a possibility of bias or favor in a judge who is sworn to administer impartial justice" (cf. supra n. 233). Unfortunately we cannot in every instance imitate the Thebans who dedicated to judges statues wanting hands, showing that justice is above bribes, though, emblematic of the Scriptural truth that "gifts blind the eyes of the wise" (Exodus XXIII, 8), we might, like them, frequently raise statues of judges with eyes closed!

III. THE TRIAL.

1. THE PARTICIPATORS.

§ 68. The idea of a regular criminal trial implies the presence of: 1, a *competent tribunal;* 2, an *accuser* or *prosecutor;* 3, an *accused.*

§ 69. For a *tribunal* to be fully competent to try criminal cases, Talmudic jurisprudence requires not only that it be legally constituted of the requisite number of duly qualified persons,[237] but also that all judges composing that number shall be amicably disposed towards each other.[238] Nor must there be on the judicial bench either a relation, or a particular friend, or an enemy of either the accused,[239] or of the

---

[237] Supra §§ 53–57; nn. 210, 236.

[238] Sanh. 29ᵃ; Maimon. H. Sanh. XXIII, 7.—When the members of a court are inimical to each other, personal feelings might prove more powerful than the most logical reasonings of their opponents, and induce them to carry on sophistical logomachies rather than argue conscientiously and earnestly on the merits of the cases before them.

[239] Cf. nn. 210, 236.—Raphall (l. c. II, p. 169 sq.) and Jost (Gesch. d. J. u. s. Sekten I, 243) assert that Simon ben Shettah presided at the trial of his own son, and that the sentence of death was passed on the youthful victim of conspiracy by the wretched father himself. We, however, cannot discover in the simple account of that trial the least allusion to Simon's presiding thereat, or his participation therein, in contravention of the explicit ruling of the old Mishnah (Sanh. 27ᵇ), according to which

no one may sit in judgment on a person with whom he is connected by the ties of blood or affinity, whether in the direct or lateral line. But here is the Rabbinic version of that affair:—
Simon ben Shettah's hands were very warm [i. e., he was exceedingly strict in his endeavor to exterminate crime, as related above, n. 108. Goaded on to desperation,] there arose a band of reckless persons who conspired [to wreak vengeance on their persecutor]. 'Let us bear witness against his son [i. e., accuse him of a crime—cf. §71] and kill him,' said they. They testified against him, and had him condemned to death. As he was taken away to be executed, they [the conspirators, either moved by conscience to confess, or gloating on the misery of their enemy, and knowing that, after the trial had proceeded to a certain stage (infra §91, n. 307), no retraction by a witness is admissible] said: 'Master, we have testified to a falsehood!' Thereupon the father wished to have him recalled [before court, that the case might be reviewed]; but *he* said: 'Father, if thou art indeed anxious to confer a benefit on thy country, render me the threshold'(to pass over me,—cmp. D. Eretz Zuta c. 1), i. e., let me die as an illustration of the universality and immutability of the law (Yer. Sanh. VI. §5, 23ᵇ bot.; Yalkut II, §688).—Is there in this plain statement any ground for assuming that Simon presided at the trial, contrary to established law? Simon was president of the great Synhedrion, a tribunal whose original jurisdiction was naturally limited to the most celebrated cases (supra n. 197); and supposing that his son was charged with the deadly sin of uttering false prophecy,—the only crime which might have brought him directly before the supreme national council (Sanh. 2ᵃ, et al.),—there was still *no necessity* for the heartbroken father to sit in judgment on him, since one-third of the whole number of members of that tribunal constituted a legal quorum to dispose of all cases coming before it (supra n. 222). Besides, Simon is really not mentioned in connection with the trial. The only time he appears on the scene is after the confession of the conspirators, when it is said: "His father wished to recall him;" but this does not say that he acted in his official capacity. He acted as a father who, seeing his son led forth to execution for a heinous crime, and hearing the witnesses by

110   THE TRIAL.

accuser,[240] or one who has himself witnessed the commission of the crime.[241]

§ 70. The only *prosecutors* known to Talmudic criminal jurisprudence are the witnesses to the crime. Their duty it is to bring the matter to the cognizance of the court, and to bear witness against the criminal.[242] In capital cases, they are the legal executioners also.[243] Of an official accuser or prosecutor there

---

whose testimony that son had been convicted, convict themselves of conspiracy and falsehood, desires to save his son from an ignominious and unmerited death.

[240] Sifre I, § 160; Sanh. 27ᵇ; Yer. Shebuoth IV. § 1, p. 35ᵇ, et al. Cf. supra n. 236.

[241] Tosefta Maccoth III (II), § 7; Rosh Hash. 26ᵃ; B. Kama 90ᵇ; Maccoth 12ᵃ.—Murder committed by a diseased person is the only exception to this rule (supra § 38, n. 143).—Common law now-a-days agrees with this rule, and "if a juror knows anything of the matter in issue, he may be sworn as a witness, and give his evidence publicly in court" (Blackstone III, 375); but anciently the doctrine was that all such evidence as the jurors had in their own conscience, by their private knowledge of facts, had as much right to sway their judgment as any evidence delivered in court. Accordingly, it has been held that, though no evidence at all be produced before court, the jury might still bring in a verdict of conviction agreeably to "their own personal knowledge, without hearing extrinsic evidence or receiving any direction from the judge" (ib. 374); thus rendering the juror at once witness and judge.

[242] Supra n. 104; infra n. 281.

[243] Infra § 121.—In Rome there were public accusers (the *quaestores parricidii* or *quaestores rerum capitalium*) whose duty it was to ferret out all crimes, and, when they discovered that a capital crime had been committed, to prosecute the offender before the proper courts. The sentence having been pronounced, it devolved upon them to carry it into execution. Their num-

is nowhere any trace in the laws of the ancient Hebrews.

§ 71. The *accused* must be a person of legal age and of sound mental and physical condition, or no indictment can lie against him.[244] From the time the accusation is lodged against him, he becomes a prisoner,[245] but is not deprived of other personal rights and privileges. An injury inflicted on him is punishable, as if it had been inflicted on any other person; and an injury done by him is equally punishable.[246] In short,

---

ber varied with time and circumstances; originally it was but two; afterwards four, and then eight; Sylla raised the number to twenty, and Julius Cæsar to forty (Fiske III, § 246; Smith 828ª).

[244] Supra §§ 45–50 and notes.

[245] Mekhilta Nezikin § 6; Sanh. 78ᵇ.—Among the classic nations, the prisons in which persons under accusation were confined, served also as the place of execution (Smith 213ᵇ; 394ᵇ). This was especially the case in Rome with the *Tullianum* or *Mamertine*, close to which were the "steps of wailing" (*Scalae gemoniae*) down which the bodies of those who had been executed, were either thrown into the forum, to be exposed to the gaze of the populace, or dragged with hooks and cast into the Tiber (ib. 213ᵇ; Fiske III, § 264, 3).—Among the Hebrews, the place of execution was at some distance from the city (infra § 117).

[246] Sifre I, § 160; Tosefta B. Kama IX, § 15.—Summary punishment of a criminal is altogether foreign to the letter and the spirit of Rabbinic law. Though his guilt is sure to cause his conviction and execution at human hands, the criminal must nevertheless not be summarily dealt with (Sifre 1, § 160; Mekhilta Nezikin § 4; Sanh. 85, et al.).—By common law the rule is that no man shall be forejudged of life or limb; and that no man shall be put to death, without being brought to answer by due process of law (Blackstone I. 133); therefore deliberately,

until the accused is duly tried and convicted, he is in the eyes of the law an innocent being.[247]

2. TIME OF TRIAL.

§ 72. Criminal cases can be acted upon by the various courts during day time only,[248] by the Lesser Synhedrions from the close of the morning service till noon,[249] and by the Great Synhedrion till evening.[250]

---

uncompelled and extrajudicially to kill the greatest malefactor, is murder (ib. IV. 178). Still it prescribes summary punishment in certain cases. Thus, a person guilty of contempt committed in the face of the court, may be instantly imprisoned, even without examination (ib. IV, 286. Cf. supra n. 143). The Athenian law allowed in certain cases—as theft, murder, ill-usage of parents—a summary process. The punishment of these cases was generally fixed by law, and if the accused confessed, or was proved guilty, the magistrate could execute the sentence at once, without appealing to any of the jury-courts (Smith 66ᵃ. Cf. infra n. 293).

[247] Cf. Sifra Kedoshim § 4; Sabbath 127ᵃ; Sanh. 32ᵇ; Sheb. 30ₐ.

[248] Sanh. 32ᵃ.—The Areopagus of Athens always held its sessions in the night and in the dark (supra n. 219).

[249] Supra § 60; n. 218.

[250] Supra § 62.—By Talmudic law there is, properly speaking, no *dies nefasti* with reference to the dispensing of justice. Even on the Sabbath the court might sit in judgment of a criminal cause (Sanh. 35ᵃ). On civil causes, indeed, the Talmud forbids all action during the Sabbath, but its reason for the prohibition: "Lest some writing will have to be done" (Beza 36ᵇ), is not applicable to criminal trials inaugurated the day before, it being improbable for such an emergency to arise, since all the writing will have been done on the first day of the trial (Tosafoth Sanh. l. c., s. v. *Liymere*). That no court was held on the Sabbath was owing to the law prohibiting executions on the

§ 73. Unless urged by extraordinary circumstances,[251] no court is allowed to act on more than one criminal case in one day.[252]

§ 74. No trial of a case involving capital punishment can be inaugurated on the eve of the Sabbath or of a festival,[253] and that for the following reason: The Rabbis viewed the interval between the passage of the condemnatory sentence and its execution as the most painful time for the convict; therefore, in order to save him all unnecessary suspense, they decreed that the execution should follow close upon the verdict.[254] But another humanitarian law pro-

---

Sabbath (Sifre II. § 221; Mekhilta Wayakhel § 1; Sanh. 35a) or after sunset (Sanh. l. c.; Yer. ib. IV § 7. p. 22b). In Rome, for the purpose of the administration of justice, the calendar marked distinctly the days (*dies fasti*) on which the praetor could hold court at any hour, and the days (*dies intercissi*) on which judicial business could be transacted at certain hours only, and the days (*dies nefasti*) on which no courts were allowed to be held (Fiske III § 229; Smith 362. Cf. supra n. 217).

[251] E. g., those mentioned supra § 9.

[252] Sifre II § 221; Sanh. 46ᵃ.—This rule not only precludes the trial on one day of two entirely different cases, but even cases of the same category (§ 30), but subject to different penalties— e. q. adultery with a priest's daughter, where the adulteress is punished with burning (§ 27), while the adulterer's penalty is strangulation (§ 29. n. 97)—must be tried separately and on different days.

[253] Sanh. 32ᵃ; Maimon. H. Sanh. XI, 2.

[254] Sanh. 35ᵃ; Maimon. H. Sanh. XII, 4.—Most ancient nations executed their criminals soon after conviction (Fiske III § 108). Blackstone (IV, 404) very warmly advocates early executions, but for utilitarian rather than humanitarian reasons. He argues: "It has been well observed that it is of great importance that the punishment should follow the crime as early as

hibits the pronouncing of a verdict of guilty, on
the day the first judiciary vote is taken.[255] If now
a criminal case is opened on the eve of the Sabbath
or of a festival, and it appears on the first vote, that
it must result in conviction, the verdict, according to

---

possible; that the prospect of gratification or advantage, which
tempts a man to commit a crime, should instantly awake the
attendant idea of punishment. Delay of execution seems only
to separate these ideas, and then the execution itself affects the
minds of the spectators rather as a terrible sight than as the
necessary consequence of transgression" (cf. supra n. 18; infra
§ 116, n. 302).

[255] Sanh. 32ª; Maimon. H. Sanh. XII, 3. Cf. infra § 100, n.
326.—A very ancient Rabbinic-legal maxim says: "Be slow in
judging" (Aboth I § 1). This the judiciary applied to all its
proceedings, but never more scrupulously than when the life or
liberty of a human being was involved. Here it was ordained
that the announcement of a verdict of guilty be postponed to
the day following its finding, in the hope of discovering in the
evidence, or somewhere else, a flaw that might turn the scale of
justice in favor of the accused (Sanh. 17ª, et al. Cf. infra § 100, n.
326). To this rule there was an exception, and one only, which
deserves a passing notice. It is the case of maladministration.
The *Zaken Mamre* (Rebellious Elder), as the Talmud styles him,
is a regularly ordained teacher, or judge who presumptuously
utters precepts, or renders decisions, contrary to the law as interpreted by the supreme authorities (supra § 54, n. 226). For
the first offense, having been duly tried and legally convicted by
the several courts, he was reproved, and reprieved during good
behavior; but for the second offense, if found guilty by the
local Synhedrion only, he was sent up to Jerusalem. There he
was detained till the advent of a high festival (cf. Deut. XVI,
16) convoked thither great masses of the people from the country, and then only was he publicly put to death (Sanh. 86ᵇ, 89ª;
Maimon. H. Mamrim III, 8. Cf. Tosefta Sanh. XI § 7).

the first mentioned law, would have to be postponed till the following day, a Sabbath or a festival; and as these are days on which no execution may take place,[256] the unfortunate culprit would have to be kept in painful suspense, death staring him in the face, for an unnecessarily long time.[257]

3. WITNESSES.

§ 75. To convict a person of a crime, Talmudic jurisprudence requires convincing proof of his guilt,[258] which must be furnished by at least two competent witnesses.[259]

§ 76. To be a competent witness the party must be, like the modern juror,[260] (*liber et legalis homo*) a free and legal person.[261]

---

[256] Mekhilta Wayakhel § 1; Yer. Sabbath VII, § 2, p. 9ᶜ; Sanh. 35ᵃ.

[257] Sanh. 35ᵃ; Maimon II. Sanh. XI. 2.

[258] Mekhilta Nezikin § 4; Sifre I § 161; Sanh. 80ᵇ. Cf. Sotah 2ᵇ.

[259] Sifre II § 148; Kethuboth 87ᵇ.—Common law requires two witnesses in cases of treason only; in almost every other cause one positive witness is sufficient (Blackstone IV, 357). But reason requires two witnesses, since a witness who asserts and an accused who denies counterbalance each other, and it requires the testimony of a third party to make a decision possible (Beccaria § 13). Montesquieu (B. XII c. III) is rightly of the opinion that "those laws which condemn a man to death on the deposition of a single witness, are fatal to liberty." By Talmudic criminal law, one witness is not only incompetent to convict a person of an alleged crime, but is also considered a slanderer, and liable to the punishment of the slanderer (cf. Pesahim 113ᵇ; supra n. 62).

[260] Their qualifications are accordingly almost identical with those of the judge (Sanh. 34ᵇ; Nidda 49ᵇ).—No legally qualified

§ 77. Therefore, the following persons are incompetent to be witnesses: Women,[262] slaves,[263] minors,[264]

---

person is exempt from the duty of bearing witness when called upon to do so, except a king of a dynasty other than that of David (Sanh. 18ª, 19ₐ; Shebuoth 31ª. Cf. supra n. 167). When the high priest appears as a witness, the king occupies a seat on the judges' bench (Sanh. 18ᵇ).

[261] Sifre II § 190; B. Kama 88ª; Sanh. 27ᵇ; Shebuoth 30ª.

[262] Shebuoth 30ª; Maimon. II. Eduth IX. 2.—Also among the Romans, women, except in cases of treason (Smith 609ᵇ sq.), were originally excluded from the witness box; and from the general policy of Athenian law, as also from the absence of any example in the orators where a woman's evidence is produced, may be inferred the incapacity of women among the Greeks. The same observation applies to minors (ib. 626ª).

[263] B. Kama 88ª; Maimon. II. Eduth IX, 4.—Only complete manumission qualified a slave for the witness stand (Guittin 39ª). Among the Greeks and Romans slaves were incompetent, except when the torture was applied (Smith 140ª). On the other hand, when a Roman slave, of his own volition, accused his master of any crime, except treason, he was, for the mere offense of committing such an act of insubordination, punished "by the sword," or, in other words, was condemned to a gladiatorial combat in the arena (Pike, History of Crime, I, p. 14). In the Attic courts of justice, as a rule, no freeman could be put to the torture; and it was considered an act of impiety to give up even an emancipated slave for such a purpose; still we find that, on some extraordinary occasions, freemen were put to the torture by a special decree of the people or of the senate, as on the occasion of the mutilated Hermes busts, and they were less scrupulous about aliens than about citizens (Smith 627ᵇ). Among the instruments employed for the torture of criminals or of witnesses, were the wheel and the rack (ib. 989ᵇ. Cf. infra n. 310).

[264] B. Kama 88ª; B. Bathra 155ᵇ.—Puberty or adulescence (supra § 49) is the age which qualifies a normal person to be a witness in a criminal case, though with reference to real estate

demented persons,[26] deaf or mute,[266] and blind men;[267] persons convicted of irreligion or immorality, or

---

majority is the required age (B. Bathra l. c. Cf. supra n. 186, 262). By common law, where a case depends on the testimony of an infant, it is usual for the court to examine him as to his competency to take an oath, previously to his going before the grand jury; and, if found incompetent, for want of proper instruction, the court will, in its discretion, put off the trial, in order that the party may, in the meantime, receive such instruction as may qualify him to take an oath (Roscoe 95). By Talmudic law, the person witnessing an act during his minority, cannot bear testimony thereof even after reaching his majority (Yer. Meguilla II § 4, p. 73^b bot.; Sanh. 52^b), for it requires that the witness be as fully competent at the occurrence of the acts as well as at the time when he appears before court in the capacity of a witness to those acts (Tosefta Sanh. V § 4, et al. Cf. infra n. 266).

[265] Tosefta Shebuoth III § 8; B. Bathra 128^a.

[266] Tosefta Sheb. III § 8; Guittin 71^a; B. Bathra 128^a.—The last three classes of persons (minors, demented persons and deaf-mutes) the Talmud generally quotes together and considers them all alike (supra § 46). The deaf mute is disqualified, because he neither can hear the court's admonition (infra § 78 sq.), nor give parol evidence (Guittin l. c. Cf. infra § 83, n. 288). On the other hand, the evidence of an emancipated slave touching facts witnessed by him before his enslavement, of a cured lunatic testifying to a fact antedating his lunacy, or of a cured deaf-mute to something antedating his defect, is accepted as valid—the legal maxim in such cases being: Whatever is seen by one of normal condition, and testified to by the party when in a normal condition, is legal evidence (Tosefta Sanh. V § 4; B. Bathra 128^a; Maimon. II. Eduth XIV. 2). By common law, "a person born deaf and dumb, though *prima facie* in contemplation of law an idiot; if it appear that he has the use of his understanding * * * is competent as a witness" (Roscoe 95).

[267] Tosefta Sheb. III § 8; B. Bathra 128^a; Nidda 50^a.

strongly suspected thereof;[268] gamblers,[269] usurers,[270] and farmers or collectors of imposts,[271] illiterate or immodest persons,[272] relatives by consanguinity or

---

[268] Rosh Hash. 22ᵃ; B. Kama 72ᵇ; Sanh. 25ᵇ sq.—The witness cannot disqualify himself by self-accusation, as by asserting that he was incompetent, because of his being guilty of a crime, or because he was suborned in this case, unless extrinsic testimony corroborates his assertion (Kethub. 18ᵇ. Cf. infra § 93). Similar is the rule of common law. A confession of having been convicted of a felony by the witness himself does not disqualify him, unless it is corroborated by the judgment of a court of competent jurisdiction (Roscoe 101).

[269] Tosefta Sanh. V § 2; Sanh. 24ᵇ.—This, however, was the case only when gambling was their regular occupation. By common law, "if the witness lay a wager that he will convict the prisoner, he is still competent, though it goes to his credit" (Roscoe 105). As wagering is in itself a crime by Talmudic law, the wagerer is necessarily disqualified *propter delictum*, and as we shall soon see (n. 274), also *propter affectum*, because he is directly interested in the conviction of the accused.

[270] Tosefta Sanh. V § 2; Sanh. 24ᵇ.

[271] Sanh. 25ᵇ.—The *publicans* were generally classed with the sinners and the heathens (cf. Mat. IX. 10; XVIII. 17; XXI. 31), and hated, not simply because they held their leases from the Roman oppressors of Judea, but because they were usually guilty of great extortion and cruelty (cf. Fiske III § 167, 1; Smith 821ᵇ sq.). Theocritus being asked, which was the most cruel of beasts, made answer: Among the beasts of the wilderness, the bear and the lion are the most cruel, but among the beasts of the city, the publican and the parasite! Hence the publicans were strongly suspected of unscrupulousness in bearing witness, and not trusted. Collectors, however, are disqualified only when actual extortion is proved against them (cf. Maimon. II. Eduth X. 4).

[272] Kiddushin 40ᵇ; Sanh. 26ᵇ.—Even eating on the public streets is, according to some Rabbis, sufficient to disqualify the one who does it.

affinity,[273] and persons directly interested in the case.[274]

---

[273] Sifre I, § 160; Sanh. 27ᵇ sq.; Yer. ib. III § 10, p. 21ᶜ.— Relationship incapacitates the witness whether it exists between him and the accused, between him and another witness in the cause, or between him and one of the judges. When there are more than the required number of witnesses, and one of them is found under such a disqualification, if all admit that they had agreed with each other to appear together as witnesses in the case, the whole party is disqualified, and the testimony of all is consequently rejected (Maccoth 5ᵇ sq.). This rule the Rabbis deduce from the Mosaic prohibition: "Thou shalt not put thy hand with the wicked to be an unrighteous witness" (Exodus XXIII, 1), arguing that, as the whole party had associated themselves with the incompetent person to bear witness in the case, none of them is any longer trustworthy in that case (cf. Sheb. 30ᵇ). The Attic law took no exception to relatives (Smith 626ᵇ), and in some countries the law punished even the nearest relatives of a criminal for not informing against him. Thus the law of the Burgundians decreed that, "if the wife or son of a person guilty of robbery did not reveal the crime, they were to become slaves. This law," remarks Montesquieu (B. XXVI. c. III), "was contrary to nature: A wife to inform against her husband! a son to accuse his father! to avenge one criminal action, they ordained another still more criminal." In Rome, the evidence of near relatives, though not excluded, did not have much weight. Common law disqualifies a person from acting as a juror, if he is related to either party to the suit, within the ninth degree (Blackstone III, 363); but it permits the nearest relations, except the lawful husband and wife, to appear as witnesses against each other (cf. Roscoe 112 sq).

[274] B. Bathra 53ᵃ; Maimon. H. Eduth XV.—A glance at this array of exceptions to witnesses must remind the reader of the "challenges to the polls of the jury" in common law, which are: *propter honoris respectum, propter defectum, propter affectum,* and *propter delictum* (Blackstone III, 361 sq.), and serve to convince him that Rabbinic jurisprudence, founded, as it was, upon

4. Cautioning Witnesses.

§ 78. The legal axiom : "The law springs from the fact" (*ex facto oritur jus*), occupies an important place in Talmudic law. The Talmud prohibits going behind the returns, saying: "The judge has nothing to guide him, save what is before his eyes,"[275] i. e. *evidence*. And as the witness is not required to swear to the truth of his evidence,[276] the Rabbis prescribe a

---

human nature and divine justice, threw every possible safeguard around the accused. The witnesses prosecute a person (supra §70); their testimony convicts him; but they must be trustworthy and disinterested witnesses, or the court may not admit their evidence. The testimony of an accomplice is accordingly not admissible by Rabbinic law, both *propter affectum* and *propter delictum*, and no man's life, nor his liberty, nor his reputation, can be endangered by the malice of one who has confessed himself a criminal. (By common law, "a conviction on the testimony of an accomplice, uncorroborated, is legal."—Roscoe 119). Therefore, too, the expectation of a benefit, though not necessarily or legally flowing from the event of the proceedings, which in modern law does not render a witness incompetent (Roscoe 104), is, according to the Talmud, sufficient to invalidate the testimony (Kiddushin 58b; Bekhoroth 29a). The witness was incapacitated when he accepted remuneration for his *testimony* though he was at liberty to accept indemnification for the consequent *loss of his time* (cf. Yer. Sanh. I §1, p. 18b top; supra §66).

[275] Sanh. 6b, et al.—Bouvier (Dict. s. v. Maxim) quotes a Latin maxim which is almost the exact rendition of ours. It reads: *Nihil habet forum ex scena.*

[276] Neither the Bible nor the Talmud imposes on the witness any oath to confirm his testimony. The divine prohibition of bearing false witness was considered by Moses and by the Jewish legislators succeeding him, as sufficient to induce people to state truths only. Later Jewish sages are of opinion that the

preliminary caution or admonition, in the course of which the witnesses, standing in the presence of the whole assembly in court, are earnestly exhorted to testify to such matters only as have come under their personal observation, and cautioned against asserting aught based on conjecture or hear-say;[277] at the same time they are forewarned that the court will subject them to close examination and searching cross-examination, and carefully weigh the evidence.[278]

§ 79. The language of the admonition addressed to witnesses in criminal cases, is of so striking and awful a nature, that we deem it not superfluous to transcribe a portion thereof. It runs thus:

Know ye that there is a vast difference between the results of trials of civil matters and those of criminal cases. In civil affairs, a man may atone for his guilt by paying the injured party an adequate sum of money; but in criminal cases the blood of the innocent and unjustly condemned, as well as the blood of

---

witness who would not tell the truth without an oath, would not scruple to assert falsehood with an oath (cf. B. Joseph H. Mishpat XXXIV, 38; Tosaf. Kidd. 43ᵇ s. v. *Hashta*). Indeed, some Jewish philosophers consider swearing injurious in itself; for he who swears is *ipso facto* suspected of lacking credibility (cf. Philo Judaeus, *De Decalogo* III; Josephus, II Wars VIII, 6; infra n. 312).

[277] So, by the Athenian law, a witness could testify to what he had seen, but not to what he had heard. When, however, he had heard anything relating to the question before court from a person who had died in the meantime, an exception was made to the rule, and what he had heard from the deceased person was admissible evidence (Smith 15ᵇ).

[278] Sanh. 37ᵃ. Cf. infra § 91.

the victim's possible issue to the end of all generations [which is cut off by his premature death], falls on the heads of the false witnesses. That such is the case clearly appears from God's rebuke administered to Cain who slew Abel, wherein we find the words: "The voice of thy brother's bloods cries unto me, &c."[279] Now, since the Lord did not say, "Thy brother's *blood*" [*Dam*], but "Thy brother's *bloods*" [*Demay*], He intended to inculcate the idea that, in slaying Abel, Cain became guilty of shedding the blood of the victim's progeny as well as of shedding the victim's own blood. Again, the fact that at the beginning God created one man only, should impress upon you the idea that whosoever occasions the loss of a single innocent life is as great a sinner as if he had destroyed a whole generation; and, on the contrary, whosoever saves a single innocent life, is as meritorious as if he had saved the world.—But these ideas must not deter you from testifying to what you actually know. Scripture declares: "The witness who hath seen or known, and doth not tell, shall bear his iniquity."[280] Nor must ye scruple about becoming the instruments of the alleged criminal's death [which cannot undo the crime]. Remember the Scriptural maxim: "In the destruction of the wicked there is joy."[281]

---

[279] Genesis IV. 10 sq.

[280] Lev. V, 1. Cf. supra n. 104.

[281] Prov. XI. 10. The object of the closing admonition is, not only to remind the honest witness of his duty to bear testimony, but also to induce him to testify even against a person tried for life, impressing upon him the idea that *qui parcit*

5. Examination.

§ 80. All examinations are conducted in public,[232] and in the presence of the accused.[233] The judges occupy their seats, the witnesses and the accused stand before them.[234]

§ 81. The general dilation having been heard, the witnesses retire from the presence of the court, only one remaining to be examined. One after the other of his associates closely follows him on the witness-stand.[235]

---

nocentibus innocentibus punit; and that, although the culprit's death will not counteract the misdeeds for which he is to be tried, his removal from the theatre of his crimes will in itself be a benefit to the public (cf. Sifre II § 187, end; supra n. 104).—The Athenians, too, considered as a part of the duty which every man owes to the state, the obligation to attend as witnesses, both in civil and criminal proceedings, and to give such evidence as one is able to give (Smith 626ᵇ).

[232] Sifre II § 149; Sanh. 30ᵃ.

[233] Sifre II § 190; Keth. 20ᵃ; B. Kama 112ᵇ.—The Talmudic rule of law being: "Testimony must not be heard, barring exceptional cases, in the absence of the party concerned" (B. Kama l. c.). Another rule of law is: "The cause of a client must not be disposed of unless he is present" (Sanh. 79ᵇ); and a third: "No man may be convicted unless he is present" (Keth. 11ᵃ, et al.). From these rules it clearly follows that outlawry for non-appearance at trial could never, by Talmudic law, be decreed against an alleged criminal, as was frequently done in Rome and in England (cf. Blackstone IV, 319 sq.). Especially are these rules directed against secret accusations which, owing to defective laws, are sanctioned as necessary evils (cf. Beccaria § 15).

[234] Sifre II § 190; Yer. Yoma VI § 1, p. 43ᵇ bot.; Sheb. 30ᵃ.— The right to examine witness is not confined to the acting

§ 82. All evidence must be direct, and not circumstantial or presumptive.[286] Be the chain of evidence ever so strong, if not all links are forged by direct eye-testimony, and that of at least two competent witnesses, the accused cannot be adjudged guilty.[287]

---

judges, but shared by the probationers also (Sanh. 41ᵈ sq. Cf. supra § 64). And this is not merely a privilege, but a duty, where the probationer sees that his superiors are mistaken. Nor must he delay in respectfully pointing out the mistake. He must at once call the attention of the court to it (Sheb. 31ᵃ. Cf. Ab. Zara 19).

[285] Tosefta Sanh. VI § 3; Sanh. 40ᵃ; Maccoth 6ᵃ.

[286] Sanh. 37ᵃ; Maimon. II. Sanh. XII, 3. In Rome a sentence of death or infamy was often founded on the slight and suspicious eveidence of a child or a servant; and the guilt of the green faction, of the rich, and of the enemies of Theodora, was presumed by the judges (Gibbon c. XLIV).

[287] Sanh. 37ᵇ, Maimon. II. Sanh. XX, 1.—As an illustration in point, the Talmud (l. c.; Yer. Sanh. IV § II. p. 22ᵇ bot.) records the following episode in the life of Simon ben Shettah. That sage once saw a man hotly pursuing another who took refuge in a deserted building. The sage followed. On entering the place, he beheld in the pursuer's hand a sword covered with blood, while before him lay the victim weltering in his own blood. Thereupon the sage exclaimed: "By my salvation, thou art the murderer of this victim! But what can I do? Thy blood is not in my hand," i. e. I cannot prosecute thee and have thee legally convicted (cf. infra n. 389).—In modern courts, *violent presumption* is admitted in evidence, and the instance selected to illustrate the nature of presumption in criminal cases is akin to, though *lighter* than the one before us; yet it is termed "violent presumption," and considered as "proof next to the sight of the fact itself" (Roscoe 12 sq.). Also by Talmudic law violent presumption is admitted as legal evidence in criminal cases, but only with reference to the *status* of the party. Thus, if a man and a woman live together, and keep

§ 83. All evidence must be given *vive voce*,[288] and in

---

with them a youth and a maiden as their children, the parties are violently presumed to stand in the relations of husband and wife, parents and children. If now it is duly proved that there was illicit correspondence between the man and the maiden, or between the woman and the youth, or between the children themselves, the guilty parties will be capitally punished for incest, though there is no other evidence to prove their consanguinal relationship (Kidd. 80ᵃ; Maimon. H. Is. Biah I. 20). On a charge of adultery, however, neither the paramour nor the alleged adulterer can be capitally punished, unless the presumed conjugal relationship is of at least thirty days' standing, and based upon the assertions of the parties themselves (Yer. Kidd. IV § 10, p. 66ᵇ bot.; Maimon. l. c. 21. Cf. B. Bathra 167ᵇ).— By common law, in a civil suit for adultery, as also upon indictments for polygamy, a marriage *in fact* must be proved; though generally, in other cases, reputation and cohabitation are sufficient evidence of marriage" (Blackstone III, 140).

[288] Yebamoth 31ᵇ; Maimon. H. Eduth III, 140.—This, as well as the next proviso, is based on the Scriptural dictum: "At the mouth of two witnesses, or of three witnesses, shall he, that is to die [by human hands], be put to death (Deut. VII. 6).—The Attic law required all testimonial evidence to be in writing, in order that there might be no mistake about the terms, and that the witness might leave no subterfuge for himself when convicted of falsehood (Smith 626ᵇ). Talmudic jurisprudence is more in consonance with the emotional nature of man, when it adopts parol evidence as the safest means of arriving at truth, believing that a man will not as readily lie in the presence of the party concerned, as he might do in a document prepared and read behind the person's back (Guittin 51ᵇ; Tosafoth ib. s. v. *Ain*. Cf. Sheb. 42ᵃ, et al.); or, as Blackstone says: "As much may be frequently collected from the manner in which the evidence is delivered, as from the matter of it" (III, 373). And the additional requirement which imposes on the official scribes the duty of writing down the testimony (cf. supra n. 201), is an additional safeguard against subterfuge and impos-

a language understood by the judges.[269] It must furthermore be deposed in the presence of the whole court,[290] and must cover the whole case.[291]

§ 84. Each witness is required to give positive answers to two kinds of questions: Main questions and Test questions;[292] while the judges are required to cross-question him closely,[293] and to be exceedingly

---

ture. A subsequent rigorous oral cross-examination, by evoking contradictions between the answers and the recorded statements of the witness, can more easily lead to the betrayal of the falseness of his testimony.

[289] Maccoth 6b; Maimon. H. Sanh. 6; ib. XXI, 8. Cf. supra n. 204.

[290] Sanh. 80b; Maimon. H. Eduth IV, 1-7. Cf. Kesef Mishneh ib. 7; § supra n. 222.

[291] Sanh. 86a; Maccoth 6b, et al.—The Bible says: "At the mouth of two witnesses, or at the mouth of three witnesses, shall the matter be established" (Deut. XIX, 15), upon which the Talmud bases the rule that each witness must testify to the whole matter, and not to part of the matter only. Thus, to constitute the capital crime of kidnapping, there must be both abduction and selling (supra n. 99). Now, if two parties of witnesses appear against the criminal, one testifying to the abduction, and the other to the selling, the criminal cannot be sentenced to death, for neither of the parties has established the *whole* matter.

[292] Sanh. 40a; Maimon. H. Eduth I, 4.

[293] The judges are not only prohibited from passing summary sentence on the culprit to whose crime they themselves were eye-witnesses (Yer. Sanh. I. § 1, p. 18b; Maccoth 12a), but must be personally ignorant of the circumstances in the case, or they may not sit in judgment thereon; for the rule is: None who may be a competent witness in the cause, may be judge of the cause (Tosefta Maccoth III. § 7. Cf. supra n. 143).—The Roman law is of the same opinion. It says:—The judge ought to proceed according to the allegations and proofs laid before

guarded in their utterances, lest the witness draw from them hints how to answer evasively.[294]

§ 85. The main questions which every witness is required to answer, relate to the *persons*, the *time*, the *place* and the *manner* of the alleged crime.[295]

§ 86. With reference to the *person*, the Talmud requires that the witnesses be certain of his identity, and of his having been duly forewarned.[296] The least doubt on this head invalidates the testimony.[297]—If

---

him, and not according to his own knowledge of the fact; for he is to judge as a public person, not as a private one, and he ought not to be judge and witness. Neither ought the lives and fortunes of men to depend upon the pretenses of his own knowledge. In such a case, the judge ought to lay aside his office for a time, and become a witness (Wood, Civil Law B. IV, c. 1).

[294] Aboth I. § 9; Aboth de R. Nathan X. Cmp. Keth. 52ᵇ, 86ᵃ; Yer. B. Bathra IX, § 6, p. 17ᵃ top.

[295] Sanh. 40ᵃ sq.; Maimon. II. Eduth I, 4.

[296] Cf. supra § 16, n. 68.

[297] Sanh. 40ᵃ; Maimon. II. Sanh. XII. 1.—The *identity* thus required is not confined to the person's being, but extends to facts also. Thus, if murder is charged, and several persons are implicated in that charge, each witness is required to identify the person who gave the last or *death-blow*, for only this one is answerable with his life for the life of the victim (supra § 43).—By common law, accomplices, or accessories before the fact, share the punishment with the principal (supra n. 128). Thus, when an indictment charges that A gave the mortal stroke, and that B and C were present aiding and abetting, even if it appear in evidence that B gave the mortal stroke, and A and C were aiding and abetting, they may all be found guilty of murder or manslaughter, as circumstances may vary the case. The stroke of one is, in the consideration of common law, the stroke of all, and the identity of the person supposed to have given the stroke is an immaterial circumstance, the

the crime charged of is murder, the identity of the
victim and of his race must be established;[298] if idolatry, the name of the idol must be given.[299]

§ 87. With reference to the *time*, the witness must
furnish the exact date of the commission of the crime.
He must name the number of the septenary in the
jubilee cycle;[300] the number of the year in the septenary; the name or number of the month in the year;

---

person giving the stroke being no more than the instrument by
which the others strike (Roscoe 83). But according to Talmudic law, such a "circumstance" is *very material*, as it might
acquit the accused of the charge of murder, though it would
render him guilty of culpable homicide (cf. supra § 36).

[298] Sanh. 40b; Maimon. II. Sanh. XII, 1.

[299] Sanh. 40a; Maimon. II. Eduth. 4. Cf. supra n. 43.

[300] Cf. Lev. XXV, 8 sq.—"By common law there is no general
statute of limitation applicable to criminal proceedings * *
In New York, indictments for murder may be found at any
time; in all other cases, indictments must be found and filed in
the proper office, within three years after the commission of
the offense" (Blackstone IV, 301 n. 1).—Nor do we know
of any general limitation to criminal prosecution by Talmudic
law; and from the fact that the witness was required to give
the date minutely (stating the number of the year in the septenary and jubilee-cycle), it would appear that the lapse of time
had no effect on guilt. Still, judging by the spirit of Talmudic jurisprudence, and seeing that by that jurisprudence personal disabilities, acquired in consequence of conviction for
crime, are removed by time and circumstances (cf. infra § 140
sq.), it may be assumed that for the most heinous crimes, especially murder, (cf. infra n. 424) there was no limitation, but for
minor crimes, if a considerable time had elapsed since the commission thereof, no prosecution could be inaugurated against
the criminal.

the day of the month and of the week; and the hour of the day.³⁰¹

§ 88. With reference to the *place*, the location must be distinctly stated, and the immediate surroundings minutely described.³⁰²

---

³⁰¹ Sanh. 40ᵃ; Maimon. H. Eduth. I, 4.—The several particulars referring to time and place, must be furnished with the greatest possible precision and certainty, and that by the whole party of witnesses. The slightest disagreement on the part of the witnesses, in regard to any one of these particulars, invalidates the entire testimony. Even where a number of witnesses greater than that required by law, as three, appear, and two agree on every point, but the third differs from them as to more than one day, or more than one hour in the day, the whole testimony is invalidated. For time and place are the only points which affect the person of the witness himself: he not being able to be at more than one spot at any one time; time and place are accordingly the only grounds on which the witness may be confuted (infra § 95) and duly punished (supra § 31), and the Talmud says: Any testimony which, owing to an intrinsic defect, is not liable to confutation, is no testimony (B. Kama 75ᵇ; Sanh. 41ᵃ, et al.).—The same is the case where only a legal number of witnesses appear, and one of them is not certain as to any one of these particulars. But when there are more than the required number of witnesses, if only two of them testify to time and place, though all the rest aver uncertainty, the charge is sustained on the testimony of the two (Sanh. 41ᵇ; Maimon. H. Eduth. II, 3).

³⁰² Sanh. 40ᵃ. Cf. infra § 90, n. 304.—By common law, while it is necessary to name the time *when*, and the place *where*, the alleged fact was committed, a mistake in these points is in general not held to be material, provided the *time* be laid previous to the finding of the indictment, and the *place* be within the jurisdiction of the court (Blackstone IV. 306). According to Talmudic law, a very material difference would ensue from a mistake in these points, as clearly appears from what is stated

§ 89. With reference to the *manner*, witnesses must set forth the principal circumstances connected with the alleged crime. If the crime charged is murder, they must state how the killing was done, and with what instrument; if idolatry, the way in which homage was paid must be described.[303]

§ 90. The *test-questions* touch those particulars which, while they are not exactly matter of prime importance, may serve to establish or to disprove the main testimony. Thus, in the case of murder, the witness is called upon to describe the dress of the victim, or of the accused, worn at the commission of the crime; or to state the color of the ground on which the crime was committed.[304]

---

in the preceding note. Moreover, suppose the witnesses to allege that the crime has been committed in the *eastern* part of a town; now, if it appears in evidence that at the stated time, they were in the *western* part of the town, whence they could not have witnessed the act, they stand confuted, and subject to the penalties of the law in such cases (Maccoth 5ª; Maimon. H. Eduth XIX, 1).

[33] Sanh. 40ª, 41ª; Maimon. H. Eduth I, 4; II, 2.—By common law, a person cannot be convicted of one species of murder, as of poisoning, when the indictment charges him with another, as of starving. But if only the concomitant circumstances are varyingly reported, "as if a wound be alleged to be given by a sword, and it prove to have arisen from a staff, or an axe, or a hatchet, the difference is immaterial" (Blackstone IV, 196). According to Talmudic law, a contradiction of this kind invalidates the whole testimony.

[34] Sanh. 32ₐ, 40ª; Maimon. H. Eduth I, 4 sq.—In the test-questions more latitude is allowed than in the principal ones. Here uncertainty does not invalidate the positive part of the testimony, even when all the witnesses manifest an equal de-

§ 91. The direct questioning is followed by a severe cross-examination which may be extended *ad libitum*, especially when a striking similarity in the language of the several statements becomes apparent.[305] Under such circumstances the effort is to perplex and abash the witnesses.[306]—After the cross-examination the wit-

---

gree of indecision; for they are not expected to take notice of such immaterial circumstances. In this, Talmudic law agrees with the rule of common law, where "if an averment may be entirely omitted without affecting the charge against the prisoner, and without detriment to the indictment. * * * it may be disregarded in evidence * * * and need not be proved" (Roscoe 84). But where the witnesses do testify to them and contradict each other, the contradiction has the same effect on the whole testimony, as contradictions in the answers to the principal questions (Sifre II. § 93; Sanh. 40ª, 41ᵇ).—How far the Rabbis went in testing witnesses is illustrated in the Talmud by the statement that once a judge tested them almost literally by an *experimentum crucis*. At a trial of a case of murder alleged to have been perpetrated near a fig-tree, a probationer required the witnesses to describe the figs: whether they were light or dark; whether they had long or short stems, thick or thin (Sanh. 40ª, 41ª. Cmp. Hist. of Susannah 54–58).—Nor were the judges always satisfied with the mere averments of the witnesses. When occasion rendered it practicable, they subjected the proofs to physical tests. Thus it is recorded that when, to prove infidelity in a woman, a prosecutor produced albumen of egg and represented it as spermatic fluid, the judge applied the *corpus delicti* to the fire, knowing that albumen coagulates under heat, while spermatic fluid does not; and by this test he exposed the impostor (Guittin 57ª).

[305] Concurrence as to facts is a *conditio sine qua non* in evidence; but similarity in expressions awakens suspicion of conspiracy and coaching (Yer. Sanh. III, § 9, p. 21ᶜ top).

[306] Sotah 8ª; Sanh. 32ᵇ.—When the judge, in spite of the apparently artless answers to his direct and cross-questions, still

ness is dismissed, and is not allowed to correct or recant any part of his testimony, even when he offers reason for his proposed correction or recantation.[307]

6. The Defendant.

§ 92. All the prosecuting witnesses having been duly examined, the court directs itself to the defend-

---

suspects that the evidence before him is not altogether ingenuous, or that some facts concerning the case are withheld, he may not render judgment in the case, and throw the responsibility for the wrong accruing to the unfortunate victim on the heads of the witnesses. He must, under such circumstances, retire from the bench, and leave the case to be disposed of by others who do not share his misgivings (Sheb. 30b; Maimon. H. Eduth XXIV, 3). This rule is based on the Scriptural command: "Keep far from a false matter" (Exodus XXIII, 7).

[307] Sifre II. § 190; Tosefta Keth. II, § 1; Sanh. 44b. Cf. Sheb. 31b.—Thus, when he avers that he was mistaken in his original statements; or that he was no competent witness, because of a disqualification in consequence of conviction for a misdemeanor (cf. supra § 77); or even when he confesses that he was prompted to prosecute by a spirit of vengeance, as was the case with the witnesses who conspired against the son of Simon ben Shettah (supra n. 239); for at this stage of the proceedings, the Talmudic rule is: What is once said, cannot be unsaid (Keth. 18a; B. Bathra. 168a; et al. Cf. infra n. 319; § 103). When, however, the witness appears to have labored under a palpable misapprehension, as when his testimony appears decidedly adverse to the party calling him, he is allowed to correct his testimony. In such cases the Talmud says: It is self-evident that no one brings witnesses to convict himself (B. Meziah 28b; H. Mishpat XXIX, 1), and that the witness certainly came with the intention of testifying in his favor (Rashi ad B. Meziah l. c.).

ant. He is encouragingly addressed,[308] and called upon to present disproving testimony.[309]

§ 93. Not only is self-condemnation never extorted from the defendant by means of torture,[310] but no attempt is ever made to lead him on to self-incrimination. Moreover, a voluntary confession on his part is not admitted in evidence, and therefore not competent to convict him, unless a legal number of witnesses minutely corroborate his self-accusation.[311] No man

---

[308] Sanh. 32b.—In modern practice, when the prisoner has put himself upon trial, the clerk of the Court says: "God send thee a good deliverance" (Blackstone IV, 341).

[309] In common law the rule formerly obtained that, on capital charges, the accused was not allowed to exculpate himself by the testimony of witnesses; and though from and after the reign of Mary I, the court gradually introduced the practice of examining witnesses for the prisoner, this examination was not held under oath, and consequently the jury gave less credit to the prisoner's evidence than to that of the prosecution (Blackstone IV, 359). It was not until the close of the seventeenth century that the admission of witnesses for the prisoner upon oath was enacted (ib. 441).

[310] Talmudic jurisprudence knows of no form of judicial torture, which was so frequently practised by the Greeks and Romans, and even among modern nations (supra n. 263).

[311] Tosefta Sanh. XI, § 1, 5; Keth. 27b; Sanh. 9b. The reason assigned for this enactment is the wish to avoid the possibility of committing judicial homicide on self-accusing lunatics, or on persons who, in desperation, wish to cut short their earthly existence, and to effect this, falsely accuse themselves of some capital crime.—By English law, standing mute, or not pleading to an indictment, amounted to a constructive confession, and the accused was thereupon adjudged guilty, and sentenced and punished, as if he "had been duly convicted by verdict or confession of the crime" (Blackstone IV, 329). And this enact-

is competent to convict himself, says the Talmud: "he is his own kin,"[312] and we have just seen that kinfolks are not admissible as witnesses. This, however, does not apply to the defense. In his own exculpation, the accused is a competent witness.[313] In short, the Talmud does not presume the guilt of the accused, and therefore considers him innocent, until the contrary is proved by competent witnesses upon whom the burden of proof rests.[314]

§ 94. The witnesses for the defense are subject to the same rules as those of the prosecution.[315]

---

ment was in itself a merciful improvement on previous practices, which compelled the prisoner to plead. He was put into a dark room, where he was denuded and laid on his back on the bare floor, and a heavy weight placed on him. Very little sustenance was allowed him during this ordeal which was known under the name of *penance*, or *pressing to death*, and sometimes continued for forty days (ib. 327). "Thus rating a man's virtue by the hardiness of his constitution, and his guilt by the sensitiveness of his nerves" (cf. Beccaria § 16).

[312] Sanh. 9b, et al. That no oath was administered to the accused is self-evident; for if, as we have seen (supra § 78, n. 276) with reference to the witness who is to be entirely disinterested (supra § 77, n. 274), the presumption is that he, who would not tell the truth without an oath, will not tell it with an oath,—how much less can it be expected that the oath will have any effect on the only interested party, the accused himself, and force from him a statement of the truth which may convict him ?! Beccaria (§ 18) justly condemns the custom of putting the accused under oath, believing that 'in most men religion is silent when interest speaks.'

[313] Sanh. 40a; Maimon. H. XIII, 1. Cf. infra § 119.

[314] Tosefta Sanh. XI, § 1; Kidd. 76b; Tosefoth Yom Tobe. ib. c. IV, § 10; Sanh. 80r. Cf. Keth. 75a; Sheb. 46b; Sanh. 32b; Arakhin 22a; Nidda 2a sq.; supra § 41.

7. Disproval and Confutation.

§ 95. Witnesses may be either disproved or confuted. They are *disproved* when conter-testimony is produced, demonstrating that the crime could not have been committed by the alleged criminal, at the time or the place stated;[316] they are *confuted* when it appears from the counter-testimony that they could not possibly have witnessed the commission of the crime.[317]

§ 96. The effect of disproval, at any stage of the proceedings, is simply negative: it condemns no one; but stops all further action on the case, and sets the prisoner free.[318]

---

[315] In fact the witnesses *for* the defense are at the same time witnesses *against* the prosecution whom, as we shall presently see (§ 97), their evidence may cause to exchange places with the defendant (Sanh. 32ᵇ).

[316] Maccoth 5ᵃ; Maimon. II. Eduth XVIII, 2.—Thus, when the prosecuting witnesses charge A with having slain B, and others appear and testify that, at the time stated, A was not at the place named, or that B has not been slain at all; or when the alleged victim of a murder himself appears in *propria persona* (B. Kama 74ᵇ; Maimon. H. Eduth XVIII, 6).

[317] Maccoth 5ᵃ; Maimon. II. Eduth XVIII, 2.—When counter-evidence proves the *alibi* of the witnesses themselves (cf. supra § 31, n. 302).

[318] Maccoth 5ᵃ, et al.—According to the scholiasts on Plato, it requires the conviction of more than half the witnesses of *falsum* or perjury, in order to obtain a reversal of the sentence passed on a convict in consequence of their testimony (Smith 628ᵃ). By Talmudic law, if one witness in a hundred is found incompetent, the testimony of the whole party is thrown out (supra n. 273), the legal maxim being: "If part of the testi-

§ 97. The effect of confutation on the case, at any time, is the same as that of disproval; but its effect on the confuted witnesses depends on the stage of the proceedings: if the confuting testimony is presented before the verdict is pronounced, it amounts to a mere disproval; but if, after the verdict is pronounced, they become subject to the penalty which their testimony, had they not been confuted, would inflict on the alleged criminal.[319]

---

mony is invalidated, the whole is invalidated" (B. Kama 73ª; Yer. Maccoth I, § 16, p. 31ᵇ).

[319] Sifre II, § 190; Sanh. 89ª; Maccoth 2ª, 5ᵇ.—Provided, however, that their testimony was in other respects valid, and sufficient to convict the accused; that all the witnesses were duly confuted (Maccoth 5ᵇ; Maimon. H. Eduth XX, 1. Cf. infra § 99); and that the confutation took place in their presence; otherwise it will amount to simple disproval (Keth. 20ª; Maimon. H. Eduth XVIII, 5). Provided, further, that confutation takes place *before the intended victim of their falsehood is executed* (Maccoth 5ª; Maimon. H. Eduth XX, 2).—The last proviso may appear paradoxical, and some critics do indeed ascribe it to "the clemency of a period which, removed from the practice of penal law, still moved in the subtilties of theory" (Geiger, Urschrift p. 140, n. 2).—But on close contemplation of the spirit of Talmudic jurisprudence, one may readily perceive that this proviso is a necessary consequence of the Rabbinic system.—A witness is not allowed to recant his testimony after the court has cross-examined him (§ 91). He may do so only as long as the court needs him, but not after it is done with him (Sifre II, § 190; Yer. Keth. II, § 3, p. 26ᵇ); then it requires outside testimony to reopen the evidence of that witness. And why this? Evidently, because the court is bound to set a limit to the liberties of witnesses, in order to preserve and enforce respect for its own authority. Now, with the execution of the condemned, the whole case closes, and the court

§ 98. When two parties of witnesses disprove each other, though the testimony of both parties is rejected and the case affected thereby is dismissed, each party, or each individual thereof, may still be trusted in other cases; but a fusion of the two parties, or a combination of individuals from both, must never thereafter appear as witnesses on the same side.[320]

---

is done with it for ever. If a court, after the execution of the convict, were to try the testimony on which he has been convicted, it could never know where and when a capital case would come to a close, or how many victims it might require to close the case, and at the same time it would publish its own incapacity, and have to try itself for a judicial murder! Moreover, the Talmudic system makes the prosecuting witnesses the only legal executioners of their convict (infra § 121). Now, supposing the court to disregard its own self-respect, and to reopen the case after the execution of the alleged criminal, and the prosecuting witnesses to be confuted,—can the court pass a sentence of death upon them? Their crime cannot be denominated murder, because they have killed their victim by order of the court (cf. Horayoth 3ᵇ, Rashi ad l.); it may be a species of culpable homicide, for which the death penalty is not inflicted (supra § 37), and the court can hence not award them punishment in kind, as the law of confutation requires (supra § 97). On the other hand, if they are duly confuted before the execution, but after the sentence of their victim, they are proved guilty of a gross attempt at misleading the court, and of malicious intent with regard to the prisoner, in reference to which the Bible says: Ye shall do unto the false witness as he *intended* to do to his brother (Deut. XIX. 19). The witness *intends to kill* an innocent man; prevent him from carrying out his felonious intention by killing him: the Biblical injunction is his death-warrant, and on the part of the court it will be a case of justifiable homicide.

[321] B. Bathra 31ᵇ; Sheb. 37ᵇ. Individually the parties are not disqualified, because, though one of the two is certainly unreli-

The confuted witness, on the other hand, is not only for ever after debarred from appearing as a witness in any case,[321] but also all evidence given by him since his participation in the case on which he is confuted, is distrusted and invalidated,[322] while he himself suffers the very injury he had intended to inflict on his fellow-man.[323]

---

able the court has no certain grounds on which to convict either; but jointly they must not appear as witnesses, because each represents the other as false, and by associating with that other he renders himself incompetent (cf. supra n. 273).

[321] Tosefta Maccoth I, § 11; Sanh. 27ª.—Akin to this is the Attic law which, in case the prosecutor fails to obtain at least one-fifth of the votes in favor of his accusation, imposes on him, in addition to a fine of 1000 Drachmae, an *atimia* which debars him from ever thereafter appearing as prosecutor in a case of the same nature as that in which he has been defeated (Smith 537ª).

[322] B. Kama 72b; Sanh. 27ª.—This exemplifies the maxim of modern law: *Falsus in uno, falsus in omnibus*. (False in one thing, false in everything).

[323] Cf. n. 318.—There are, however, cases in which the sentence passed on the victim of false testimony, is not executed on the confuted witness, but is substituted by flagellation. These are: A false charge of corruption of Levitical blood—as that of being the son of a marriage between a priest and a divorced woman (cf. Lev. XXI, 13-15), or a *Halutzah* (a widow who has loosed the shoe of her brother-in-law,-cf. Deut. XXV, 7-10)—is preferred against a priest, which would disqualify him and his descendants from officiating in the Temple. In this case, if the intended injury were inflicted on the confuted witness, his innocent children would necessarily share the infamy with him, and that is against the law (cf. § 133, n. 401). Again, confuted witnesses escape their appropriate punishment, when they have falsely testified against a person that he has committed accidental homicide, and that he is consequently

§ 99. Witnesses are not subject to the penalty of confutation, unless all of them are duly confuted. But when an interval, longer than necessary, has elapsed between the hearing of one portion of them and the beginning of that of the other, only those suffer the penalty who have been the direct subjects of confutation, while the rest are exempt from it,[324] although the testimony of all is rejected, if a single one of the whole party is confuted.[325]

---

subject to exile (§ 23); or when they accuse one of having escaped from penal servitude (§ 22); or when they accuse him of being under sentence to pay a fine for a homicide committed by one of his animals (n. 129).—Neither is the witness who is confuted in a case of adultery against a priest's daughter, punishable as she would be, had the charge been sustained—by burning (supra § 27). He is punished, as the adulterer, by strangulation (Maccoth 2ᵃ. Cf. supra § 29). Nor is posthumous hanging superadded to the penalty of stoning, when the witness is confuted in a matter of idolatry or of blasphemy (cf. infra § 130).

[324] Maccoth 5ᵇ sq.; Maimon. H. Eduth XX, 8.—With reference to disproval or to confutation, the law does not follow majorities, but the order of succession. The last party is the victorious party. Therefore even if the first party of witnesses numbers vastly more than the second, the second is still preferred, and confutes or disproves the testimony of the greater number (Maccoth l. c.; Maimon. l. c. XVIII, 3. Cf. Sanh. 27ᵃ). If a third party thereupon appears and disproves or confutes the second, the second stands convicted, while the first is vindicated; and so one party may succeed another in endless rotation, and the court is bound to believe the last and, with it, its predecessors whose evidence its testimony corroborates (Maccoth 5ᵃ; Maimon. l. c. XX, 6). The principle underlying this rule is akin to to that underlying the Roman maxim: *Ponderantur testes non numerantur* (Witnesses are weighed, not counted). [325] Cf. supra n. 318.

8. The Deliberations.

§ 100. Only the finding of the court in the prisoner's favor disposes of the case on the day of the examination. Therefore if, after hearing both sides, the court finds the delation not fully sustained, the prisoner is at once set at liberty; but if he cannot be acquitted immediately, the case is adjourned to the next day,[326] and the court meanwhile enters on deliberation.[327]

---

[326] Sanh. 32ª, 34ª; et al.—The object of this postponement is, to allow the first impression made on the judges to wear off, and to afford reason time to see clearly the path of justice, which might lead to an acquittal (cf. supra n. 255). The only crime not allowed this advantage is instigation to idolatry (§ 26). In this case no postponement is granted, for no mercy may be shown (Tosefta Sanh. X, 11. Cf. supra n. 37; infra n. 333).

[327] Sanh. 40ª; Maimon. II. Sanh. XII, 3.—The court is the representative neither of the state nor of the prisoner, but of the majesty of justice which represents both the state and the prisoner; and justice being blind and impartial, no counsel or advocate is allowed to either side (Mekhilta Kaspa, § 20. Cf. *Meir Ayin* a. l.),—the Rabbis basing this prohibition on the Scriptural dictum (Ex. XXII, 8): "Before the judges shall come *the word of both parties*)," but not of counsel who, by their plausible argumentations, might mystify the judges and cause them to stray from justice.—If the legal fraternity of to-day find this low estimate of their usefulness strange and unwarranted, let them look back to the Talmudic age, when the *synegoroi* and *advocati* flourished in Greece and Rome, and perverted judgment in both countries. Nor was this idea confined to the Rabbis. When King Ferdinand, a thousand years after the close of the Talmud, sent out colonies to the Indies, he provided that no lawyers should be carried along, lest law-suits should become ordinary occurrences in the new world, and he

§ 101. The deliberations must be opened with an argument for the defense,[328] and by one of the younger judges.[329] A simultaneous and unanimous verdict of guilty rendered on the day of trial has the effect of an acquittal.[330]

§ 102. Probationers are allowed to participate in the deliberations, provided they incline to the side of

---

evidently judged with Plato that lawyers are the pests of the country! (Cf. Montaigne, Essays III, c. XIII).—But whatever the Rabbinic opinion be of so important an institution as counsel avowedly is, the procedure of Rabbinic jurisprudence is certainly more consonant with justice, and therefore with the welfare of society, than was the civil law, and after it the law of England, which in capital cases allowed counsel to the prosecution, but not to the defense (cf. Blackstone IV, 359; supra n. 309).

[328] Sifre I, § 12; Sanh. 32ᵃ, 40ᵃ.

[329] Sanh. 32ᵃ, 36ᵃ; Maimon. II. Sanh. XI, 6. Lest the chief, or any of the seniors having given his opinion, the juniors might be tempted to acquiesce, if only out of respect for seniority (Tosefta Sanh. VII, § 2. Cf. Rashi Sanh. 32ᵃ s. v. *Min Hatzad*).

[330] Sanh. 17ᵃ; Maimon. II. Sanh. IX, 1.—Contrary to reason as this rule may appear, it is founded on Rabbinic humanity and as a necessary consequence of Rabbinic law. We have just seen that, for very good reasons (n. 326), a verdict of guilty must not be rendered on the day of examination; but where all suddenly agree on conviction, does it not seem that the convict is a victim of conspiracy, and that the verdict is not the result of sober reason and calm deliberation? In such a case it is hardly probable that, even after the interval of the required adjournment, the court will endeavor to find reason for mitigation. All the judges give up the prisoner as lost, and there will be not even one to plead his cause, as the law provides there should be (Sanh. 29ᵃ); and as every irregularity in the proceedings operates in favor of the prisoner, he is, in the case before us, set at liberty.

the accused. If any one of them rises to speak for the prosecution, he is at once silenced.[331]

§ 103. Witnesses are precluded from arguing on the case to which they have testified, even when they would argue in favor of the accused;[332] while the defendant himself may argue in his own behalf, and when he does not avail himself of this privilege, others must do it for him.[333]

§ 104. The judge who is vacillating in his opinion needs give no reason for his indecision;[334] but those who express decided opinions, must furnish the grounds for their opinions,[335] which the secretaries carefully enter on record.[336]

---

[331] Sanh. 40ᵃ; Maimon. H. Sanh. X, 8. The probationer advances to the judicial bench, whence he delivers his argument. If his argument proves untenable, he remains among the judges for the rest of that day only; but if it is clever, and serves to save the life of the prisoner, he remains there for ever after as an active member of the court (Tosefta Sanh. IX, § 3; Sanh. 42ᵃ).

[332] Sanh. 33ᵇ, 40ᵃ; Maimon. H. Eduth V, 8. For their arguments would affect their own testimony (Sanh. 34ᵃ), which must not be reopened by themselves after the cross-examination (supra § 91, n. 307).

[333] Sanh. 29ᵃ; Maimon. H. Sanh. XI, 5. Except for the instigator to idolatry (cf. n. 37).

[334] Sanh. 17ᵃ; Maimon. H. Sanh. VIII, 3. Cf. infra § 107, n. 344.

[335] Sanh. 34ᵃ; Maimon. H. Sanh. X, 1.

[336] Sanh. 34ᵃ, 36ᵇ, et al.; Maimon. H. Sanh. XII. 3. Cf. supra n. 201.—The object of recording the arguments will appear presently (§§ 106, 107).

9. The Verdict.

§ 105. The members of the court vote *viva voce*,[337] and the majority of votes determines the verdict. A majority of one is sufficient for acquittal, but it requires a majority of at least two for conviction.[338]

---

[337] Sanh. 34ª, 40ª. The only exception is the mishap stated in § 107.—In Athens the judges gave their decision by means of white or black pebbles: the former for acquittal, and the latter for conviction. As the court always sat in the dark (supra n. 219), the white pebbles were distinguished by holes bored into them. Two urns were used: one of wood to receive the white votes, and the other of brass to receive the black ones (Fiske III, § 108; Smith 770ª).

[338] Sanh. 2ª, 32ª; et al. Thus: if the Lesser Synhedrion (§ 53) is divided on a question, eleven members being in favor of conviction and twelve of acquittal, the prisoner is at once pronounced not guilty and set at liberty; but when, per contra, eleven are in favor of acquittal and twelve of conviction, there can be no effective verdict, and recourse must be had to the probationers (§ 109), for it requires a majority equal at least to the legal number of witnesses competent to convict (Tosefta Sanh. III, § 7; Mekhilta Kaspa, § 20).—The French law was the same in this particular, and Montesquieu (B. XII, c. III) warmly commends it. He says, " The Greeks and Romans required one voice more to condemn, but the French law insists upon two. The Greeks pretended that their custom was established by the gods ; but this more justly may be said of ours." While the learned annotator to Blackstone (III, 376, n. 37) strongly favors the rule that a presentment or conviction should not be effective unless approved by at least twelve men, he is strongly opposed to the unanimity required of a jury. He is of opinion that the unanimity of twelve men, so repugnant to all experience of human conduct, passions and understandings, could hardly in any age have been introduced into practice by a deliberate act of the legislature."

§ 106. In counting the votes the following particulars must be observed. When the records show that more judges than one have advanced one and the same argument, though each supported it by different Scriptural dicta,[339] their opinions are considered together as one.[340] Father and son, teacher and pupil,[341] count also as one.[342]

§ 107. If, after having advanced a tenable argument for acquittal, the probationer becomes suddenly disabled from further participation in the debate, the records speak for him, and his recorded opinion counts a vote in the prisoner's favor;[343] while the judge who

---

[339] Cf. supra n. 33.

[340] Tosefta Sanh. III, § 8; Sanh. 34ª. For the Rabbis argue that the Bible is too concise to contain clear statutes on all possible cases (cf. Berakhoth 5ª; Sanh. 87ª; Yer. ib. IV, § 2, p. 22ª bot.), but that it is a kind of mnemotechnic *index rerum* to the vast system of divine laws which are detailed in the Rabbinic literature (cf. Yer. Berakhoth I, § 7, p. 3ᵇ bot. et al); and while each of its expressions is therefore a firm basis to at least one law, no two of them refer to one and the same thing under like circumstances (Erubin 21ᵇ; Sanh. 34ª, et al.).

[341] As stated above (n. 210) father and son are not eligible in one and the same court; our case can therefore happen only when the one is a member of the court and the other a participating probationer (cf. §§ 102, 108). As to teacher and pupil, they are not allowed to sit on the same bench, as long as the pupil actually requires the teacher's assistance, and are therefore counted as one; otherwise the pupil is counted as an independent person (Sanh. 36ᵇ; Maimon H. Sanh. XI, 7).

[342] Sanh. 36ª; Maimon H. Sanh. XI, 7. But this is the rule when their opinions support the same side, not when they disagree (cf. Tosefta Sanh. II, § 1).

[343] Sanh. 34ª; Maimon H. Sanh. X, 3. If, however, the mishap occurs before he has duly established his opinion, though

is undecided and wavering is considered as absent, and therefore not counted.[344]

§ 108. When the court is so divided that no effective verdict for acquittal can be given on that day, it adjourns to the next day. In the meanwhile the judges may partake of food, but must drink no wine whatever. They may retire from the court-room, but not to rest. In the privacy of their closets they must, either by themselves or with some colleagues, continue to study the questions at issue. Early the next morning they must again be in their seats at the place of meeting, and proceed, in the manner described, to dispose of the case.[345] In rearguing the

---

he may have expressed himself as favoring acquittal, his opinion does not count (Sanh. 43ª; Maimon. l. c. 4).

[344] Sanh. 40ª; Maimon II. Sanh. IX, 2. Even if he states his reasons for vacillating, giving arguments pro and con, which he is not required to do (§ 104), he cannot be considered as present, so long as he is undecided about the verdict (Sanh. 17ª; Maimon. l. c. VIII, 2 et al. Cf. infra n. 348).—In Rome the judices voted by ballot. Each one was provided with three tablets, on one of which was marked A = Absolvo; on the second, C = Condemno; and on the third, N. L. = Non liquet, and a majority of these ballots determined the condemnation or acquittal of the accused (Smith 552ᵇ).

[345] Tosefta Sanh. IX, § 1; Sanh. 40ª. All the arguments must be restated. If any one who has spoken in favor of acquittal becomes confused, the secretaries extricate him by means of the records; but if he is one who has argued in favor of conviction, no such assistance is rendered him. He is left to extricate himself as best he can (Tosefta l. c.; Yer. Sanh. V, end, p. 23ª top); and when it is proved by the records that he now argues from a different standpoint, though still on the side of conviction, the case must be adjourned for another day (Sanh.

points, any one who has previously expressed himself as favoring conviction, but subsequently changes his opinion, may state his reasons for the changes; but he who has spoken in favor of acquittal, if he changes his opinion, is not allowed to give his reasons.[346]

§ 109. When, on recounting the votes, it appears that no effective verdict can be found by the acting judges, their number is increased or supplemented by two probationers.[347] If these do not reach a deci-

---

[34a]. Cf. Yer. 1. c.).—During the thousand years following the close of the Talmud, which contains hundreds of such humane laws, the world branded the Rabbinic system of laws as barbarous and inhuman, at a time when the English courts did not suffer the prisoner accused of a capital crime, to exculpate himself by the help of witnesses (supra n. 309). How consistent and just!

[346] Sanh. 34a, 40a. But he must vote with those whom he conscientiously believes to be in the right.

[347] Sanh. 17a, 40a; Maimon II. Sanh. IX, 2. When the opinions of the members of the court are so divided as to constitute a majority for conviction, but that majority consists of one vote only (supra § 105), the court is simply increased by the addition of two supernumeraries; but when one of the original twenty-three judges is not clear on the question and, therefore, undecided as to the verdict (supra n. 344), though all the others are of one and the same opinion, there is a virtual deficiency in the required number of judges, wherefore the court must be supplemented.—As to the time at which this process is resorted to, it might appear, from Sanh. 40a, to be the second day after the formal examination, and Rashi (ad. l. c.) so interprets that passage; but, from Tosefta Sanh. IX, § 1, and Sanh. 35a, it clearly appears to be the day immediately following that on which the examination closed, and Maimonides (l. c.) so understood it.—By the old English law, a verdict by the grand assize had to be approved of by at least twelve members; and if twelve did not

sion,³⁴⁶ the process of increasing or supplementing is again resorted to, and this is, under similar circumstances, repeated either until a decisive majority is secured, or until there are on the bench as many judges as constitute the Great Synhedrion—seventy-one.³⁴⁹

§ 110. If after reaching the number of seventy-one, the court continues unable to find an effective verdict,³⁵⁰ the entire court remains in session and continues to discuss the points of variance, until one of the participants changes his opinion, when the ver-

---

agree, the assize was afforced, *i. e.* others were added till twelve did concur (Blackstone III, 376, n. 37).

³⁴⁸ This may happen either when the supernumeraries are divided on the question, thus making thirteen for conviction and twelve for acquittal; or when the court stands eleven to eleven, with one undecided, and the suppletories are divided, thus making twelve against twelve. On the other hand, when the original court stands twelve for conviction and eleven for acquittal, or eleven to eleven with one undecided, and the supernumeraries vote together for conviction; or when the court stands twelve to eleven, and the supernumeraries are divided, one voting with the twelve for conviction, and the other being undecided and not voting at all, the verdict of the majority holds good. But when the original twenty-three are divided, there being twelve on one side and eleven on the other, and one of the supernumeraries votes with the minority for acquittal, and the other does not vote at all, thus causing a tie of twelve against twelve, the prisoner is acquitted (Sanh. 17ᵃ; Maimon. ib. IX, 2).—By Grecian law, too, an equal division of votes was equivalent to an acquittal (Smith 770ᵃ).

³⁴⁹ Sanh. 40ᵃ; Maimon. H. Sanh. IX, 2. The Great Synhedrion itself was not to be increased under any circumstances (Sanh. 42ᵃ; Maimon l. c., 3).

³⁵⁰ For reasons stated in notes 347 and 348.

dict is carried by the requisite majority.[351] But if after a long and thorough discussion, the requisite majority cannot be secured, each side remaining firm in its convictions and unchangeable in its opinions, the chief of the court declares the case "drawn," and the prisoner is discharged.[352]

§ 111. When a verdict is arrived at, the accused is brought before the bar,[353] and the chief of the court declares it. • If that verdict is in the prisoner's favor, acquitting him of the charge, he is at once liber-

---

[351] Sanh. 40a; Maimon. II. Sanh. IX. 2.—In such cases the defense has great advantages, and a verdict of guilty is hardly any longer probable; for the party that has once spoken for the defense, if he changes his opinion, is not allowed to speak for the prosecution, or even to state his reasons for the change (§ 108), while the deserter from the ranks of the prosecution is allowed to state his reasons for the change, and, speaking now for the defense, he may carry others with him, by convincing them of the guiltlessness of the accused or of some irregularity in the trial, which makes a conviction illegal (Sanh. 17a; Maimon. l. c.). Another advantage of the accused is the rule debarring the party who has expressed himself as being undecided, from voting with the convicting side, even after he is convinced that conviction is in consonance with justice (l. c.), because the postponement of the verdict is intended to produce results favorable to the accused (supra n. 326), and is not allowed to cause him injury.

[352] Sanh. 42a; Maimon. H. Sanh. IX, 2.—In Rome also it was the duty of the presiding magistrates to pronounce the sentence of the judices; in the case of condemnation, to adjudge the legal penalty; of acquittal, to declare him acquitted; and of doubt, to declare that the matter must be further investigated (Smith 552b).

[353] Sanh. 79b; Maimon. II. Rozeah IV, 7; II. Sanh. XIV, 7.

ated;[354] if, on the contrary, he is found guilty, then he is straightway led forth to execution.[355]

---

[354] Sanh. 40ᵃ; Maimon. H. Sanh. XII, 3.

[355] Sanh. 42ᵇ sq. Cf. supra, § 74, n. 254. The *Zaken Mamre* is an exception to this rule (cf. supra n. 255).—As the Talmud, like the civil and common law (cf. Roscoe 575), considers the embryo in the womb *pars viscerum matris* (Sanh. 80ᵇ, et al.) and, therefore, as not having individual existence, a pregnant woman is not reprieved; but the embryo is first killed within her, and then she is executed. When, however, the woman is about to be delivered, a respite is allowed (Arakhin 7ᵃ; Maimon. l. c.. 4 .— Blackstone (IV, 395) speaks of a case on the island of Guernsey. where a woman big with child was burned; and when, through the violence of the flame, the infant sprang forth at the stake. and was preserved by the by-standers, the priests who assisted at the sacrifice, after some deliberation, cast it back into the fire as a young heretic.—As to the interval between the sentence and the execution, there formerly was a law in England, prescribing that the judge, before whom any person is found guilty of wilful murder, shall pronounce sentence immediately after conviction, unless he sees cause to postpone it; and shall, in passing sentence, direct the convict to be executed on the next day but one; and that during this short but awful interval between the sentence and the execution, he shall be kept isolated and sustained with bread and water (ib. 202).—By Rabbinic law the verdict implies the sentence, since nothing is left to the discretion of the court; the punishment for every crime being prescribed by statute (supra §§ 21-29). Fines and flagellations are exceptions, but only as to the amount of money (supra n. 148) and the number of stripes (infra n. 421). And if the great commentator (l. c. 377 sq.) claims it as "one of the glories of our English law, that the species, though not always the quantity or degree of punishment is *ascertained* for every offense," what glory might not the Rabbinic system claim, which ascertains the *degree* as well as the *species* of punishment (cf. n. 23)! Nor were Grecian courts invested with discretionary powers in awarding

§ 112. All the participants in the debate are strictly enjoined not to divulge the opinions of the different members of the court, nor the names of those who voted for or against the accused.[356]

§ 113. On the day on which a human being is condemned by their verdict to capital punishment, the judges are not allowed to partake of any food or drink.[357]

10. Reversal of Judgment.

§ 114. A verdict of conviction may be reversed by the trial court, but a verdict of acquittal can, under no circumstances, be reversed.[358]

---

punishment, for also in Greece the law determined the punishment according to the nature of the crime (Smith 770a).

[356] Sifra Kedoshim § 4; Sanh. 29a. The Talmud (Sanh. 31a) records the instance of one who, having been found guilty of a violation of this rule decades after the occurrence, was expelled from the court-house as a slanderer.

[357] Sifra Kedoshim, § 6; Sanh. 63a. If the trial takes place on a half holiday, when fasting is not allowed, the verdict is not pronounced till near sunset, and the execution takes place immediately thereafter (Moed Katon 14b).—A Spanish nobleman resented an insult offered him by a guardsman of Sixtus V. Without any such intention on the part of the nobleman, the recounter resulted fatally for the guard, and the Pope ordered the unfortunate homicide to be whipped to death. This barbarous execution took place under the windows of the papal residence and was witnessed by the Pope. As soon as life became extinct, Sixtus ordered in his dinner, gleefully adding: "This act of justice has given me an excellent appetite!"—Was he governed in this procedure by the "inhuman laws" of the Rabbis?!

[358] Sifre II, § 144; Sanh. 32a. Though the trial was conducted, and the verdict of guilty arrived at, in obedience to all the rules

§ 115. If a convict who has escaped from one court is brought before another, the latter is not competent to review his case, but must see that the judgment of the trial court be carried out, provided the original witnesses or prosecutors are present.[359] But if the

of Rabbinic judicial procedure, if sufficiently new evidence in favor of the convict is found (cf. infra § 119), or if the verdict is discovered to rest on a mistake of law, or if even the convict himself declares that he has something to say in his own favor (§ 120), the court is bound to reopen the case, and afford the convict a chance for vindication and deliverance. But when, on the contrary, the party stood his trial and was found not guilty, he must not again be brought in jeopardy for the same offense, though his guilt might now be established on new and conclusive evidence. And even when the judges themselves discover that their verdict of acquittal was founded on a mistake of law, that verdict cannot be revoked.—This rule is founded on the Biblical injunction: "The innocent and the righteous slay not" (Exodus XXIII, 7), which the Rabbis construe thus: The innocent, though found guilty, and the one found righteous, though really guilty, slay not (Mekhilta Kaspa, § 20; Sanh. 33b). —An exception to this rule is the instigator to idolatry. If he is once adjudged guilty, he is executed; and if declared innocent, he must be retried and convicted, when new evidence is discovered sufficient to convict him (Sifre II, § 89; Sanh. 33b. Cf. supra n. 326).

[359] Maccoth 7a; Maimon. H. Sanh. XII, 7. Where the fugitive from justice is a convict for murder, any two witnesses of the declaration of the condemnatory verdict are competent to compass his execution at the instance of any court (Maimon. l. c. Cf. Sanh. 45b).—By Athenian law, a convicted murderer, if found within the limits of the state, might be seized and put to death; and whoever harbored or entertained any one who had fled from his country to avoid capital punishment, was liable to the same penalties as the fugitive himself (Smith 134b). But

conviction took place before a foreign court, and the escaped convict is brought before a Palestinean tribunal,[360] the verdict of the foreign court is set aside, and the convict is granted a new trial.[361]

---

no murderer, even if he escaped after conviction, could lawfully be killed or even arrested in a foreign country (ib. 770^b).

[360] The Palestinean courts were considered higher than those of other countries (Maccoth 7^a, et al.).

[361] Tosefta Sanh. III, § 11; Maccoth 7^a.

IV. THE EXECUTION.

1. BETWEEN LIFE AND DEATH.

§ 116. Believing that the interval between conviction and execution is the most terrible period in the life of the convict, the Talmud ordains that the execution take place before sundown [362] of the very day on which the verdict is pronounced.[363]

---

[362] Sanh. 34ᵇ sq.; Maimon. II. Sanh. XV, 7.

[363] Sanh. 32ᵃ, 35ᵃ: Maimon. II. Sanh. XIII, 1. Cf. supra § 74, n. 254.—As the execution of the criminal was not looked upon by the Hebrews as a retribution for his crime, nor as making amends for the mischief done; nor yet as a vindication of the majesty of the law, or as satisfying the abstract demands of justice;—as, in short, the great aim of penal justice was to warn the future rather than to avenge the past (supra n. 184), and as death generally is considered by the Rabbis as an expiation for misdeeds (cf. Yoma 85): the Rabbinic law did not permit a spirit of vengeance or of retaliation to embitter the last hours of the convict. On the contrary, strict as was the law, and vigilant as were its guardians, every possible consideration was bestowed upon the unfortunate victim of folly, which the Talmud assumes every offender to be (Sotah 3ᵃ), and every possible alleviation of his necessary pains and sufferings was afforded him (cf. infra § 120). Hence the haste in which the execution followed the sentence. Besides, the shortness of the time elapsing between the passing and the execution of the sentence is in itself very useful (supra n. 18); since the shorter the interval between the crime and its penalty, the stronger and the more lasting is the impression made on the human

§ 117. The place of execution is located outside of the city limits,[364] and at a considerable distance from the court-house.[365]

§ 118. As the convict is led forth towards the scaffold, a flag-bearer is stationed at the entrance of the court-house, and, at some distance from him, a rider is placed, while a herald marches in front of the procession, loudly proclaiming the name of the convict, his crime, where and when committed, and the names of the prosecuting witnesses, at the same time inviting any and every one knowing reasons why the sentence should not be executed, to appear and declare them.[366] If any favorable testimony comes to light, the flag-bearer gives the signal, and the equestrian hastens to

---

mind by the association of the two ideas, the commission of the crime and the paying of the penalty, and the more involuntarily will the one be generally considered as the cause and the other as the necessary and infallible effect (cf. Beccaria § 19).

[364] The betrothed maiden convicted of adultery, and the idolator suffer their respective penalties in the city where they committed the crime; and the former, even at her father's residence, when the crime is laid there (Sifre II, § 139, 148; Keth. 44ᵇ sq.).

[365] Sanh, 42ᵇ, Maimonides (H. Sanh. XII, 3) puts the distance at 6000 paces.—The object of locating the place of execution far from the court-house, is twofold: first, to avoid the appearance of the judges' participating in the execution (cf. infra n. 369); and, secondly and especially, to afford the convict a last chance for meeting some circumstance that might lead to a rehearing of his case (Sanh. l. c. Cf. § 118).

[366] Or the judges themselves, who remain in session, may discover some error in their judgment (cf. supra n. 358).

bring the convict back before the court, who hear the new testimony and judge thereof.[367]

§ 119. The convict's own declaration that he has to make a statement in his own favor is sufficient to cause a temporary stay of proceedings, until after he is heard by the court; and if no favorable result is gained, a repetition of his request to be reconducted before the court must likewise be heeded.[368] After that, two scholars[369] accompany him; and when he again applies for a reconsideration of his case, he is obliged to state his reasons to his learned escort; if these consider them of sufficient weight and importance, he is returned to court, and heard and judged as before; if not, he is led on to execution.[370]

§ 120. When the procession arrives within ten paces from the scaffold, the convict is exhorted to make a general confession of his sins, but not necessarily of the crime for which he is to suffer the penalty.[371] Thereupon a mixture of wine and olibanum is administered

---

[367] Sanh. 43a; Maimon. H. Sanh. XIII, 1.—Except in the case of the instigator to idolatry (supra n. 358).

[368] For it is assumed that the convict's embarrassment and confusion, incident to the awful ordeal of the trial, prevented him from arguing clearly and pleading effectually at the proper stage of the proceedings (Sanh. 43a).

[369] Not from among the authors of the verdict, who, for reasons stated (n. 365), do not leave the court-house until after the execution (Maimon. H. Sanh. XIII, 4).

[370] Sanh. 42a; Maimon. H. Sanh. XIII, 1.—He is not prevented from bidding farewell to his relatives and friends (Semahoth II, § 9).

[371] Sanh. 42b; Maimon. H. XIII, 1. The formula of the confession is very simple and concise. "May my death be an expiation for all my sins" is all that the convict is expected to

to him that he may fall into a stupor, and not realize the painful close of his earthly career;[372] and when he is brought still nearer to the fatal place, he is divested of nearly all his clothes, and thus led on to the spot.[373]

2. The Executioners.

§ 121. Talmudic jurisprudence provides for no official executioners.[374] The witnesses to the crime pros-

---

say. No justification of the verdict is sought at his mouth. On one occasion a convict, in sight of the scaffold, asserted his innocence, saying, instead of the usual formula: "If I am guilty of the crime for which I am about to die, may my death not atone for my sins; but if I am innocent thereof, may my death be an expiation for all my sins, and may the court and all Israel not be held responsible for my untimely and unmerited death, but may the false witnesses who compassed this judicial murder never find pardon." When this confession was reported to the court, the judges began to doubt the justice of their verdict. To their sorrow, they had no legal ground upon which to base a reversal of their verdict (cf. supra n. 358), but they admitted that a terrible responsibility rested on the witnesses (Sanh. 44b; Yer. ib. VI, § 4, p. 23b bot.; Tosefta ib. IX, § 5).

[372] Sanh. 43a; Maimon. II. Sanh. XIII, 2.—Little more than one century ago, Blackstone (IV, 377) ascribed to "the *humanity* of the English nation" the fact that there were "few instances (and those accidental or by negligence) of any person's being embowelled or burned, till previously deprived of sensation by strangling!"

[373] Sifra Emor § 19; Sanh. 45b.—A woman is not deprived of her clothes, her sex protecting her against the indignity (cf. infra n. 395).

[374] In Athens, it was the duty of the *Thesmothetae* to see that the sentence was executed, and of the *Eleven* to execute it

ecute the criminal and execute him.[375] When they find themselves unable to execute the sentence of the court, the by-standers are obliged to do it for them;[376] but when their inability is the result of some mishap which has occurred since the trial, the prisoner escapes the sentence, and is liberated.[377]

3. THE CONSUMMATION.

§ 122. Arrived at the place of execution, the convict, who has gradually been prepared for the closing

---

(Smith 770a). In Rome the *quaestores parricidii* were the public executioners as well as the public accusers (ib. 828a), while the *carnifex* executed slaves and foreigners (ib. 217a). To the spirit of Talmudic jurisprudence it is repugnant to appoint a man specially to take another's life.

[375] Sifra Emor, § 20; Sifra II. § 151, et al.; Sanh. 45b, et al.

[376] Sifra Kedoshim, § 8; Sifre II. § 89, 151, et al.; Sanh. 45b, et al. While the public was allowed to witness the execution (Sifra Emor, § 20; Sifre II. § 240, et al.), no one was allowed to lay hands on him or otherwise abuse him (cf. supra n. 126), unless the occasion absolutely required it,—as when the convict resisted, and the legal executioners, the witnesses, were not strong enough to cope with him (cf. infra n. 395). Thus was precluded the possibility of an infuriated mob's wreaking vengeance on a fellow-being, criminal though he was (cf. Sanh. 44a).

[377] Sanh. 45b; Maimon. H. Sanh. XIV, 8. If the convict, however, is a murderer, he must not be allowed to escape his doom, but the by-standers must execute him.—Blackstone (IV, 316) says: "The ancient usage was, as late as Henry the Fourth's time, that all the relations of the slain shall drag the appellee to the place of execution: a custom founded upon the savage spirit of family resentment which prevailed universally through Europe."

scene, is pinioned,[378] and the execution of the sentence,—*stoning, burning, decapitation* or *strangling,* [379] whichever may be the necessary and statutory consequence of the verdict,[380]—is proceeded with. That is done in the following manner:

§ 123. STONING.—The witnesses, having placed their convict on a high platform or scaffold, precipitate him to the ground.[381] If instant death is not produced by the fall, the witnesses hurl upon his prostrate body a

---

[378] Sanh. 49ᵇ; Maimon. H. Sanh. XIV, 1.—Any one duly convicted of a crime which renders him liable to different modes of death at once; or one who, convicted of one capital crime, commits another of greater malignity, is punished with the death to which the more heinous crime made him subject (cf. supra §§ 17 and 25). Thus when one is guilty of illicit commerce with a married woman,—for which the penalty is death by strangulation (§ 29),—he is punished with burning, if that woman is his wife's mother, (§ 27). Again, if one standing convicted of false prophecy (§ 29), in the presence of the court (cf. Tosafoth Sanh. 81ᵃ, s. v. *Wenigmar* supra, n. 143) commits blasphemy (§ 26), he is punished with stoning (Sanh. 81ᵃ; Maimon. l. c. 4. Cf. supra § 17; infra § 127.

[379] For the respective subjects of these penalties cf. supra §§ 26-29; but it will presently appear that the execution of the sentence under the Talmudic dispensation, is not the same as it was under the purely Mosaic system. From that system have been preserved in the Talmudic system only the technical names of the deaths, but not the modes of the application of the respective deaths.

[380] Cf. supra n. 355.

[381] *Precipitation* was practised by the most ancient nations. The Greeks precipitated the convict into a pit, which was a noisome hole with sharp spikes at top and bottom (cf. supra n. 86).

heavy stone; and only when that is not sufficient, the by-standers throw stones at him until he is dead.[382]

§ 124. BURNING.[383]—The witnesses secure the culprit so as to render him unable to move; then his mouth is forced open by means of a cord wrapped in a soft cloth,[384] and tightly drawn around his neck, and then some molten lead is poured down his throat.[385]

---

[382] Sifre I, § 144, et al.; Sanh. 45ª.—These steps were prescribed by the Rabbis in order to prevent, as much as possible, the mutilation of the convict's body. The application of the Mosaic ordinance: "Thou shalt love thy neighbor as thyself" (Lev. XIX, 18), the Rabbis maintain, must be extended beyond the limits of social intercourse in life, so that even the pronounced criminal may share its benefits; and although the law justly claims his life, the spirit of love and compassion must be manifested towards him by rendering his death decent, —*i. e.* by abstaining, if possible, from sending him to the felon's grave, bearing disfiguring marks of violence (Sanh. 45ª, 52ª, et al.).

[383] Whenever this penalty was inflicted, it was carried out in the literal sense of the term, and among some nations in a most horrible way. Among the Romans, the convict was wrapped in a garment covered with pitch, and then set on fire and burned (Fiske III, § 264. 3).—MacFarlane (Empire of Japan, Book V) tells, on the authority of travellers, that a similar custom obtains in Japan. There the convict is enveloped in a close-fitting shirt, made of reeds, to which fire is applied; and while the poor victim, distracted by the flames, runs and leaps about in his agony, which is called by the pleasant name of the "Death-dance," the spectators laugh and applaud, as at a dance in the theatre.

[384] That no marks be left on the body (cf. supra n. 382).

[385] Sanh. 52ª; Maimon. H. Sanh. XV, 3. According to some Rabbis, the mixture was an alloy of lead and tin (Yer. Sanh. VII, § 2, p. 24ᵇ; Maimon. l. c.). On the other hand, the Talmud preserves an account of an execution at the stake, which a

§ 125. DECAPITATION.—The convict having been fastened to a post, his head is severed from his body by a blow with a sword.[386]

§ 126. STRANGLING.—The convict having been carefully secured, a cord wrapped in a soft cloth is drawn around his neck until all breath leaves his body.[387]

§ 127. When, after due trial and conviction, those convicted of different crimes, and consequently under sentences of different modes, of death, are so intermixed that the executioners are unable to distinguish one from another,—all undergo the death of the least criminal.[388] When a convict succeeds in hiding him-

---

sage asserted that he had witnessed in his early childhood, during the last years of Judea's second commonwealth; but as no one is competent to bear witness to what he has seen in his minority (supra n. 264), no rule of procedure could be established on his authority (Tosefta Sanh. IX, § 11; Sanh. 52^b). And when the same authority averred that he had seen a similar execution in his riper years, the Rabbis remarked that the court so ordering it was an ignorant court, or consisted of Sadducees (Sanh. l. c.).

[386] Sanh. 52^b; Maimon. H. Sanh. XV, 4.

[387] Sanh. 52^b; Maimon. H. Sanh. XV, 5. With the exception of the deadly mixture, this is the same as burning (§ 124), and is the penalty of all offenses for which the Bible awards death at human hands, without defining the manner of the death. It is considered the least painful of all (Mekhilta Nezikin, § 5; Sanh. l. c., et al.).—The Persians had a singular punishment for great criminals. A high tower was partly filled with ashes, into which the culprit was thrown. The ashes were continually stirred up by means of contiguous and surrounding machinery, and the dust therefrom gradually suffocated him (cf. II Macc. XIII, 5).

[388] Sanh. 79^b; Maimon. H. Sanh. XIV, 6. Cf. supra n. 378.

self amid a crowd of people and he cannot be duly identified, the penalty is altogether remitted.[389]

4. Posthumous Ignominies.

§ 128. In order to render the crimes of idolatry and blasphemy more repugnant to the masses of the people, the punishment for them is rendered more ignominious by the superaddition of *hanging*.[390]

§ 129. Hanging, as part of the punishment for the crimes named, is a *posthumous* superaddition to stoning;[391] and although it is intended as an insult to the

---

[389] Sanh. 79ᵇ; Maimon. II. Sanh. XIV, 7. If a case of this kind occurs before the trial, even when there are only two persons present and one of them is beyond all suspicion of crime, there can be no prosecution, unless the criminal can be fully identified by eye-witnesses (Sanh. 80ᵃ. Cf. supra n. 287).

[390] Sifre II. § 221; Sanh. 45ᵇ; Maimon. II. Sanh. XV, 6.—In Rome, hanging was one of the several modes of punishment for treason (Smith 754ᵇ); but in England, it was one of a series of punishments inflicted for the same offense. Here the criminal was drawn to the gallows, and not carried or walked; he was then hanged by the neck and cut down alive; his entrails were thereupon taken out and burned while he was still alive; then he was beheaded, and his body divided into four parts and left to the King's disposal (Blackstone IV, 92).

[391] Under the Talmudic dispensation no punishment was attended with insult, except that for these crimes (cf. supra n. 362); and never was an execution attended with any of those tortures and horrible mutilations which have disgraced the jurisprudence of so many polished nations before and since the close of the Talmud. What a chapter of horrors is that describing the martyrdom of the seven brothers for strenuous adherence to their ancestral religion (II Macc. VII)! How terrible were the fiendish torments inflicted by Rufus, in the name of

criminal, the exposure of his suspended body must not

Roman law, on the Jewish Martyrs! R. Akiba was flayed alive with iron pincers (Berakhoth 61ᵇ); another Rabbi was enshrouded in a parchment scroll containing the Pentateuch, and slowly roasted upon a pyre of green twigs, while wet wool was put on his chest to prolong the agony of death (Ab. Zara 18ᵃ). Breaking on the wheel, impaling, exposing to wild beasts, and crucifixion,—in which life and consciousness and excruciating pain were prolonged not unfrequently to the third day, and sometimes even to the seventh,—were among the delectable sights at Roman executions; while the Persians practised a form of execution *by the boat*, which combined all the horrors an oriental imagination could suggest, and from describing which an occidental pen revolts. Mithridates, with much difficulty, found relief in death after being confined in the boat for seventeen days (Plutarch, Life of Artaxerxes). And coming down the vista of time to the last century and to England, we meet with numerous circumstances of terror, pain and disgrace superadded to the actual death-penalty; and yet Blackstone glories in the clemency of the English law! In summing up the several modes of punishment practised in England and in his days, he remarks (IV, 377): "Disgusting as this catalogue may seem, it will afford pleasure to an English reader, and do honor to the English law, to compare it with that shocking apparatus of death and torment to be met with in the criminal codes of almost every other nation in Europe." If Blackstone had good reason for exulting in the humanity of the English law as it was constituted in his days, a little over a century ago, how much more right have the Jews to glory in the Talmudic laws which are confessedly as high above the English laws in humanity as in age! Here we not only see no torturous and lingering punishments, but even the swiftest method of death, if death must be inflicted, is deprived of its horrors and pains (cf. § 120), while posthumous insults are exceedingly rare, and those inflicted but of momentary duration. Man is endowed with the image of his Maker—argues the Talmud; he

be protracted.[392] The convict's hands are joined above his head, and by them he is suspended from a gibbet,[393] but immediately thereafter taken down.[394]

§ 130. Only the party duly convicted of idolatry or blasphemy, is the subject of this ignominy, but the confuted witnesses to the alleged crime do not share it.[395]

§ 131. The bodies of executed criminals must be buried soon after the execution,[396] but not in the sepul-

---

must therefore not be exposed to disgrace (Sanh. 46ᵇ. Cf. infra n. 393).

[392] In Rome the bodies of executed criminals were usually exposed to the gaze of the populace, either before the prison, or on certain stairs, called *scalae gemoniae* (Smith 213ᵇ). In England the heads of those executed for treason were exposed on the pikes of the executioners, or from the tower, and often the dismembered body was nailed up in different parts of the city.

[393] The gibbet must be an artificial one, easily removable out of sight; and not a stationary one, as a tree rooted in the ground, which would require cutting down before removal, or if left standing in its place would serve as a constant reminder of a human being's disgraceful end (cf. n. 391).

[394] Sifre II, § 221; Sanh. 46ᵃ, sq.; Maimon. II. Sanh. XV. 7. The gibbet as well as the instruments used in the execution are buried out of human sight, in the neighborhood of the criminal's grave (Sanh. 45ᵇ; Maimon. l. c. 9).

[395] Sifre II, § 221. Cf. supra § 97.—Nor is this superaddition inflicted on female convicts (Sifre ib.; Sanh. 45ᵇ sq. Cf. supra n. 376).—By English law in Blackstone's days, the punishment for treason in woman was different from that inflicted on man (n. 390).—"For as the decency due the sex forbids the exposing and mangling their bodies, their sentence (which is full as terrible to sensation as the other) is to be drawn to the gallows, and there to be burned alive" (Blackstone IV. 202).

[396] Sifre II, § 221; Sanh. 46.—It was the general custom among the Hebrews, as among other Eastern nations, to bury their

chres of their families.[397] They are interred in cemeteries especially devoted to such purposes.[398]

§ 132. The relatives of executed criminals are not allowed to wear outside marks of mourning for them;[399] but are to call on the prosecuting witnesses and the court, and, kindly saluting them, manifest their personal abhorrence of the crime, and approval of the verdict.[400]

§ 133. No sentence carries with it the least change in the status of the convict's children,[401] or confiscation

---

dead as soon after the occurrence of death as the necessary preparations permitted. A postponement of the rite, except for purposes of dignifying the occasion, was considered sacrilegious. In Rome the remains of criminals were, after exposure (supra n. 295 and 392), dragged with hooks and cast into the Tiber; and in England, no executed criminal could be interred before his remains were publicly dissected (Blackstone IV, 202).

[397] Family sepulchres were usual among the Hebrews.

[398] Tosefta Sanh. IX, § 8; Sanh. 46ª.—The community provides two cemeteries: one to receive the remains of those executed by stoning or burning, and another for the decapitated or strangled. After the thorough dissolution of the flesh, the naked bones may be disinterred and buried in the general Jewish cemetery.

[399] As baring of feet, dressing in black, rending the garments (cf. Moed Katon. 14ᵇ sq., et al.; Maimon. II. Abel V, sq.; supra n. 37).—Nor were relatives, under such circumstances, allowed to mourn among the Romans (Smith 754ᵇ).

[400] Sifre Maimon. § 1; Sanh. 46ª.

[401] Sanh. 27ᵇ; Nidda 50ª; et al. Cf. supra n. 323. Plato is of the opinion that, instead of punishing the innocent children of a convict, they ought to be commended for not having followed their parent's examples (Montesquieu, B. VI, c. XX); and this opinion is shared by the Pharisees of old (cf. Josephus, IV Ant. VIII, 39).—How much and how justly do we congratu-

of his property.[402] All his hereditaments descend to his heirs.[403]

---

late ourselves on that principle of our constitutional law, that no criminal attainder shall work corruption of blood! Yet this principle was embodied in the constitution framed by Moses, although the opposite doctrine prevailed in the governments of the most polished nations of antiquity. His statute is expressed with characteristic clearness and brevity: "The parents shall not be put to death for the children, neither shall the children be put to death for the parents; every man shall be put to death for his own sins" (Deut. XXIV, 16). This principle Moses incorporated into his code, in the face of prejudice, common opinion, immemorial usage, and the sentiment of inexorable and insatiate revenge (Wines 262). And the Talmudists followed his example of justice and humanity, in the face of the opposite doctrine among the cotemporaneous legislators of other nations. Among the Greeks and the Romans, the posterity of those who were put to death by the people, or were convicted of certain infamous crimes, such as theft, inherited the infamy of their ancestors (Smith 479a, 534b.) The Macedonian law extended even the capital punishment of treason, not only to the children, but to all the relations of the delinquent: and, of course, their estates also were forfeited, as no man was left to inherit them (Blackstone IV, 383). But among the Hebrews, only the natural taint, such as results from *mesalliance*, descended to the offspring or recoiled on the father (Lev. XXI, 9–15). No one is criminally responsible, according to Talmudic jurisprudence, for the crimes of another. It is true, the Rabbis declare "all Israelites responsible for one another" (Sanh. 27b; Sheb. 39a); but this is in a moral sense only. When one can preserve another from committing a crime, and does not avail himself of his power, he is responsible *before Heaven* for the omission. There exists among Israelites a sort of "Frankpledge" to preserve the peace and morality of society; but it does not go so far as to include suffering human punishment for, or with, one another.

[402] Arakhin 6b; Maimon. H. Arakhin I, 14. Although with reference to amercements (cf. supra n. 148) for injuries inflicted

5. Minor Punishments.

§ 134. Exile, as the penalty for accidental homicide,[404] means confinement in the city of refuge for life,[405] unless the reigning High Priest dies in the

---

by him after his conviction, he is considered dead as soon as sentence of death is pronounced against him, he may nevertheless dispose of his property as he sees fit. In cases of treason, however, all his effects are forfeited to the civil government (Tosefta Sanh. IV, § 6; et al).—The forfeiture or confiscation of property for treason was universal among ancient, and is almost so among modern nations; but for other offenses too the laws of many nations confiscated the real estate of the attainted (cf. Blackstone IV, 383 sq.); and even when confiscation was not included in the penalty, the attainted had not the right of transferring or transmitting property (ib. 382). Thus a banished person (or a professed monk) was accounted absolutely dead in law, therefore all his rights were extinct, and his next heir could at once enter on his estate (ib. I, 132).

[403] Tosefta Sanh. VI, § 6; Sanh. 48b).—In Germany, by the famous Golden Bull (copied almost *verbatim* from Justinian's code), the lives of the sons of such as conspire to kill an elector are spared, as it is expressed, by the emperor's *particular bounty*. But they are deprived of all their effects and rights of succession, and are rendered incapable of any honor, ecclesiastical or civil: "to the end that, being always poor and necessitous, they may forever be accompanied by the infamy of their father; may languish in continual indigence; and may find their punishment in living, and their relief in dying" (Blackstone IV, 383).

[404] Cf. supra § 23, n. 76, § 35.

[405] Sifre I, § 160; Tosefta Maccoth III, § 5; Maccoth 11b. No amount of money can shorten it or commute it (cf. supra n. 95).—Among the Greeks where murder was commonly punished with banishment, either voluntarily sought or expressly

meantime; then the refugee is considered purged of his unpremeditated offense, and therefore at liberty to return home.[406]

§ 135. On his way [407] to the city of refuge, the fugi-

---

decreed by public sentence, banishment extended over but one year, and even that could be commuted to a fine (Fiske III, § 37. Cf. supra n. 123).

[406] Num. XXXV, 25; Sifre I, § 160; Tosefta Maccoth III. § 5; Maccoth 11a. He may then resume control of his property as before the unfortunate accident, but he is not restored to his former offices of honor (Sifre l. c.; Maccoth 13a.)—Various reasons are assigned for allowing the fugitive to return home on the death of the high priest. Maimonides (More III, c. 40) believes the death of the pontiff to have been the termination of individual mourning, inasmuch as it is natural for man to drown the recollections of his personal grief in the similar or worse sorrows of the general public; and since the death of so august a personage as the high priest, was considered a great calamity to the whole Jewish people, it plunged every man in deep mourning, and made the "avenger of the blood" (supra n. 95) forget his own bereavement, even in sight of the human author thereof. Others believe it a kind of amnesty generally extended to criminals on the accession of a new ruler, spiritual or temporal, so that the joy of the occasion may be universal (cf. Luzzatto ad Num. l. c.). Still others think the death of the high priest to be in itself an atonement for unintentional bloodshed (Yer. Yoma VII, § 5. p. 44c top). It is perhaps for this reason that, when one is found guilty of accidental homicide during the interim between the death of the one high priest and the accession of the other; or when he accidentally kills the high priest himself; or when the high priest himself is found guilty of that offense, the exile may never leave the city of refuge, not even after the death of the succeeding high priest Sanh. 18a sq.; Maccoth 11b).

[407] The roads leading to the several cities of refuge must always be kept in good condition, so that no impediment bars

tive is protected by an escort furnished him by the court;[408] and once within the city limits, he is secure against molestation.[409] If a misfortune befalls him in his new home similar to that which forced him

---

the fugitive's progress. Twice a year the authorities are bound to have the roads thoroughly inspected, and, when necessary, repaired, while guideposts must be placed at all cross-roads to direct the fugitive's steps towards his goal, and thus prevent him from going astray and falling into danger (Sifre I, § 159, et al.; Tosefta Maccoth III, § 5; Maccoth 10ª sq.).—As to the cities themselves, they must be provided with all means necessary to sustain human life, but must not be very large and populous, or centres of commerce and industry, lest they draw too many people into their midst, and thus afford the avenger an opportunity for covertly entering the city and killing the fugitive. Nor must they be too small to afford protection, or too limited to afford accommodations (Sifre II. § 180; Tosefta l. c., § 8 sq.; Maccoth l. c.). which must be furnished gratuitously (Maccoth 13ª, et al.).

[408] Tosefta Maccoth III, § 5; Maccoth 9b.—In case death overtakes him before he reaches his destination, his body is carried thither; if after he arrives, he is buried there. In either case, his remains may be brought home on the death of the reigning high priest (Maccoth 11b).

[409] Sifre I, § 160; Maccoth 11b. If he intentionally passes the city limits, the avenger may slay him with impunity; but when he inadvertently oversteps them, his slayer is subject to the penalty of homicide, or of murder, as the case may be (Maccoth l. c.).—By the Attic law it was unlawful to do any injury to the fugitive, either on his leaving the country or during his absence (Smith 770b). Still, exile does not seem always to have protected him from death at the hands of the avenger. Instances are met with in which fugitives are represented as wanderers over the earth and, though in foreign lands, as being haunted by the fear of the vengeance of the kinsmen of the slain (cf. ib. 134b).

to desert his old one, he must remove his habitation from that quarter of the town in which it is located to another, but he must not leave the city.[410] If he does, it is at his peril.[411]

§ 136. PENAL SERVITUDE may be imposed on man,[412]

---

[410] Sifre II. § 181; Maccoth 12b.—Among the Greeks, if a man, after going into exile for unintentional homicide, and before appeasing the relatives of the deceased (cf. supra n. 123), was charged with having committed a murder, he was brought back in a ship to the harbor at Phreatto in the Piraeus, and there pleaded his cause on board ship, while the judges remained on land. If he was convicted, he suffered the penalty for murder; if acquitted, he was returned to his place of exile to suffer the remainder of his sentence (Smith 135a, 769b).

[411] Maccoth 11b; Maimon. H. Rozeah VII, 8.—By the laws of Athens, a convicted murderer, if found within the limits of the state, might be seized and put to death; and whoever harbored or entertained any one who had fled from his country to avoid capital punishment, was liable to the same penalties as the fugitive himself (Smith 134b). Similar was the law in England, where returning from transportation, or being seen at large in Great Britain, before the expiration of the term for which the offender was ordered transported, was a capital offense Blackst. IV, 132).

[412] Cf. supra § 22, n. 75. But he must not be sold publicly, "upon the auction stone," or to a non-Israelite (Sifra Behar §7; Sifre II, § 118; Mekhilta Nezikin § 1; Kidd. 20a. Cf. supra n. 75). The Greeks had regular auction sales of slaves on the first of every month, usually announced by a crier, standing on what was called the "vender's stone" (Fiske III, § 99; Smith 881a). The Romans exposed their slaves from scaffolds in the markets, and tablets were suspended from their necks, stating their country, age, character, &c. (Fiske l. c. § 323). Both the Greeks and the Romans sold their slaves to the highest bidder, native or foreign.

but not on woman,[413] and for a period of not more than six years.[414]

§ 137. As regards the position of the convict, it may be said that, although his master could compel him to perform all such work as he had been accustomed to

---

[413] Sifre II, § 118; Sotah 23ª.—The Roman law made a slave of the free woman who held commerce with a male slave (Smith 212ᵇ).

[414] Exodus XXI, 2; Mekhilta Nezikin, § 1; Sifre II, § 118; Kidd. 17ª. If the servant was able to repay his master for the unexpired term in proportion to the price paid for him, he could by so doing regain his liberty at any time (Lev. XXV, 49 sq.; Sifra Behar § 7); and if the year of the jubilee occurred during the term, the servitude ceased of itself (Lev. l. c. 39 sq.). If, owing to physical disability, the slave could not work for part of the term, that was the master's loss, and did not militate against his right to emancipation either at the termination of the six years or at the beginning of an intervening release year (Mekhilta l. c. § 2; Sifre l. c.). Nor could he be sold for less than his actual market value, or when worth more than the thing stolen (cf. supra § 22), without regard to the mulctuary additions (cf. Exodus XXII, 1-3.—Mekhilta l. c. § 12; Kidd. l. c.).—Slavery was a very old institution, and so deeply rooted in the economy of nations as to appear to be natural,— but Moses interdicted all but two kinds of slavery among the Jews: the voluntary enslavement of the necessitous (Lev. XXV, 39 sq.), and the enforced servitude of the felon (Exodus XXII, 3). Moses thus prepared the way for the total abolition of the institution, at least in as far as the person of the Jew was concerned (cf. Wines 267). The Rabbis, by their restrictive enactments based on the spirit of his legislation, carried his philanthropic measures further, rendering the enforced servitude of a Hebrew highly impracticable (cf. n. 416), and, when imposed, the severity and inhumanity which characterized the institution among other nations were not allowed to be practised even upon a convict.

do while free, no menial labor could be imposed on him,[415] and he was in all respects to be treated with due consideration as a human being and a brother.[416]

§ 138. FLAGELLATION [417] is administered by the public servitor, [418] with quadruple leathern straps, [419] on the

---

[415] Sifra Behar § 7; Sifre II. § 118; Mekhilta Nezikin § 1. E. g., attending the master to the bath, fastening or unfastening his sandals, washing his feet, or any other labor usually performed by the regular slave; for the Bible (Lev. XXV, 39) says: "Thou shalt not compel him to labor as a bondsman." Nor may he be turned by his master into a servant of the public, as a tailor, a baker or a barber, unless that was his original vocation.—The Roman slave could be employed in every conceivable manner, and usually performed the most degrading services (Fiske III, § 322).

[416] Sifra Behar § 7; Mekhilta Nezikin § 2; Kidd. 20ᵃ. Thus, he was to be fed from his master's own table, clothed and housed respectably; and, in general, his position was not to be rendered in the least uncomfortable. These rules are based on the Scriptural dictum referring to the slave, which says (Deut. XV, 16): "It is pleasant unto him with thee," and seem to have been carried so far that it came to be said: "He who buys a Hebrew slave, buys himself a master" (Kidd. l. c.; ib. 22ᵃ).—Among other nations, the condition of the slave was very hard, he being considered a chattel rather than a person (cf. Fiske III. § 322; Smith 883ᵃ), and usually treated with extreme cruelty (Fiske l. c. § 99). The master had unlimited power over his slave, extending even to life and death (Fiske l. c. § 63).

[417] Cf. supra § 21. n. 74.

[418] "Who must be endowed with more mental than physical vigor," that he may not strike too hard or on a dangerous spot (Maccoth 23ᵃ; Maimon. M. Sanh. XVI, 9), or that he may know when to stop, in case the convict grows weak under the lash (cf. Maccoth 22ᵃ sq.; Maimon. l. c. XVII, 2). If the convict happens to be one of his parents, he must not participate

bare body of the convict who, in a reclining position, is tied by his hands to a post.[420] Thirty-nine is the highest number of lashes that may be administered for any one offense.[421]

§ 139. If after being pinioned, the convict succeeds in escaping, or if the lash breaks at the second stroke, the sentence is considered executed, and the prisoner is discharged.[422]

---

in the execution of the sentence (Sanh. 85b; Maimon. H. Mamrim V. 13).

[420] Among the Romans, flagellation was inflicted on a criminal as a prelude to crucifixion, or sometimes on a slave to gratify the caprice or cruelty of his master. The whip used to punish slaves was knotted with bones or heavy indented circles of bronze, or terminated by hooks, when it was aptly called a scorpion (Smith 445a).

[42'] Sifre II, § 286; Maccoth 22b.—In Sparta, the offender received this punishment (*whipping* or *goading*) as he was driven through the city (Fiske III, § 128).

[421] Tosefta Maccoth V, § 12; Sifre II, § 286; Maccoth 22a.—As the spirit of moderation and clemency pervades all Talmudic penal laws, this punishment likewise is not allowed to be carried to extremes. Moses prescribed forty stripes as the highest number (Deut. XXV, 3); but the Rabbis took off one. When the convict's life is thought to be endangered by this number, a less number is apportioned, which must not be increased, even when it subsequently appears that he could stand the full count (Tosefta l. c. § 13; Maccoth l. c.). And as the lash is applied over the shoulder-blades and chest, the number of stripes must be divisible by three; if inadvertently a number not a multiple of three is apportioned, it must be reduced to render it divisible. Thus if the court sentences one to receive twenty stripes, he receives eighteen only (Tosefta l. c. § 12; Maccoth l. c.; Maimon. l. c. 2).

[422] Maccoth 23a; Maimon. H. Sanh. XVII, 5 sq. Cf. supra § 121. If, however, the lash breaks at the first stroke, the sentence is not considered executed.

6. REHABILITATION.

§ 140. Persons disqualified from bearing witness, because they have been convicted, or are violently suspected of misconduct,[423] may be rehabilitated either by submission to the sentence of the court, or by changing their mode of life, so as to manifest unmistakable evidence of genuine reformation.

§ 141. Those convicted of a misdemeanor, the penalty of which is flagellation,[424] are rehabilitated either after receiving their sentence, or after giving an earnest of sincere repentance;[425] *usurers*, after reimbursing their payees the ill-gotten rates, and promising never more to take usury even from a non-

---

[423] Cf. supra § 78.

[424] Cf. supra n. 74.—Of a pardoning power no trace is found in Talmudic law, while, on the contrary, with reference to atrocious crimes against society, the Rabbis explicitly forbid even a commutation of the statutory sentence (Mekhilta Nez., § 10, et al. Cf. supra n. 405). This especially applies to bloodshed, where, even if the "avenger" is willing, no remission of the prescribed punishment is admissible (supra n. 95), for the Rabbis argue that the life of man belongs to God, and only the law of God may dispose of it (cf. Maimon. H. Rozeah I, 4, and sources).

[425] Yer. Sotah II, § 1, p. 17ᵈ; Maccoth 23ᵃ. "Having submitted to the ruling of the law, he is thy brother as before," says the Talmud. Hence an officer having been found guilty of a trespass, is not removed from his post, however exalted, if he submits to the sentence of the court; but a chief of a Synhedrion, or a master of an academy, sentenced to flagellation, is removed from his office, for his subordinates or disciples would no longer respect him (Yer. Sanh. II, § 1, p. 19ᵈ bot.; ib. Horayoth III, § 2, p. 47ᵃ).

Israelite;[426] *gamblers*, after voluntarily destroying their apparatuses, and promising in the future not to engage in such occupation even for mere pastime; *suspects* of all kinds, after withstanding great temptations to do the very things of which they are suspected.[427]

---

[426] Sanh. 25b; Maimon. H. Eduth XII, 5. Cf. Maimoniana ad locem.

[427] Sanh. 25a sq.; Maimon. H. Eduth XII, 6 sq.

MAXIMS AND RULES.

§ 142. "Human laws are born, live and die," but a maxim, once ushered into existence, is endowed with a perpetual lease of life. Its form is often so altered as to be irrecognizable, but its spirit continues to live. Many a modern legal maxim which enjoys a wide circulation and has won a fortune of renown for its reputed author, is in reality nothing more than old currency cast in a new die—the gold of Moses or Solomon remodelled and embellished with the royal insignia of Constantine or Justinian; and we have reason to believe that many a maxim brought into the world by a Hillel or an Akiba is now current under the superscription of a Coke or a Blackstone.[428]—The following

---

[428] The production of a few Talmudic maxims with their more modern analogues will, we trust, convince the reader of the probability of our assumption. The rule of common law, *Nullus commodum capere potest de injuria sua propria* (no one shall take advantage of his own wrong), which Bouvier (Dict., s. v. Maxim) can trace back no further than to Coke, has, fifteen hundred years before that jurist, prompted the Talmudists to go beyond their own rules, and to impose extraordinary restrictions and amercements on parties who might otherwise have profited by their personal wrongs (cf. Hallah II, § 7; Yer. ib., p. 58ᵈ; Yeb. 92ᵇ; B. Kama 38ᵃ, et al.).—To Coke Bouvier ascribes the maxim: *Quando aliquid per se non sit malum, tamen si sit mali exempli, non est faciendum* (when any thing in itself is not evil, and yet may be an example for evil, it should not be done). Many things, indifferent in themselves,

are some of the most important maxims and rules, culled from the jurisprudence of the ancient Hebrew sages.

A majority of one is sufficient for acquittal, but it requires a majority of at least two for conviction.

A man is his own kin.

A minor has no discretion.[429]

---

are forbidden by the Rabbis, only because they might serve as examples for evil, or as the Talmud expresses it, *Mippene marith ayin* (for appearances sake.—Cf. Sabbath 64^b; Beza 9^a; Ab. Zara 12^a, et al.).—Leonard is credited with the authorship of the maxim: *Judici satis poena est quod Deum habet ultorem* (It is punishment enough for a judge that he is responsible to God). A younger contemporary of R. Judah I (cf. Appendix) said, "When a judge sits in judgment, he should feel as if a sword were pointed at him and hell were open beneath him" (Yeb. 109^b; Sanh. 7^a).—In an English law book—we cannot recall which—we have seen an English jurist advancing the idea that 'a judge who is sued and, by the judgment of the court, is made to disgorge money, ought to be judge no longer.' This moral maxim which is much older than the oldest writer on Common Law and of Rabbinic construction, serves well to illustrate the evolutionary character of some maxims. The Talmud (B. Bathra 58^a) records the fact that R. Bannaa, in his capacity as associate judge in Palestine, under Roman Government, had it altered to its present form. Originally it read: "The judge who is sued ought not to be called judge," to which the Rabbi objected as being unreasonable and dangerous, since it afforded the enemies of the judge easy means to have him removed, and he proposed to amend it so as to bring it within reason and right. His argument was declared cogent, and the maxim in its present form was the result.—But enough. In the subjoined analogues culled from Bouvier (l. c.), most of which are thought to be not older than Coke or Littleton, the reader will find further proof.

[429] Hence he is *doli incapax*, and not amenable to capital punishment (cf. § 50; n. 183).

A person deserves not the title of *Man* before reaching the age of twenty-five years.

A simultaneous and unanimous verdict of guilty acquits.

A single accuser deserves to be treated as a' slanderer.[430]

A Synhedrion executing one human being in the course of every seven years is a murderous tribunal.

A verdict of conviction may be reversed, but not one of acquittal.[431]

A verdict of guilty may not be rendered on the day of trial.

All evidence must be direct, and not circumstantial or presumptive.

All Israelites are responsible for one another.[432]

An equal division of the Court on a verdict is an acquittal.

As Moses sat in judgment without the expectation of material reward, so also must every judge act from a sense of duty only.

Be slow in judging.[433]

By punishing criminals the world is benefited.

---

[430] *Unius omnino testis responsio non audiatur* (Let not the testimony of a single witness be heard at all), was the maxim in Civil Law where, in most cases, two witnesses were required.

[431] *Nemo debet bis vexari pro eodem causa* (No one ought to be twice vexed for the same cause), is the maxim of modern, as it was of the Roman law.

[432] Applied to moral and religious, but not to civil or criminal affairs (cf. n. 401).

[433] *Judicia in deliberationibus crebro maturescunt, in accelerato processu nunquam* (Judgments frequently become matured by deliberation never by hurried process).

Collisions with a deaf-mute, or an idiot, or a minor, are always disadvantageous.

Crimes committed under duress are not punishable.[434]

Cross-question the witness closely.

Death atones for sins.[435]

Divulging the individual opinions of judges is slander.

Drink not and thou wilt not sin.[436]

Each witness must be qualified to testify to the whole case, and not only to part thereof.

Evidence must be heard directly from the mouth of the witnesses, and not through an interpreter or written document.

Extraordinary times legalize extraordinary punishments.[437]

Fine and flagellation are not imposed together for the same offense.[438]

For conviction it requires a majority of not less than the minimum number of witnesses competent to sustain an accusation.

Having submitted to the judgment of the law, the man is restored to his status as thy brother.

---

[434] *Ejus nulla culpa est cui parere necesse sit* (No guilt attaches to him who is compelled to obey. Cf. supra n. 47 and 168).

[435] Only for such sins as are offensive to God alone. Offenses against man must be atoned for otherwise (cf. sources quoted in n. 363).

[436] *Omne crimen ebrietas et incendit et detegit* (Drunkenness inflames and reveals every crime).

[437] *Crescenta malitia crescere debet et pœna* (Vice increasing, punishment ought also to increase).

[438] *Nemo bis punitur pro eodem delicto* (No one can be punished twice for the same misdemeanor).

He who buys a Hebrew slave buys himself a master.
He who gives the death-blow is alone responsible.
He who swears is *ipso facto* suspected.
If one witness is found disqualified, the whole party is disqualified.
Immodest behavior is a bar to the witness-stand.[439]
Judges must be exceedingly guarded in their utterances, lest the witnesses learn from them how to answer evasively.
Kill him who unlawfully attempts to kill thee.[440]
Let justice pierce the mountain.
Let the incorrigible die while in a state of comparative innocence, rather than live and go from bad to worse.[441]
Make a hedge around the law.
Man is to live, and not to die by the observance of law.
Man's life belongs to God, and only according to the law of God may it be disposed of.
Neither honor nor insult the remains of the suicide.
No man convicts himself.[442]

---

[439] *Qui accusat integræ famæ sit* (Let him who accuses be of clear fame).

[440] *Quodcunque aliquis ob tutelam corporis sui fecerit jure id fecisse videtur* (Whatever one does in defense of his person, that he is considered to have done legally. Cf. supra n. 113).

[441] *Nemo prudens punit ut præterita revocentur, sed ut futura præveniantur* (No wise man punishes that things done may be revoked, but that future wrongs may be prevented. Cf. supra n. 184).

[442] *Allegans suam turpitudinem non est audiendus* (One alleging his own infamy is not to be heard. Cf. § 93).

No man is considered guilty until after he is duly proved to be so.

No man may be condemned unless he is present.

No man produces witnesses to convict himself.

No man sinneth unless attacked by idiocy.

No mercy may be shown where that is contrary to justice.

No one is a competent witness whose knowledge of the facts is based on hearsay or conjecture.[443]

No one is responsible for the crimes of another.[444]

No punishment may be inflicted for transgressions not accomplished by bodily action.[445]

None, but the legal executioners, may execute the convict.

None who may be a competent witness in a cause, may be judge of the cause.[446]

One court may not try two capital cases in one day.

Part of the evidence being invalidated, the whole is invalidated.[447]

---

[443] *Testis occulatus unus plus valet quam auriti decem* (One eye-witness is worth ten ear-witnesses).

[444] *Nemo punitur pro alieno delicto* (No one is to be punished for the wrongs of another. Cf. n. 401).

[445] *Les lois ne se chargent de punir que les actions exterieures* (Laws do not undertake to punish other than outward actions). But other authorities say, *In atrocioribus delictis punitur affectus licet non sequater effectus* (In more atrocious crimes, the intent is punished, though the effect does not follow).

[446] Cf. supra n. 143. 293.

[447] *Falsus in uno falsus in omnibus* (False in one thing, false in every thing).

Relations and interested persons may not act as judges.[448]

Self-accusation does not convict.

Self-accusation of misdemeanors involving fines exempts the culprit from paying the fine.[449]

Similarity in expressions between witnesses awakens suspicion of conspiracy and coaching.

Testimony must not be heard in the absence of the party concerned.

Testimony to which the law of confutation cannot be fully applied deserves not the name of testimony.

The blood of the victim of false testimony and that of his lost progeny falls upon the heads of the witnesses.

The act of breaking in is the burglar's death warrant.

The cause of a party may not be disposed of in his absence.

The convict must not be kept in suspense.

The drunkard is responsible for his actions.[450]

The end of a period is considered as the beginning thereof.

The hour legalizes extraordinary rigor.[451]

---

[448] *Nemo sibi esse judex vel suis jus dicere debet* (No man ought to be his own judge, or to administer justice in cases where his relatives are concerned).

[449] *Cum comfitente sponte mitius est agendum* (One making a voluntary confession is to be dealt with more mercifully).

[450] *Qui peccat ebrius, luat sobrius* (He who offends when drunk must be punished when sober. Cf. supra § 48).

[451] *Crescenda malitia crescere debet et pœna* (Vice increasing, punishment ought also to increase).

The judge has nothing to judge by but what is before his eyes.[452]

The judge not voting is considered absent.

The judgments for which the judge was paid are void.

The law does not punish for injuries occasioned through fortuitous circumstances.[453]

The less punishment is discharged in the greater.

The person witnessing an act during his minority is not competent to testify thereto, even after reaching his majority.

The public servitor must be possessed of more mental than physical vigor.

The robe of the unfairly elected judge is to be respected not more than the blanket of the ass.

The scholar's popularity with the masses is not always the reward for righteous bearing; often it is the consequence of his failing to notice vices and rebuke them.

The suborned witness is despised even by his suborner.

The Supreme Judge does not punish a person of less than twenty years.

The votes of father and son, or of teacher and pupil, in the same court, are counted as one.

---

[452] *Non refert quid notum sit judici, si notum non sit in forma judici* (It matters not what is known to the judge, if it is not known to him judicially).

[453] *Casus fortuitus non est sperandus, et nemo tenetur divinare* (A fortuitous event is not to be foreseen, and no person is held bound to divine it. Cf. supra § 35).

The witness must be fully competent at the time when the crime is committed as well as when he appears to testify to the crime.

The witnesses for the defense are accusers of the prosecution.[454]

The word of the parties to the suit, and not that of counsel, shall be heard by the judges.

There is no agency in crime.[455]

Thine own life may be dearer to thee than that of thy neighbor.[456]

Thoughts are not punishable.[457]

What the witness has once said he may not unsay.

Whatever one observes while in a normal state, and testifies to when in a normal state is legal evidence.

When one can prevent a crime and does not, he is responsible before Heaven.[458]

When the judge is, like a king, well provided for, he will establish the peace of the land on justice ; but when, like the priest, he must rely on gifts for his subsistence, he will overthrow it.

Where Heaven sees fit to condone, human tribunals may not punish.

---

[454] *Reus excipiendo fit actor* (The defendant by a plea becomes plaintiff).

[455] *Quod per me non possum, nec per alium* (What I cannot do in person I cannot do through the agency of another. Cf. n. 155).

[456] *Ignoscitur ei qui sanguinem suum qualiter redemptum voluit* (The law holds him excused who chose that his blood should be redeemed on any terms.)

[457] *Cogitationis pœnam nemo patitur* (No one is punished for his thoughts.—Cf. n. 36).

[458] *Qui non obstat quod obstare potest facere videtur* (He who does not prevent what he can, seems to commit the thing).

Where there are officers to enforce the judgment, there judges can act, but where there are no officers, there can be no judges.

Whosoever compassionates a human being obtains compassion from Heaven.

Whosoever preserves one worthy life is as meritorious as if he had preserved the world.

Whosoever will not tell the truth without an oath, would not scruple to assert falsehood with an oath.

Wisdom increases with age.

CONCUSION.

§ 143. In the foregoing pages, an analysis is offered of the system of criminal jurisprudence, as it is preserved in the Talmud and other ancient Rabbinic writings. In its spirit and its letter, in its substance and its form, it is eminently considerate and humane, if not always practical. It very favorably compares with the codes of the most civilized countries of our day, and by far surpasses the systems of Greece and Rome, after which the former are often modelled. The lofty spirit of the Mosaic legislation, which has confessedly exercised an influence, benign as extensive, wholesome as permanent, over the doctrines of mankind, breathes through it all ; and although in following up their own maxim : " Make a hedge around the law," the Rabbis built up—to use Dean Stanley's expression—"elaborate explanations, thorny obstructions, subtile evasions, enormous developments, till the Pentateuch was buried beneath the Mishna, and the Mishna beneath the Guemara," they never for a moment lost sight of the dignity of man and the principles of humanity, of the rights of the individual and the welfare of society, of the majesty of justice and the divine attribute of clemency.

§ 144. The authors of this system of criminal jurisprudence, the ancient Jewish scholars, legislators and judges, who paid so much regard to human life, who fought so bravely and so successfully against every outrage on human dignity, in the face of all contemporaneous class-legislation and atrocious tyranny—as, I believe, I have abundantly demonstrated in these pages,—these very Hebrew sages are the so much decried Pharisees whom, for nearly two thousand years, the Christian world has stigmatized as "cruel, vindictive, sanguinary." If I have succeeded in, at least partly, proving that they do not deserve such opprobrious epithets; if I have succeeded in awakening in some breast a just determination not to condemn so great and so important a literary repository as the Talmud, before examining its contents, I am amply repaid for my labor, and can close with Wines's exclamation: "Thanks be to God for that rainbow of promise, with which the civil polity of Moses has spanned the political heavens!"

APPENDIX.

THE TALMUD.

The following sketch appeared originally in the *South Atlantic* Monthly (July and August, 1878). As a fit supplement to the Criminal Jurisprudence which is preserved mainly in the Talmud, it is here reprinted, with some few additions, but without material alterations.

THE TALMUD.

The most ponderous work in ancient or modern literature is that comprising the teachings of the ancient Hebrew sages, and known as the *Talmud*. This gigantic compilation[1] has a peculiar history of its own, and by it the old adage, *Habent sua fata libelli* (even books have their peculiar fates) has been well illustrated. How checkered has been its career during the last fourteen centuries,—how diversified its course since Rabh Ashi and Rabh Abina compiled and systematized it! While at times it excited praise and admiration, and attracted to its almost inexhaustible stores of wit and wisdom the most cultivated minds of whole generations, it was, at others, but too frequently made a target for poisonous arrows, held up to mockery and to derision, and repeatedly proscribed, confiscated or destroyed. Influenced by hierarchical fanaticism, the enemies

---

[1] Modern editions of the Talmud, including the most important commentaries, consist of about 3000 folio sheets, or 12,000 folio pages of closely printed matter, generally divided into 12, or 20 volumes. One page of Talmudic Hebrew intelligibly translated into English would cover three pages; the translation of the whole Talmud with its commentaries would, accordingly, make a library of 400 volumes, each numbering 360 octavo pages.

of free conscience, of free religion and of free thought, in France, in Italy and in other European countries, condemned the Talmud as heretical, and consequently sentenced it to the ignominious end of the heretic. This was especially the case during the dark Middle-Ages, when prelates, from their thrones, thundered forth anathemas against every idea which did not exactly coincide with their own, and, by means of inflammatory bulls and edicts, caused all books named in the voluminous "Expurgatory Index," to be burned publicly. Among them was not only the Talmud,[1] but even the Bible, written or printed in the original tongue.

Paradoxical as this may seem, yet it is a fact that those learned divines who raised their voices against "the 'heresies' of the Talmud," were, as a rule, entirely ignorant of the real contents of the Talmud, and condemned it solely on hearsay or on the basis of some quotation, generally ill-selected, mutilated and distorted.[2] Indeed, some of those "defenders

---

[1] Within a period of less than 50 years—and these forming the latter half of the sixteenth century,—it was publicly burnt no less than six different times, and that not in single copies, but wholesale, by the wagon-load. Julius III issued his proclamations against what he grotesquely calls the "Gemaroth Talmud" in 1553 and 1555, Paul IV in 1559, Pius V in 1566, Clement VII in 1592 and 1599 (cf. Deutsch, The Talmud, London *Quarterly Review*, Oct., 1867).

[2] "It is easy to make quotations which may throw an odium over the whole. But fancy if the production of a thousand years of English literature, say, from the 'History' of the venerable Bede to Milton's 'Paradise Lost,' were thrown together into a number of uniform folios, and judged in like manner; if

of the faith" did not even know that the Talmud is a collection of books. Henricus Segnensis, a pious monk, having heard a great deal about the heretical Talmud, took it to be a person, and swore that he would ere long have *him—the Talmud!*—put to death by the hangman!—And, although we live in an age far advanced and greatly enlightened, when scholars regard every literary production, religious or secular, as part and parcel of human learning; although modern theologians and Orientalists study the Talmud not merely with the intention of refuting some of its doctrines, but often with that of bringing to light some of its vast stores of knowledge; although this great work is frequently referred to in almost every branch of science, particularly in theology, Biblical criticism, and in sacred geography,—yet even to the majority of literary men it continues to be "as a sealed book," known by name only.

In the following pages we propose to furnish sketches of the lives of some of its foremost authors, of the course of its composition and compilation, as well as a bird's eye view of its contents.

I.

The Mishnah.

The origin of Talmudic lore is, like "the origin of Common Law, as undiscoverable as the head of the

---

because some superstitious monks wrote silly 'Lives of Saints,' therefore the works of John Bunyan should also be considered worthless. The absurdity is too obvious to require comment" (Alexander, *The Jews*).

Nile." Rabbinism claims for it hoary antiquity, asserting that it was synchronous with the proclamation of the Decalogue.[1] This antiquity some ascribe to the whole mass of traditional laws,[2] others to the principles only upon which the Rabbinic disquisitions are based.[3] But whether its origin is coeval with Moses,[4] or not, certain it is that traces of traditions are to be met with at an early stage in Israel's history, and Ezra is their reputed foster father who, in conjunction with his coadjutors, the men of the Great Assembly (*Ecclesia Magna*), delivered them to the mass of the people on their return from Babylonian captivity.[5]

The age of Ezra and his associates, as well as that of their immediate successors, is known as the age of the *Soferim* (scribes), which ended with Simon Justus (about 200 B. C. E.) and was followed by that of the *Hakhamim* (wise men, scholars) or *Zugoth* (pairs, *duumviri*). In the schools of this age the "Oral Law" received remarkable impetus and development. The heads of these schools were: Antigonus of Sokho; Jose of Zereda and Jose of Jerusalem, Joshua ben Perahia and Nittai the Arbelite, Judah ben

---

[1] Sifra Behuckothai, end; Berakhoth 5a; Megillah 19b.

[2] Yer. Hagiga I. § 8, p. 76d; Ex. R. c. 47.

[3] Ex. R. c. 41.

[4] It is claimed that thousands of oral rules (*Halakhoth*) were buried with him (Temurah 16a).

[5] Succah 20a, et al.—Farrar says: Ezra "carried on the silent revolution in Jewish conceptions of which the last eight chapters of Ezekiel are the indication, and which find expression also in the book of Chronicles" (Hist. of Interpretation, p. 52).

Tabbai and Simon ben Shettah, Shemaiah and Abtalion. Each of these contributed his share towards enlarging the sphere of the oral law, which, however, reached a most flourishing stage at the time of the rise of the rival schools of Hillel I and Shammai, in the reign of Herod. The sayings, teachings, doctrines, elucidations, decisions of these schools were delivered orally, and in the progress of time became so numerous and extensive that, according to the statements of later Talmudists,[1] between six hundred and seven hundred books could be made of them. They followed each other so promiscuously that it was an utter impossibility to retain them in one's memory, or to refer to them at will. Hillel therefore collected and assorted them, and arranged them in proper order, reducing the whole mass to six books or orders.[2]

Hillel, the Great.

Notwithstanding that a great accumulation of literary matter is said to have come down to Hillel, but little that is authentic has come down to us from his predecessors. He may be, and generally is, considered the first whose critical and paleographical remarks on the Bible have been transmitted in his name. They were originally either noted down on the margin of his scrolls, or delivered orally, and preserved in the memory of generations and ages down to the eleventh cen-

---

[1] Hagiga 14ª.
[2] Beth Habehirah ad Aboth; De Lates, Shaare Zion; Yuhasin s. v. Hillel.

tury, when they were collected and arranged, together with those of other sages, under the title of *Masorah* (tradition).

According to Hillel, two sources poured forth an unbroken stream of oral law. The first of these was *tradition*, transmitted from mouth to mouth, from generation to generation, its authenticity guaranteed by the trustworthiness of those who delivered it.[1] But as

---

[1] The existence of some traditional elucidations of Biblical precepts, in the early days of Israel's commonwealth, is argued from the necessity arising from the abstruseness of many a Biblical ordinance, as well as from the varied and intricate situations of life. A few examples will suffice to illustrate this.—The Bible (Lev. XVI. 29; ib. XXIII, 27 sq.) ordains that on the tenth day of the seventh month (the Day of Atonement), all Israelites shall *afflict* their souls, but it does not state by what process this affliction shall be accomplished. Tradition declares it to be the suspension of all carnal enjoyment, especially of eating and drinking, i. e. *fasting* (Sifra Emor c. 14; Yoma 74b). Again, the Bible (l. c. XXIII. 40) prescribes that, 'on the first day of the Feast of Booths, fruit of the *hadar* tree be taken;' but it does not define the genus of the tree. Tradition—supported by the various meanings of the term *hadar* (which is generally rendered *goodly, ornamental,* but by changing its punctuation may be made to correspond to): growing at the *waterside, perennial, ovate*—declares it to be the one called *Ethrog* (citron, *citrus medica.*—cf. Josephus III Antiqu. X, 5; XIII. XIII, 5), which possesses all these characteristics (Sifra l. c., c. 16; Succah 35a). And again, the Bible (l. c. XXIII. 3) prohibits all manner of work on the Sabbath day, but does not define what work means. Moreover, as if to render the riddle more difficult of solution, the Bible explicitly mentions several engagements as forbidden (Ex. XVI. 29; ib. XXXV, 3; Num. XV, 32). Wherefore it requires some tradition to tell us which works are forbidden, and tradition does it. Tradition counts

this consisted of finished transactions, of schemata complete in themselves and incapable of expansion, and therefore insufficient for the varied and intricate situations of life,[1] necessity suggested another source: rules by means of which new *Halakhoth* (decisions) could be deduced either from some Scriptural allusion, or from former decisions, based on tradition or on Scripture. He accordingly elaborated seven hermeneutic rules, by the application of which a Mosaic law might be variously explained, and statutes and ordinances, answering the requirements of every age and condition, deduced therefrom. These rules are: 1, The inference from major to minor, and *vice versa*, from minor to major; 2, The inference from agreement or similarity of phrases used in different texts; 3, The inference from the principal idea underlying one Scriptural verse, or two verses; 4, The inference from the contrast existing between the general description of a subject and its specified particular; 5,

---

the number of times that the term *Melakhah* (work) is repeated in the Pentateuch, and finding it to be thirty-nine, and corresponding to that of the different forms of work practised in raising the Tabernacle, declares that all forms of work practised on that occasion and numbering thirty-nine, are forbidden on the Sabbath (Sabbath 49ʰ; ib. 73ᵇ; Yer. ib. VII, § 2, p. 40ᵇ bot.).

[1] Cf. Jurisprudence, n. 33. We all know by experience, that a law, though very minutely and exactly defined, may yet be susceptible of various interpretations, and question upon question is sure to arise when it comes to be applied to the ever-varying circumstances of life. Hence we find Moses himself perplexed as to the proper term of the law in certain cases Num. IX. 8; ib. XV. 33).

From a particular expression followed by a general one; 6, The inference from a correspondence of circumstances; and 7, By induction from the context.[1]— Thus Hillel gave a peculiar cut and cast to Judaism, perfecting and firmly establishing its judicial character; at the same time he created a particular theory, a kind of Jewish theology, or more correctly a *nomology* (science of the religious law).[2]

By the application of his own rules, Hillel established a proviso, which suspended an express Biblical precept. According to the Bible (Deut. XV, 1-2) the creditor was bound to release all his outstanding loans of money at the end of every seventh year, termed *Sh'mittah* (=release). In the course of time, however, this precept became impracticable, detrimental to the welfare of society in general, and of those whom it intended to benefit in particular. The poor man stood in need of money-loans which the capitalist refused to grant, lest the Shemittah year will find the loan not repaid, and oblige him to relinquish his claim. In order to obviate this danger threatening the economy of the country, Hillel established a new law, to

---

[1] Aboth de R. Nathan XXXVII.—These rules were, about a century later, increased by R. Ishmael to thirteen; and still later R. Elazar b. Jose added nineteen more, making a total of thirty-two.—One of the Rabbis ridiculed the application of the inference from major to minor by suggesting the following paralogism: If the marriage with one's own daughter is prohibited, although the marriage with her mother is legal, how much more should it be unlawful to marry another man's daughter, the marriage with her mother—a married woman—being strictly forbidden! (Derekh Erctz Rabba I).

[2] Graetz IV, c. 1.

wit: If the creditor, before the beginning of the Sh'mittah year, enters his claim at a regular court, then shall the Sh'mittah year not extinguish the debt.[1] This law he derived from the Scriptural dicta instituting the Sh'mittah. "This is the manner of the *Sh'mittah* (release) : Every creditor that lendeth shall release." In this passage, reasons the sage, the term release occurs twice ; in the first instance it applies to the release of land, in the second to that of money. But since the same term is used in both instances, its operation too must be the same in both instances. Hence we infer that the prime intention of the law was to make it dependent on the soil ; as long as one is bound to release the soil, *i. e.*, as long as the Jewish law governs the land, so long is one bound to release loans ; but when the law of release is not applicable to land—as when Judea is under Roman rule—it no longer has validity with reference to personal property.[2]

The study of the law was taught by Hillel to be of paramount importance. His favorite maxims were : "He who doth not increase his knowledge, diminisheth it ; he who doth not study, deserveth death, and he who useth the crown of the law [for his personal aggrandizement] will perish."[3] Nor did he merely advocate these ideas ; he exemplified them in

---

[1] Its effect was the same as is that of the modern law suspending the operation of the "Statute of Limitation", where suit had been entered prior to the expiration of the time within which the law does not consider a debt extinguished.

[2] Shebiith X. §§ 3-5 ; Guittin 36ª.

[3] Aboth I. § 13.

himself. Although he labored under great difficulties, he persevered until he gained admittance into colleges, and succeeded in advancing in his studies. It is related that when he first came from his native country, Babylon, to Jerusalem, he was so poor that he was obliged to resort to manual labor and drudgery for means of subsistence. His small earnings (a *tropaïcon* per diem) he expended partly for food and partly in admission fees to the door-keeper of the academy, where Shemaiah and Abtalion instructed their pupils. On a certain winter-solstice day he failed to find work; and as he could not pay the required entrance fee, the door-keeper would not admit him into the college. But so eager was Hillel to hear the two great teachers, so quenchless was his thirst for the knowledge of the law, that he stood near the window attentively listening, without taking notice that a heavy fall of snow had commenced. At length his limbs, numbed with cold, failed him, and he fell insensible to the ground, where his body was soon covered by the snow. As the heap thus formed before the window obscured the light, it attracted Shemaiah's attention, and on examining the cause, Hillel's apparently lifeless body was discovered. He was carried into the hall, and attended to until he revived and accounted for the occurrence.[1] After this he had no more trouble with college door-keepers. The chiefs admitted him as a regular listener to their lectures, and provided for his bodily need as well.

---

[1] Yoma 35b. Ever since, the Rabbis say, the ignorant poor are condemned by his example.

Endowed with extraordinary talent and keen faculties, Hillel rapidly acquired great stores of knowledge, and became one of the highest authorities on traditional law. Indeed, he soon surpassed the great teachers of his day, and rose to be a renowned master. Once an important religious question was debated in the college, and, of all the sages, Hillel alone was in possession of authentic traditional information bearing on the subject, and his declaration settled the question. Thenceforth he was looked upon as the most prominent figure in the academy, and the greatest pillar of oral law. He was ultimately elevated to the presidency of the Synhedrion,[1] in which office he continued for a considerable number of years, to the end of his useful and glorious life.

That Hillel was held in high esteem was owing not alone to his great erudition and progressive spirit, but also to his excellent character and friendly disposition. "Be of the disciples of Aaron: loving peace and pursuing it; love all men, and thus bring them under the influence of the law",[2] was his rule of con-

---

[1] Pesahim 66ª, Yer. ib. IV. § . p. 33ª. Later sages therefore compare him to Ezra, for, like him, he recalled the law to the memory of his people (Succah 20ª).

[2] Aboth I, § 12.—His patience is illustrated by the following anecdote. A man wagered four hundred *dinars* against an equal sum that he would provoke Hillel to anger. He hastened to the sage's residence, on a Friday afternoon, while the Rabbi was preparing himself for the Sabbath, and unceremoniously approached the bath-room and called, in a loud voice, "Is Hillel here? Is Hillel here?" without even adding the title. The Prince, for such was he in Israel, dressed himself quickly, and

duct, and by it he attracted to himself a numerous following, even from among the "strangers." Here

meeting the intruder, kindly inquired, "What is thy desire, my son?" Whereupon the stranger replied, "I wish to ask you a question." "Go on, my son; ask." "Well," said the intruder, "I desire to know why the Babylonians have pointed heads?" To this Hillel answered, "It is, indeed, a very important question. The fault lies with their foolish and ignorant midwives." With this the Rabbi returned to his occupation, while the man left the apartment, but soon returned, again crying, "Where is Hillel? Where is Hillel?" Again the Rabbi wrapped himself in his cloak, and, on perceiving the same man, inquired, "What now, my son? What is thy wish?" "I came for an answer to the question, why the Thermedeens have weak eyes?" "This is a very important question, my son. The reason of this phenomenon is that they live in sandy regions, and the wind drives the sand into their eyes and makes them dull." Disappointed for the second time, the tempter departed, but soon re-entered, with his usual unceremonious inquiry, "Where is Hillel?" whom he asked to explain the reason why the Africans have broad feet. The Rabbi again magnified the importance of the problem, and then replied, "It is because they live on marshy land and walk barefooted."

"I might ask you," continued the stranger, "many more questions, but fear that you will grow angry." Hillel adjusted his cloak, seated himself and said, "Whatever question thou hast, ask." "Art thou," indignantly queried the stranger; "art thou he whom people term the Prince of Israel?" and having received an affirmative reply, continued, "Well, I wish that, if thou art indeed the same, there may not be many like thee in Israel!" "And wherefore, my son?" inquired the Rabbi, calmly. "Because," answered the disappointed wagerer, "I have lost on thy account four hundred dinars," and then related the entire story. Hillel still retained his equanimity, and dismissed his tempter with the admonition to control himself

are some illustrations. A heathen, desirous of obtaining divine light, applied to Shammai, Hillel's deputy in the Synhedrion,[1] for information on religion. "How many laws have the Jews?" asked he. "Two," replied the sage: "a written law—the Pentateuch, and an unwritten law—the traditional." The stranger expressed his desire to embrace Judaism, but would not accept the oral law; whereupon Shammai grew angry, and abruptly dismissed him. He made the same proposition to Hillel, and was admitted into the fold of Israel, but, by the patience of the sage, he was soon induced to accept the oral law also. Hillel taught him the letters of the Alphabet in their proper order, and afterwards reversed them, when the surprised proselyte remarked, "Thou hast not thus taught me before!" To this Hillel rejoined, "Why didst thou accept the former order of the letters? was it not because thou didst believe in my method of teaching? Well, thou must also believe me when I teach thee the oral law." The argument proved convincing, and the heathen accepted the oral traditions.

On another occasion a heathen, who had heard of the costly garments which decked the High Priest, was desirous of becoming a Jew, provided he should afterwards be appointed to the Pontificate. He, too, unbosomed himself to Shammai, but was repulsed. He applied to Hillel, and was accepted. Hillel then began

---

in the future, and to remember that he might lose many times four hundred dinars, and still not succeed in making him angry Sabbath 31; Aboth de R. Nathan XV.

[1] Cf. supra § 55.

to instruct him in the law, on the plea that, as the Prince must perfect himself in war tactics, before he can ascend the throne, so every one is obliged to acquaint himself with the laws of, before he can be elected to the office of the High Priesthood. When they reached the passage (Numbers 1, 51), "The stranger that cometh nigh shall be put to death," the proselyte inquired to whom this applies, and received in answer, "Even to King David! Only the descendants of Aaron may be elevated to that position." The proselyte was convinced of the unreasonableness of his aspirations, and abandoned the idea.

A third, who, like the former two, was repulsed by Shammai, applied to Hillel for admission into the Jewish covenant, provided he could be instructed in the laws of that religion in as short a time as he could stand on one foot. "Whatever is hateful unto thyself," said the patient sage, "do not unto thy fellow-man.¹ This is the essence of the law; the rest is but its commentary." [2]

Thus did Hillel the Great devote his mind and his heart to the elucidation and expansion of the oral law, and his energies and mental acquisitions to the promotion of the best interests, both temporal and spiritual, of his fellow-beings. He graced the patriarchal office for a period of forty years; he lived beloved, and died mourned by all. He was the founder of a dynasty of *Nesiim* (patriarchs, princes),[3] who

---

[1] Cf. Matt. VII, 12. Philo Judaeus quotes this maxim among the unwritten laws of Judaism (cf. Grætz III. p. 224).

[2] Sabbath 31ᵇ; Aboth de R. Nathan XV.

[3] Cf. supra n. 199.

successively presided over the deliberations of the Great Synhedrion, or chief council of the Jews, for upwards of four hundred years (10–425 A. C.). There was, however, a short interregnum which deserves our notice. It was that of one of his youngest disciples,

R. Johanan ben Zakkai,

whom personal merit, no less than peculiar circumstances, elevated to the patriarchate some sixty years after the demise of the great master who had predicted a blessed future for him.[1]

R. Johanan, in his advanced age, saw the last rays of the setting sun of Judea's independence, and the first rays of Israel's new epoch. As early as the closing years of the second commonwealth, R. Johanan's fame had spread; he occupied an exalted position in the Synhedrion, and directed an important academy:[2] his affability, which rivalled that of his great master, attracted to him the noblest and best sons of his people,—in short, R. Johanan was deservedly popular and highly respected. But his noblest achievements and his undying fame date from the new epoch of which he himself was the creator.

During the protracted siege of Jerusalem, R. Johanan belonged to the conciliatory party, and often counseled the zealots to open the gates to the Romans, and make peace with them. "Why," cried he, "will

---

[1] Succah 28a; Yer. Nedarim V § 7. p 39b.
[2] Cf. Pesahim 26a; Yer. Megillah III. § 1, p. 73d.

you expose the city and the temple to destruction by
fire, and the people to death by sword and famine?"
Unfortunately fanaticism ruled the day, and the
spirit of independence could not brook to his sage advice. He therefore escaped from the besieged city
into the camp of the besiegers, and from its general
he obtained permission to establish himself and his
school in the neighboring town, Jabneh or Jamnia.[1]

---

[1] Gittin 56ª, sq; Aboth de R. Nathan IV. The circumstances
attending his escape and settlement in Jamnia are thus described in the Talmud: Seeing his conciliatory counsel contemned, and danger daily increasing, he resolved upon repairing to the general of the besiegers and interceding for the
people; he hoped that his efforts might save something from the
inevitable wreck. But how evade the ubiquitous eyes of the
Zealots who would permit no one to leave the city? An expedient suggested itself. He unbosomed his fears and his hopes
to the chief of the Zealots—a nephew of his, and with the
chief's connivance a plan was concocted by which the flight
might be effected. The Rabbi was reported sick, and only his
most trusted disciples were permitted to wait on him. After
the lapse of a few days, he was reported dead, and awaiting
burial. He was placed in a coffin, and a piece of carrion put
at his side, that the cadaverous odor might help to deceive the
prying sentinels. Thus encased, he was carried forth towards
the cemetery which was beyond the walls of the city, followed
by a great concourse of mourning people, among whom was
his relative, the chief. Arrived at the city gate, the procession
was stopped by the guard who hesitated to let the coffin pass, and
prepared to examine its contents; but here the chief interfered,
and would not permit 'the remains of the beloved Rabbi in Israel
to be violated,' and so obtained permission for the pall-bearers
to pass on with their burden. Once outside of the city, R.
Johanan was released from his confinement, and he proceeded
to the Roman general, by whom he was received very kindly.

Here he took up his abode, and with a heart full of anxiety, though equally as full of pious resignation, he awaited the results of the great struggle. He had foreseen and openly predicted the consequences of the rule of the Zealots; still, when the news arrived that the city had fallen and the temple had been reduced to ashes, he rent his garments and mourned, as for the death of a near relative. But he did not despair. Seeing that his disciples indulged in lamentations and fasting, the aged master comforted himself and them, saying, "Alas, it is true that we have lost the place of expiation; the temple wherein the sacrificial rites have been practised is no more,—but we have a substitute for it all: humanity is still left to us, and this is even more pleasing to God than all the sacrifices, as the prophet says: 'I desire charity and not sacrifice,'"[1] and thus he suggested the way for the eventual accommodation of Judaism to the altered political circumstances of the Jews.

But Judaism was disjointed, and required reconstruction. Deprived of its central points of gravity— the national Temple and the national Council,—it was rent into fragments, and threatened with extinction.

---

and given leave to ask a favor. He did not hesitate long, but instead of asking a personal favor, he preferred the modest petition to be permitted to open a school at Jamnia, which the general readily granted. The Rabbi thereupon retired to the neighboring town Ramea, there to await the issue of the stirring events. Soon after the fall of Jerusalem he repaired to Jamnia, and opened his school which proved mightier than the Roman sword.

[1] Hosea VI. 6; Aboth de R. Nathan l. c.

R. Johanan's first effort was therefore to re-establish the authoritative body that should, as heretofore, deliberate upon measures, and legislate according to the exigencies of the times; and, with that end in view, he convoked in his new home a Synhedrion which was invested with all the supreme religious authority, and with the judicial functions which its predecessor in Jerusalem had possessed.[1] The Talmud enumerates nine regulations adopted by R. Johanan, no doubt, with the concurrence of the Synhedrion, whose acknowledged chief he was. Most of these referred to the abrogation of such ordinances as had lost their significance after the destruction of the Temple; but he retained many customs commemorative of Temple-life.[2] Thus Jamnia became the religious centre for the scattered remnants of the faithful in Israel, and R. Johanan ben Zakkai the preserver of Israel's law and unity.

R. Johanan was justly regarded as the personification and living representative of the oral law. The *Halakhah* (custom, decision, rule) which constituted the trunk of the law; the *Midrash* (interpretation), which formed the roots that suck the elements of life from the word of Scripture; the *Talmud*, the wide-spreading branches which embraced all this, as well as the *Agadah* (homilies), the blossoms that enlivened the colorless subject-matter of the law by their brilliant tints and sweet fragrance, —all these constituent parts of the oral law the master treated

---

[1] Except the *jus gladii*. Cf. supra p. 225.
[2] Rosh Hashanah 31ᵃ; Sotah 40ᵃ. Cf. Graetz IV. c. 1.

in his lectures,[1] and elaborated therefrom the breath of life, which revived the torpid national body, and infused into it new vigor and energy.[2]

Politically also, R. Johanan was an important agent, a shield to the incipient congregational life which he had newly created. His kind, benignant character, in which he so greatly resembled his teacher Hillel, was manifest in his dealings with every man. It is said of him that he anticipated every one he met, even a pagan, in tendering cordial greetings.[3] This uniform kindness and peaceful disposition of the Jewish leader may have been instrumental in inducing the two Flavian emperors, Vespasian and Titus, to relax their rigor and to inflict no extraordinary persecutions upon the Judean congregations.[4]

How long R. Johanan continued in the presidency of the Synhedrion, cannot be accurately ascertained.

---

[1] Berakhoth 17^a.

[2] Graetz l. c.

[3] Berakhoth l. c.—In his interpretations of Scripture he was guided by the same liberal spirit. The zealots of his day were wont to expound Biblical texts to the prejudice of other nations, but he invariably interpreted them to their advantage. Thus the Solomonic saying (Prov. XIV. 34): "The kindness of nations is sin," which his contemporaries explained as meaning that 'the kindness which the pagans show to Israel is accounted to them as sin, since they merely do it in order to mock us by their conscious power.'—R. Johanan expounded in a philanthropic sense: "The kindness of the nations is a sin-offering [the term *Hatath* used in the verse, means either sin or sin-offering]; as the sin-offering atones for Israel, so charity and benevolence atone for the Gentiles." (B. Bathra 10^b).

[4] Graetz l. c.

Though he is said to have reached the age of one hundred and twenty years,[1] he must have been advanced in years, even beyond the furthest limit set by the Psalmist,[2] when he left Jerusalem, as he has been a pupil of Hillel. Consequently not many years were vouchsafed him to steer the ship of Israel on the troubled waters at the beginning of the Christian Era. He died on his bed, surrounded by his disciples, and his parting blessing to them was, "May the fear of God have as much influence upon your conduct as the fear of man."[3]

Together with R. Johanan, a number of bright stars formed a galaxy that illumined the field of the law, and the spirit of the great master, which influenced his disciples, was by them transmitted

---

[1] Sifre II, § 357; Yalkut § 967.

[2] Psalm XC, 10.

[3] Berakhoth 27b.—The Solomonic maxim (Eccl. IX, 8): "Let thy garments be always white; and let not thy head lack ointment," he applied to the duty of man to be at all times prepared to answer the call of death, and illustrated this by the following parable: A certain king once invited his courtiers to a feast, without naming the exact hour at which they were expected to come. The prudent among them dressed and ornamented themselves early in the day, and repaired to the vicinity of the palace, thinking that at court but little time would be required for preparations, and they might be called in at any moment. The heedless, on the contrary, thought that much time would be consumed in the preparations for the feast, wherefore they turned to their usual avocations. Suddenly the king gave the signal for his invited guests to enter, and take their seats around the festive board. Those who were fully equipped for the occasion were heartily welcomed, while the negligent experienced the royal displeasure (Sabbath 153a).

to subsequent generations. He was succeeded in the presidency of the Synhedrion by R. Gamliel II, who very seldom deviated from the path laid out by his illustrious sire, Hillel I, and followed by his teacher and predecessor. R. Eliezer, R. Joshua[1] were numbered among the most prominent members of his council, and with him they zealously labored to

---

[1] Besides being learned in the law, and skilled in debate, (cf. Hagiga 5ᵇ; Nedarim 50ᵇ; Bekhoroth 8) he was familiar with astronomy, and this knowledge saved R. Gamliel and his retinue from death by starvation. The simple Talmudic story of that occurrence runs thus: R. Gamliel, accompanied by R. Joshua, set out on a voyage. Each took along his own provisions, but R. Joshua carried with him a store larger apparently than the journey required. The captain of the vessel, misled by a star, steered in the wrong course, and thereby prolonged the journey. R. Gamliel's provision gave out, and he was astonished to find his companion provided with food sufficient to supply his wants. R. Gamliel enquired for the reason that had prompted the Rabbi to lay in so great a supply of provisions, whereupon R. Joshua informed him that he had foreseen the reappearance of a star which appears but once in seventy years, and by which mariners are easily deceived. 'This star, according to my calculations, would be due some time during our journey, and I provided myself for the emergency.' (Horayoth 10ᵃ).—Modern scholars suppose that "star" to have been Halley's Comet which, according to the computation of the mathematician whose name it bears, takes about 76 years to return to its perihelion. It last appeared in 1835, and the hero of our story having flourished during the patriarchate of Gamliel II, it is assumed that the journey was taken in the year 87 A. C. The only difficulty in identifying this comet with the star is the Rabbi's given mean time of its periodic reappearance: 70 instead of 76 years; but the ancients usually delighted in round numbers, and 70 was frequently on the lips of the Talmudists.

preserve the traditions received from their predecessors, and to elaborate new *Halakhoth*. But the former was not always on friendly terms with R. Gamliel, and was ultimately banished from his college.[1] R. Joshua, on the other hand, who had inherited the forgiving disposition of R. Johanan, lived in peace with the president of the Synhedrion, and when the latter died, he managed, for a time, the administration of the spiritual affairs of the people. He, too, enjoyed the confidence of the Roman government, and employed his influence for the advantage of his people.[2]

These were the leading spirits of this generation of *Tannaim* (scholars, teachers). The other prominent members of the council were: R. Zadok, Dosa ben Harkinas, Jose the priest, Simon ben Nethaniel, Eleazar ben Arakh. They established schools at different centres of Jewish population, and taught the law. The greater their troubles, and the severer their trials, the closer did they cling to their national literature, the only relic saved from the wreck of Israel's glorious past.

In the next Tannaitic generation we meet with such names as R. Tryphon, R. Johanan ben Nuri, R. Ishmael ben Elisha, who elaborated the seven hermeneutic rules of Hillel I into thirteen, and R. Jose the Galilean, the father of R. Eleazar who extended them further to thirty-two;[3] but the most gifted and best known of them all was

---

[1] B. Mezia 59ᵃ.
[2] Graetz l. c.; ib. c. 3.
[3] Cf. supra. p. 196.

R. Akiba ben Joseph.

In his early years he had been, like Moses before entering on his great mission, a shepherd of flocks, and had obtained the hand of his wealthy master's daughter, at a price which bought fame as well as happiness—application to study.[1] He entered school with the earnest purpose of acquiring knowledge, and he succeeded. At first, it is true, his slumbering faculties would not awaken, but after continued efforts, his genius was aroused, and soon he became the equal, and gradually the superior of the master-minds of his age. Indeed, it is stated that his teacher himself, R. Eliezer was silenced by his arguments.[2]

The great fame of R. Akiba rests upon his peculiar methods in expounding scriptural dicta and systematizing the Halakhoth. Until his day the Halakhah was either "suspended by a hair,"[3] not having had

---

[1] Kethuboth 62ᵇ sq.; Nedarim 50ª. The sources relate that young Akiba was employed as shepherd by Kalba Sabua, but his modesty drew upon him the affectionate regards of the rich man's daughter. She opened her heart to him, and promised him her hand under the condition that he would acquire a knowledge of the law of which he was at the time profoundly ignorant. He agreed, and soon departed for school. For years he studied and then taught, while his betrothed suffered great privations, having been banished from the house of her hard-hearted father because of this alliance; but when he returned to claim her, and came accompanied by admiring disciples, the father not only relented, but presented him with half of his possessions, and thus made an end to the privations of his daughter and her husband.

[2] Yer. Pesahim VI. § 3. p. 33ᵇ bot.

[3] Hagiga 19.

sufficient mnemonic support in Scripture, or a dead treasure, incapable of growth and development. It had no foundation, except in tradition; no stronghold, save the memory. R. Akiba put new life into it, and made it a living mine from which, by a correct application of the means at hand, new treasures could at all times be dug. To give it more validity, he inaugurated the system of establishing decisions, no longer on the plan of a majority vote, but on the suggestive word of the written Bible text. He argued that the composition of the *Torah* (Pentateuch), especially in its judicial (Halakhah) parts, differs from that of every other written book. The human writer uses, besides the words necessary to express his ideas, certain turns, tropes, repetitions, embellishments, redundancies—certain *forms* which are almost superfluous. In the Torah, on the contrary, nothing has been inserted for the sake of mere form, but all is substance. In the Sinaic code there is nothing superfluous, not even a single letter. Every peculiarity of expression, every expletive, every mark, must, therefore, be regarded as a significant hint pointing to the establishment of certain truths, or certain legal rules. The Halakhoth thus received Scriptural authority, and controversies were thereby, to a great extent, obviated. Indeed, it was admitted that the oral law would have fallen into desuetude, had not R. Akiba furnished it with such strong support.[1]

---

[1] Sifre II, § 48.—R. Tryphon, formerly his superior, now reverentially addressed him: "whosoever forsakes thee, forsakes eternal life, for what has been forgotten by tradition thou

But this was not all that R. Akiba accomplished. His labors extended also in another direction. His attention was attracted to the inefficient method by which the traditions were imparted to the students, and he sought to remove the difficulty. Hitherto there had been no system in the manner in which the Rabbis held forth, and it required many years of constant attendance on the lectures, and of close application to study, as also an extremely retentive memory, to retain the whole mass of Halakhoth, communicated without any connection or regularity. Whatever decision occurred to the teacher's mind while at his desk, that he imparted to his hearers, without reference to antecedents or sequents, and this made it excessively difficult for the disciples to remember it. To assist the memory, R. Akiba grouped all the Halakhoth systematically. He classified the decisions, first, according to their subject-matter, so that all the laws concerning the Sab-

---

restorest by thy method of interpretation" (ib. I. § 75; Yalkut Num. ? 725); and R. Joshua, although wary on these subjects, could not repress his admiration. "Would," said he on one occasion. "that the eyes of R. Johanan ben Zakkai were reopened, so that he might assure himself of the groundlessness of his apprehension lest a Halakhah be some day relinquished, because it has no support in the word of Scripture; behold. R. Akiba has found the necessary support!" (Sotah c. V. § 2. Cf. Yer. ad l., p. 20ᵇ bot.). With such and similar effusions did R. Akiba's contemporaries hail his new method, as the commencement of a new era in the interpretation and the application of the Scriptural text (cf. Menahoth 29ᵇ; Num. R. c. 19); and at his death his disciples lamented that "the arms of the Law had been broken, and the springs of wisdom closed" (Sotah 49ʰ).

bath or of marriages, for instance, formed one *Masekhta* (*textus*, treatise); and each Masekhta he subdivided according to the number of the subjects treated. Thus, for instance, were placed together: *Four* are the principal causes of injury to property; *five* classes of men are precluded from apportioning the heave-offering; *fifteen* women absolve their husbands from the leviratical marriage; *thirty-six* transgressions are punishable by excision.[1] Of this classification by R. Akiba into sections and numbers it was said that he had provided the law with hooks and handles, as it were, for the memory.[2]

This systematic compilation by R. Akiba was called *Mishnah* (from the late Hebrew, *Shanah*—to study), especially known as *"Mishnah de R. Akiba"* (among Christian writers, the *Deuterosis* of R. Akiba); it is also known as *Mekhiltah, Mekhillin,* or *Middoth* (all of which terms mean measures), "probably on account of the numbers which were used as connecting links." This collection was, in the course of time, invested with so great an authority that it often superseded its predecessor, the *Mishnah Rishonah* (earlier Mishnah) of Hillel.[3]

Meanwhile R. Akiba's fame spread far and wide, and attracted to his school hundreds of eager students. The number of his hearers is variously and extravagantly stated, the most modest account bringing it down to three hundred; and, although the Roman

---

[1] Yer. Shekalim V, § 1, p. 48ᶜ.
[2] Aboth de R. Nathan XVIII.
[3] Cf. Graetz l. c., note 8, and sources.

government fixed the penalty of death upon every one who would give instruction in Jewish lore, R. Akiba did not cease to spread the knowledge of the Oral Law until he was thrown into prison, from which only a martyr's death freed him.[1]

After the death of R. Akiba and the repeal of the Hadrianic edicts against the Jews, (about 140 A. C.),

---

[1] Cf. supra n. 391.—As he continued preaching and teaching publicly, Papus ben Judah asked him once: "Akiba, fearest thou not the wrath of the government?" Thereupon R. Akiba replied by citing the following parable:

One day a fox was walking along the river-side, and observed the fishes shooting to and fro in great confusion. He inquired for the reason of this commotion, and was informed by the aquatic animals that it was because they feared the perils of nets and hooks, which were constantly thrown out for them. Thereupon the fox invited the terrified fishes to leave their watery homes, and to follow him into his habitation, where, under his protection, they could live in safety and peace. To this the fishes replied, "Art thou the same whom all regard as the wisest of all beasts? Thou art certainly not wise, but foolish! If, while living in the water, our natural element of life, we have reason to fear, how much more dangerous would it be for us to be on dry land, which itself is death to us?" The Rabbi continued: "Thus it is with us in these times of persecution. If our life is imperilled when we are studying the law, which is the source of a happy life, how much greater must our danger be when we neglect to study the law!" Shortly after this dialogue, R. Akiba and Papus were arrested by the minions of their Roman persecutors. The two met in prison, and the latter, in despair, exclaimed, "Happy art thou, O Rabbi Akiba, who art here for the cause of the law; but wo to me, who am imprisoned for having pursued a vain course." (Berakhoth 61b).

his surviving disciples, who had fled during the persecutions, returned to Palestine, and reorganized the council for the administration of their inherited laws. They were seven in number, and their names were, R. Meir, R. Judah ben Ilai, R. Jose ben Halafta, R. Johanan the Sandalar, R. Simon ben Johai, R. Eleazar ben Shamua, and R. Nehemia.[1] They repaired to the plain of Rimmon, where they began to deliberate on certain seasonable observances, when a dispute arose among them anent a traditional law. This at first threatened to extinguish the sacred flame kindled by their martyred teacher; but it soon subsided and only inspired them to be more careful in the future, and more zealous in prosecuting the still incomplete work of collating and arranging the scattered Halakhoth. They convoked an assembly of the learned in Usha, and re-established the Synhedrion whose sessions had, for a time, been interrupted by the Roman persecutions. Of this Synhedrion R. Simeon ben Gamliel II was Nasi, R. Nathan, the Babylonian, was *Ab-Beth-Din*, and R. Meir, *Hakham*.

R. MEIR

was the most influential, because the most gifted personage of this generation. His high-soaring mind, sterling character, and profound erudition early gained for him the friendship of his preceptor, R. Akiba, by whom he was ordained with the title Rabbi; but, on

---

[1] Yer. Hagiga III. § 1. p. 78ᵈ top.
[2] Horayoth 13ᵇ. Cf. supra § 55.

account of his youth, he was not recognized as an independent leader of a college until after his re-ordination by R. Judah ben Baba.[1] It is probable that the youthful scholar meant to criticise this undue respect for mere age, without regard to true merit, when he said: "Look not at the flask, but at that which is contained therein: there may be a new flask full of old wine, and there may be old flasks in which there is not even new wine."[2]

R. Meir[3] followed closely in the foot-prints of his great preceptor, R. Akiba, in his treatment of the Halakhah. He employed the hermeneutic, exegetical rules transmitted by his predecessors to substantiate a legal decision or to annul one; and continued the work of

---

[1] Supra n. 225. The seven disciples of R. Akiba just enumerated were ordained on that occasion.

[2] Aboth IV, § 27. Indeed, he had good reason for taking offense at the slight, for his contemporaries themselves were forced to admit (Erubin 13ᵇ) that Rabbi Meir had no equal in his generation, and that his authority would sway the decision of the colleges, were it not for the fact that his real opinion could not be ascertained. He was wont to argue questions pro and con, and cite analogous cases and inferences illustrating both sides of the subject, the affirmative and the negative, and thus left his hearers in the dark as to his true opinion. Perhaps he did this simply to avoid manifesting partiality to one or the other opinion, which, in the Speaker of the Synhedrion, might have influenced the actions of his constituents (cf. supra n. 329).

[3] His original name, the Talmud says, was Miasa or Moïse (Greek pronunciation of Moses), and Meir was applied to him metaphorically, "because he *enlightened* [*Meir* being a derivative from the Hebrew term meaning *light*] the mind's eye of the wise men" (Erub. 13ᵇ. Cf. *Yuhasin* s. v., and Rabbinowitz D. S. ad l.).

R. Akiba in the formal arrangement of the Mishnah. The isolated fragmentary parts of his teacher's compilation he united into a whole, supplied deficiencies, and gave every part a name corresponding to its subject-matter. His mode of teaching drew around him a large number of pupils, and his cultured wit distinguished him as one of the greatest fabulists of his age. On the jackal alone, the favorite figure of Oriental fiction, he is reported to have written three hundred fables, with which he relieved the dry and unpalatable study of the Halakhah, and by which he illustrated interesting *Agadoth* (homilies), whose province it was to give the free and unconstrained interpretation of Scripture, the exposition of history, the representation of the past and future of Judaism, as well as the institution of inquiries concerning the object and significance of laws and the search after abstract moral truths. Of all his allegorical illustrations of Biblical texts only three fragments are preserved, which the great Talmudical commentators, *Rashi* and *Mcharshaa*, interweave into one.[1]

R. Meir was married to Beruria (or Valeria), the learned daughter of R. Hanina ben Tradion, whose opinions on the Halakhah were honorably mentioned by R. Judah;[2] and in her he found 'a help meet unto him.' Both were modest in their behavior and re-

---

[1] Sanhedrin 38ᵇ sq.

[2] Tosefta Kelim, part II, c. 1, § 6, ed. Zuck. Former editions erroneously have Joshua instead of Judah. Her attendance on the lectures of the Rabbis is said to have been very frequent (Pesahim 62ᵇ).

signed to their fate,[1] but Beruria even more so than

---

[1] The Midrash (Prov. XXXI) preserves the following touching illustration of their pious resignation:—On a certain Sabbath afternoon, while R. Meir was at college engaged in expounding the law, his two sons, both lovely youths and of uncommon depth of mind, suddenly died. Unwilling to sadden her husband's heart on the Sabbath by the sorrowful intelligence, his wife conveyed the corpses to her bed-chamber, where she had them tenderly laid on a couch, and covered over with a white coverlet. When, in the evening, Rabbi Meir came home and inquired as to the whereabouts of his children, the grief-stricken mother evasively answered that they were not far off; and placed before him food and drink. After he had pronounced the benediction customary at the close of the Sabbath, his wife requested permission to ask a question, which he readily granted.

"A few days ago," said she, "a person intrusted a treasure in my safe-keeping, and now he claims it back. Shall I return it to him?"

"This is a strange question," answered Rabbi Meir, "which my wife should never have thought it necessary to ask. What! wouldst thou hesitate to restore to a stranger his own?"

"No!" replied she. "But I thought it best not to restore the treasure before I had acquainted thee with the affair."

She then led him to the death-chamber, and approaching the bier, removed the coverlet from the dead bodies. The sight appalled him, and in a mournful voice he began to lament: "Ah! my sons, my sons! the light of my eyes! I was your father, but ye were my teachers in the law."

The mother turned away and wept bitterly. At length she tenderly took her husband's hand into hers, and said: "Rabbi, didst thou not teach me that we must not be reluctant to restore that which is intrusted to our keeping! The Lord hath given, the Lord hath taken away, blessed be the name of the Lord!"

"Yes, blessed be the name of the Lord!" echoed the resigned Rabbi; "and blessed be his name also for thy sake, for thou hast truly comforted me."

her famous husband. When on one occasion the Rabbi, mercilessly plagued by a wicked neighbor, was provoked to anger, and uttered a wish that the sinner would be removed from this world, Beruria reproved him, saying, Not so, my husband; the Psalmist did not pray, that the sinners [*hoteim*] be consumed out of the earth, but 'that sins [*hataim*] be consumed out of the earth, and then there would be no more wicked people.'[1] Pray, not for the destruction of the person, but for the reformation of his heart.

Among R. Meir's colleagues the most noteworthy was R. Simon ben Johai, who survived all the rest, and who presided over the academy at Tekoa, in Galilee. He had a number of disciples, and became the only authority for the succeeding age. After the example of his coadjutors, he too compiled a Mishnah collection under the name of Middoth, which contains an abridged selection from that of R. Akiba.[2]

Another of R. Meir's colleagues, R. Jose ben Halaftha, was the first systematic Rabbinic historian. He vigorously applied himself to that field, uncultivated in his times, and as the result of his labors left a chronological history, based on the Bible, and continued from the creation to the Bar-Cokhba insurrection (135-138), which he styled *Seder Olam* (Order of the World), and which was designed to throw light on certain obscure data in Holy Writ, and to fill up the gaps by tradition. He also compiled a Mishnah

---

[1] Psalm CIV. 35; Berakhoth 10ᵃ.
[2] Gittin 66ₐ; Sanhedrin 86ᵃ.

collection, known under the Greek appellation *Nomi-kon* (Compendium of Laws).[1]

A third collection was at this time accomplished by R. Nathan of Babylon, vice-president of the Synhedrion at Usha. This compilation is known under the name of Aboth d' R. Nathan.

It was during the lives of these Tannaim that great disturbances arose between the disciples of the different schools, composing the Synhedrion under the patriarchate or presidency of R. Simon ben Gambiel II. A rival Synod was established and presided over by R. Hanina at Nehar-Pakod, in Babylon, which threatened to sever the religious bond of union that united all Israel under one Council. It was, however, not of long duration. The Palestinean Synhedrion did not brook a rival authority which divided the unity of Judaism into Oriental and Occidental factions. R. Isaac and R. Nathan were therefore despatched thither by the patriarch R. Simon, with instructions to exert their utmost endeavors to effect a dissolution of the new tribunal; and their mission was crowned with success. R. Hanina at first resisted the entreaties and remonstrances of the delegation; but discovering that the efforts of his opponents had made a deep impression on his constituents, who no longer sympathized with him, he submitted, and declared the first Babylonian Synhedrion dissolved.

Not so easily were the domestic disturbances quelled. Bitter feelings were engendered in the breasts of R. Na-

---

[1] Erubin 51ª; Gittin 67ª.

than and R. Meir, the Vice-President and the Speaker of the Usha Synhedrion, against the Patriarch, who, in their absence, had introduced peculiar rules by which the dignity of his office should be distinguished over those of his assistants. This irritated the two dignitaries, and they conspired to have him deposed. Their conspiracy, however, was betrayed and frustrated. Still, dissension continued to increase, and found a home among the various schools and manifested itself in heated discussions of the Halakhah. Indeed, the discord in the decisions of those days was so marked, as to make it appear as if there were really two *Toroth*, instead of one only,[1] upon which Rabbinic enactments could be based. When, therefore, after the death of R. Simon II, his son,

R. Judah I,

commonly styled *Hackadosh* (the Holy) or simply *Rabbi*,—succeeded to the patriarchate (170 A. C.), his earliest and most strenuous efforts were directed towards effecting a reconciliation between the contending elements, and codifying the Halakhoth, scattered in the memories of the Rabbis, into one digest, and thus to unify the law.

Of R. Judah I it was said that, since Moses, knowledge and authority had not been joined in one person as they were in him.[2] His wealth, too, was fabulously great, and gave rise to the assertion that his

---

[1] Erubin 51ᵃ; Gittin 67ᵃ.
[2] Sanhedrin 36ᵃ; Gittin 59ᵃ.

equerry was richer than the Persian King.¹ But this he employed in ameliorating the condition of the suffering poor. When in the reign of Marcus Aurelius, a terrible famine visited Palestine, R. Judah opened his vast granaries and distributed food, at first to the learned only, but afterwards among all classes indiscriminately.² Thus richly endowed with natural and worldly gifts, he wielded an authority which grew from day to day, and finally became so great that it made him dictator of all Palestinean Jewish congregations, and extended his sway even over his Babylonian co-religionists.³ No religious decision was valid without his sanction,⁴ and no disciple could be ordained without his approval.⁵

R. Judah did not maintain everything in the Jewish religion in *statu quo*, but zealously labored to harmonize the law with the requirements of the times and of the ever varying circumstances. When, owing to the accumulated misfortunes which succeeded the Bar-Cokhba insurrection, the laws concerning the release-year and the tithes became very oppressive on the impoverished people, R. Judah exempted from these laws the frontier towns, which, though under Judean religious surveillance, did not constitute part of Judea proper; and when his own relatives remonstrated against this enactment, which abrogated an old established custom, he replied, "My predecessors have left

---

¹ Sanhedrin 36ᵃ.
² Sabbath 113ᵇ; B. Mezia 85ᵃ.
   B. Bathra 8ᵃ.
⁴ Sanhedrin 5ᵇ.
⁵ Cf. supra n. 215.

this measure for me that I might show my undisputed authority."[1] Many other ameliorations he introduced, and, guided by the change of circumstances, he abolished customs and ceremonies sanctioned by age.

But neither his wealth and his benevolence, nor his authority and legislation, gained for him the fame which his literary labors did. His intellectual capacities early won for him the love and esteem of his teachers and colleagues, and already in his youth was he promoted by his father and the college to the first rank of the disciples;[2] and his talents, as well as the versatility of his learning—for he did not confine himself to the opinions of a single school, but drew knowledge from all sources,—enabled him to furnish impartial decisions and to complete the collection of all Halakhoth (189). Since the first collection by Hillel had been made, the subject matter of the law was greatly increased by the several schools. New cases, partly derived from old ones by the hermeneutic rules, and partly from Scriptural texts on R. Akiba's plan, swelled its volume and made it impossible any longer to learn and to teach orally. Besides, the Israelites of his times moved about from one place to another in quest of freedom, and adopted the languages of the countries of their dispersion, wherefore great fears were entertained that, in the course of events, the traditional law, which was in the possession of comparatively few only,[3] would fall into oblivion. Taking all

---

[1] Hullin 6ᵇ.

[2] Cf. B. Mezia 44ᵃ, et al.

[3] It must be borne in mind that we speak of the *traditional* or *oral* law. Until the days of Rabbi Judah nothing of the tra-

this into consideration, R. Judah I resolved to come to the rescue. He examined every opinion impartially, and fixed the decision according to majorities, thus summing up the labors of hundreds of sages and of years: "The Oral Law had been recognized by Ezra; had become important in the days of the Maccabees; had been supported by Pharisaism; narrowed by the school of Shammai, codified by the school of Hillel, systematized by R. Akiba, placed on a logical basis by R. Ishmael, exegetically amplified by R. Eliezer, and constantly enriched by successive Rabbis and their schools. *Rabbi* put the coping-stone to the immense structure."[2] He arranged the heterogenous mass of upwards of 4000 traditional *Halakhoth or Mishniyoth*, (precedents, doctrines) into six *Sedarim* (categories, orders) which he subdivided into sixty-three *Mesikhtoth* (treatises), and then into five hundred and twenty-three *Perakim* (fragments, chapters). But although R. Judah endeavored to effect a systematic grouping of the various laws under their proper titles, he did not invariably succeed, partly because the matter was too heterogenous to be harmonized, and partly, because he wished to retain the existing order and division.[3] It is therefore almost impossible to give

---

dition was allowed to be written down, and all Halakhoth were imparted by the teacher to his disciples by word of mouth. It is true that to assist the memory memoranda were occasionally drawn up by teacher or pupil, but they were left in the possession of their owner. They were kept in secret, wherefore they were called *M'gilloth S'tharim* (Secret Scrolls).

[2] Farrar, History of Interpretation.

[3] Graetz IV, c. 12.—Maimonides and others, notably Frankel (*Hodegetica in Mishnam* p. 254 sq.) labored to find in Rabbi's

a complete analysis of the work, and we content ourselves with simply furnishing a general one of the

ORDERS

which be named after the principal matters they respectively treat of.

Order I, *Zèraim* (seeds), treating of Agrarian Laws: Benedictions said over the earth's productions; Tithes, Heave-offerings, Release-year, Prohibitory Mixtures in plants, animals and garments. This Order consists of eleven treatises.

Order II, *Moed* (feasts), treating of the Sabbath, festivals and fast days, as also of the ceremonials and sacrifices for these days. This Order consists of twelve treatises.

Order III, *Nashim* (women), treats of betrothals, marriages and divorce, and of vows and obligations. This Order contains seven treatises.

Order IV, *Nezikin* (damages), treats, in the main, of civil and criminal law, and of the laws concerning idolatry. This Order contains ten treatises.

Order V, *Kadashim* (holy things), speaks of the various sacrifices and of all the Temple service, as

---

compilation a certain systematic order; but the Talmud itself says: "There is no regular order in the Mishnah" (B. Kama 102ª; Ab. Zara 7ª). That this, is the fact, the attentive reader will doubtlessly have discovered ere this, by simply glancing at the references in our compendium for which, although it treats of a single branch of Rabbinic lore, the material had to be gathered from almost all the treatises of the Babylonian and the Palestinean Talmudim, and also from their contemporaneous Rabbinic compilations.

also of the dimensions of the building and its appurtenances. This Order contains eleven treatises.

Order VI, *Taharoth* (purification), treats of the different ways and means required for the cleansing of the defiled person or thing, the leper, for instance, or a vessel which was under one roof with a human corpse. This Order contains twelve treatises.

This compilation is known under the title of MISHNAH, without any qualifying epithet designating its compiler. It comprises the earlier collections (*Mishnah Rishonah*), as well as later Halakhoth, and, although Rabbi may not have intended it so, it nevertheless became the sole standard, and attained exclusive authority, superseding that of its predecessors in all cases where differences of opinion appeared. As time rolled by, and circumstances changed, Rabbi found it necessary to revise his compilation, and make such alterations as rendered his work more compatible with the requirements of the age.[1]

Thus was at last the Traditional, or Oral Law, which had been floating in the air, as it were, during four centuries, brought to a close, and established on a firm basis.[2] "The Mishnah, at the side of the Holy Scriptures, became the principal source of intellectual stimulus and inquiry; it supplanted at times even the Scriptures, and sustained its exclusive authority.

---

[1] Cf. B. Mezia 44ᵃ; Ab. Zara 52ᵃ.—The Palestinean colleges, however, seem to have adhered to the original edition, and only the Babylonians adopted the revised one.

[2] But whether Rabbi wrote down his Mishnah or arranged it orally, is as yet a mooted question.

It became the spiritual cement, which kept together the disjointed members of the Jewish nationality, and rendered the visible bond dispensable." Henceforth it formed the mental centre of the sages and scholars of Israel, but nothing was allowed to be added thereto.

After the publication of the Mishnah by R. Judah I, his younger contemporaries proceeded to collect the Halakhoth, omitted by the patriarch, partly because they lacked legal force, and partly because they appeared as special elaborations under general formulas. Of these the principal collections are the *Tosephta* (supplement) of R. Hiya and R. Oshia; *Baraitha* or *Mishnah Hitzona* (external Mishnah, Apocrypha); *Mekhilta* of R. Ishmael; *Sifra* and *Sifre debe Rabh;* all of which are composed in the spirit of R. Akiba's principles,[1] but they are not as authoritative as Rabbi's collection.

On his death-bed (210 A. C.) Rabbi appointed his eldest son, Gamliel III, as his successor in the patriarchal dignity, and his son Simon he named for the the office of *Hakham.*[2] With the death of these, the line of Tannaim (Mishnahists)[3] ended, and was suc-

---

[1] Sanhedrin 86ª. et al.

[2] Kethuboth 103ᵇ.

[3] Maimonides, in his "Preface to Seder Zeraim," counts ninety-one Tannaim in whose names Halakhoth are recorded in the Mishnah, and thirty-seven who are mentioned only in connection with certain events, or as ethical teachers. There were, however, more than one hundred and twenty-eight Rabbis engaged in the composition of the subject matter of that great work. but their names are not given, the editor of the compilation having traced the traditions no farther back than to Simon

ceeded by that of the *Amoraim* (lecturers, interpreters), the commentators on the Mishnah.

II.

THE GUEMARA.

The younger contemporaries of Rabbi and the survivors of his immediate successors now assumed the task of continuing the chain of the Oral law, not, indeed adding aught to the complete collection of the Mishnah, but commenting upon it, and drawing logical inferences and new decisions from it. The study of the Scriptures was now almost suspended, and the Amoraim occupied themselves mainly with the cultivation of the Traditional law. They were told that, 'while the study of the Bible is a meritorious avocation, the application to the Mishnah is more important and meritorious,' and acted accordingly.[1] The Mishnah was to the Amoraim what the Bible had been to the Tannaim: a text-book of mnemonics. They made the brief, and, not unfrequently, obscure contents of the Mishnah the subject matter of their diligent study and discussion. They dissected it, commented upon it, and gave it a new dress, almost a new form. And as they did not confine themselves to the simple dissertations of the Mishnah, but gradually asserted their independence of the laws laid down by

---

the Just, and many of those which had been the subjects of discussion, he transmitted anonymously.—In his "Talmudic *Roll of Honor*," now in preparation, the author will furnish a list of Tannaim, comprising more than twice as many as stated by Maimonides.

[1] B. Mezia 33ᵃ.

their predecessors, and transgressed beyond the limits of their texts, a new sphere of activity was opened to them, assuming very large proportions; and the result of their labors was subsequently compiled under the name of *Guemara* (discussion, complement, doctrine: the term *gamar* answering to either.)

The representative Amoraim of this generation (225-280) were in Palestine: R. Hiya the Elder, compiler of the Tosefta, Bar Kappara, R. Isaac the Elder, Levi ben Sisi, R. Hanina, R. Oshia the Elder, coworker in the compilation of the Tosefta, R. Judah II, the patriarch, R. Johanan; and in Babylon: R. Shila, Abba bar Abba, Abba Arekha.

These, together with their coadjutors, studied and taught. In their public lectures they were wont to expound their themes in an undertone to the *Meturgeman* (interpreter), who pronounced them aloud to the assembled hearers.[1]

The Amoraim, like the Tannaim, endeavored to point out and thoroughly explain every precept in the

---

[1] Sanhedrin 7b. It is related that on one occasion, the patriarch appointed a favorite of his, though an ignorant man, as public lecturer, and assigned to him R. Judah ben Nahameni as Meturgeman. R. Judah strained his ears to gather up the whispered sayings expected on such occasions; but it was in vain. The lecturer knew not how to begin or what to say. Chagrined by this abuse of the patriarchal authority, the Meturgeman poured forth his biting sarcasm upon both the patriarch and his protege. Quoting a Biblical passage (Habakkuk II, 19), he exclaimed: "Woe unto him who saith to the wood, 'Awake!' to the dumb stone, 'Rouse up!' Can this one teach? Behold, he is encased in gold and silver, but there is no spirit in him." This recalled the patriarch to his senses, and we meet no more with such cases.

Bible. R. Simlai numbered all the ordinances and traced them to principles. He says:[1] "Six hundred and thirteen commandments were delivered to Moses at Sinai; of these, three hundred and sixty-five, corresponding to the number of days in the solar year, are negative ordinances, and the remaining two hundred and forty-eight, corresponding to the number of limbs in the human body, are positive. King David, however, reduced them to eleven, as follows: 1. To walk in integrity. 2. Do justice. 3. Speak truth. 4. Avoid slander. 5. Refrain from doing evil to a neighbor. 6. Do not revile thy friend. 7. Despise the wicked. 8. Revere the God-fearing. 9. Abide by an oath. 10. Not to take usury. 11. Not to take bribe.[2] The prophet Isaiah condensed these into six, to wit: 1. To do justice. 2. Speak truth. 3. Despise the gain of oppression. 4. Withhold thy hand from bribery. 5. Stopping the ear against hearing of blood (i. e. evil communications which may result in bloodshed). 6. Closing the eye against all evil.[3] Then came the prophet Micah and summed them up in the following three, viz: 1. Do justice. 2. Love kindness. 3. Walk humbly with God.[4] Again, Isaiah (II) compressed them into two, viz: 1. Observe justice. 2. Practice benevolence.[5] Finally came the prophet Habakkuk, and reduced all com-

---

[1] Cf. supra, § 11.
[2] Psalm XV.
[3] Isaiah XXXVIII, 15.
[4] Micah VI, 8.
[5] Isaiah LVI, 1.

mandments into *one,* viz: The righteous liveth in his fidelity.[1]

It was at this time that Babylonia began gradually to move to the front of Jewish history, and to become a second "Land of Israel."[2] The Jewish leaders of this country became inured to profound meditation and research. A spirit of deep inquiry and ceaseless activity pervaded them all. They refused henceforth blindly to submit themselves to the traditions, or to accept them upon mere authority; but sought for every Halakhah the "Why?" and "Wherefore?" and at times carried their independence so far as to cite the Mishnah, and even the Scriptures, before the tribunal of *Sabarah* (Logics).[3] As in the days of Rabbi Judah I, aspiring Babylonians had flocked in considerable numbers to the Judean academies, so they now either returned to their native land and took the lead of colleges, or Palestinean youth attached themselves to the Babylonian seats of learning. Nehardea, Pumpeditha, Sura, and other chief cities, were studded with colleges (called *Sidra*), and filled with students. Sura alone, which for upwards of seven hundred years continued to be the principal repository of Jewish learning, numbered twelve hundred pupils, under the rectorship of Abba Arekha who, as the editor of the Mishnah before him had been surnamed *Rabbi*, so he now was named *Rabh*, teacher, and who, like his great master in former years, maintained the poor among

---

[1] Habakkuk II, 4.
[2] Cf. Gen. R. c. 17.
[3] Cf. Berakhoth 6ᵇ, Yeb. 72ᵇ, ib. 76, et al.

the students at his own expense, deriving the means from his own estate, which he cultivated himself.[1]

Rabh's name became widely known, even outside of Babylon, and his authority was recognized throughout the land. It once occurred that he officiated as Meturgeman to R. Shila, the lecturer not knowing him. He expounded the Mishnah in a manner displeasing to R. Shila, who remonstrated with him; whereupon he remarked, "The dulcet sound of the flute, which is pleasing to the noble ear, is not pleasing to the uncultivated taste! I have ever thus interpreted this passage before R. Hiya (whose interpreter he had formerly been), and he approved of it." R. Shila, surprised at finding in his Meturgeman the great teacher, humbly apologized, and invited him to take the seat of honor.[2]

The next Amoraim generation comprised such men as patriarchs R. Gamliel IV, and R. Judah III; R. Eleazar ben Pedath, R. Ami, R. Assi, R. Hiya ben Abba and his brother, R. Simon, and R. Abbuha, in Palestine; R. Huna in Sura, R. Judah in Pumpeditha, and R. Hasda in Kaphra, in Babylonia. These, and after them their successors, both in Palestine and Babylon, carried on the work of learning and teaching, criticising and commenting upon the Mishnah for a considerable length of time; but, like their predecessors, the Tannaim, they delivered their dissertations orally.

The Rabbis ascribed to the Talmud a higher origin than human ingenuity. They declare that the pre-

---

[1] Kiddushin 12^a; Yebamoth 52^a.
[2] Yoma 20^b.

cepts (laid down in the Bible) were, together with their elucidations (recorded in the Talmud), received from Sinai. This theory they base on the following Scriptural passage: "I will give to thee the tablets of stone, and the law and the commandment, which I have written to teach them,"[1] which they explain as follows: By "the tablets" we are to understand *the ten commandments;* "the law" means *the written law* (the Pentateuch); "the commandment" represents *the Mishnah;* by the words "which I have written" are meant *the prophets and Hagiographa;* and the expression "to teach them" means *the Gemara.*[2] Agreeably to this the Mishnah teaches that Moses had received the entire law from Sinai. He delivered it to Joshua, by whom it was transmitted to the Elders, who communicated it to the prophets, and the latter bequeathed it to the men of the Great Synod.[3] Elsewhere the Rabbis explain the method by which the contemporaries of Moses learned the law. After Moses himself had received the Mishnah directly from the Almighty, Aaron entered, and was instructed in it by him. Aaron thereupon retired to the right of his teacher, and gave place to his sons, who also heard the law explained by Moses. These, too, took seats to the right and left of Moses, and heard him explain the law to the Elders, who also retired to one side, when the public at large was instructed. Aaron accordingly had by this time heard the law explained

---

[1] Exodus XXIV, 12.
[2] Berakhoth 5ᵃ. Cf. Megillah 19ᵇ, and parallel passages.
[3] Aboth I, 1.

four times; his sons thrice; the Elders twice, and the congregation once. Moses then retired and left Aaron to repeat, in the hearing of all, the law as explained to him, and to retire at the close thereof. His sons did likewise, and after them the Elders; thus each one had the opportunity of hearing every law four times before assuming to teach the same to others.[1]

The mode of teaching followed by the Rabbis was similar to that practised by Socrates. One propounded a question, another made a reply. The validity of the answer was questioned by comparing it with Halakhoth, apparently differing in their verdict. Explanations were then made, reasons given and discussed, arguments offered and authorities cited pro and con, and the decisions arrived at by the majority of the college, were adopted as laws. In this way and by the application of the hermeneutic, exegetical rules, matter to an enormous amount was gradually accumulated; but, like the Mishnah before its completion by R. Judah, it was not systematically arranged, and was therefore extremely difficult to memorize. To obviate this, R. Johanan, rector of the academy at Tiberias, collected the scattered debates and decisions, and arranged them in due order according to the Mishnah, and thus laid the foundation of the compilation known under the name of *Talmud Yerushalmi* (Jerusalem or Palestinean Talmud), and completed in the fourth century.[2] Of this Gemara

---

[1] Erubin 54ᵇ.

[2] Great differences of opinion exist among lexicographers, touching the date of this compilation, and it is extremely diffi-

only thirty-nine treatises are now extant, the last two Orders (Sedarim) having been lost. The Mishnah is published very often by itself; but the Gemara, being considered a commentary thereto, is never printed without the text. These two *together* constitute the Talmud.

The Babylonian Jews did not accept this work as authoritative. The Amoraim of the different Babylonian colleges which grew in importance as the Palestinean declined, continued to labor in the sacred field for a long time after the publication of the Talmud Yerushalmi, until R. Ashi, rector of the college at Sura, whom his contemporaries declare to have been the equal of R. Judah I in authority and knowledge,[1] attempted (427) to make a new and complete compilation. He died, however, in the midst of his work, and left it to his successors to carry out his plan. The work was completed by Mar and Meremar about the year 500, and published under the name of *Talmud Babli* (Babylonian Talmud), to distinguish it from the similar Palestinean collection. The Babylonian Gemara comments on only thirty-six treatises of the Mishnah, almost all Gemara on the first and sixth Orders being missing; still it is nearly four times as large as its predecessor, and is the Talmud *par excellence*, being highest in authority in all matters admitting of a difference of opinion.

---

cult to decide with precision. Buxtorf places it at about 230; David Ganz at 270; while Maimonides, Abarbanel and Elias Levita would have it at 370.

[1] Gittin 59ᵃ; Sanhedrin 36ᵃ. Cf. supra p. 222.

The Talmud, as the reader of the foregoing pages may now judge for himself, is a library in itself. "It is a microcosm, embracing heaven and earth." It treats on civil and religious law, on history, mathematics, astronomy,[1] medicine, metaphysics, theosophy. It passes from law to myth, from jest to earnest; it is replete with chaste diction, legendary illustration, beautiful imagery, apposite quotations, touches of pathos, bursts of genuine eloquence, finished rhetoric, graphic description. Now and then the dry subject matter of the Halakhah is relieved by flashes of wit, sallies of humor, strokes of sarcasm, amusing expressions or comparisons.

Some maintain that, in the days of the Talmudists, the position of the Hebrew woman in social and domestic life was not better than that of a slave. The student of the Talmud, however, finds no authority for such a charge. One or two illustrations, quoted from among the numerous passages in the writings

---

[1] We have already seen (supra p. 209) how R. Joshua foresaw the reappearance of a comet, and so saved himself and R. Gamliel I from starvation. R. Gamliel himself, too, is represented as an expert astronomer in his day (Rosh Hashanah 24ᵃ), and that he made use of something like the telescope (Erubin 43ᵇ). Rabh's colleague, Samuel, said of himself that, except as as to the "tailed stars" (comets), the courses of the heavenly bodies were as familiar to him as Nehardaa, where he lived (Berakhoth 58ᵇ).—In our age, when the sciences are so assiduously, successfully, and almost universally cultivated, all this may not be considered extraordinary, but these Rabbis lived some seventeen hundred years ago, when the most refined nations were still ignorant of the erratic movements of the planets.

of the Rabbis, will disabuse the minds of those who have been laboring under this false impression.

On certain days of the year the Jewish maidens, all clad in white, that the poor and the rich might appear without distinction, went out to the vineyards, formally invited the young men to join them in the dance, and half in jest, half in earnest, demanded their hands in marriage. These candidates for matrimony stated their various claims as best they knew how. Those endowed with personal beauty dwelt upon that; the children of noble birth praised high descent, and spoke of the great influence true aristocracy has on strict fidelity; while those who could boast of neither beauty nor noble blood, dilated on the transitory character of these personal advantages and the endurance of morality.[1]

This alone is sufficient to show that, unlike the Eastern woman of the other races, the Jewish woman did not lead a life of seclusion, but could freely move in society, and take part in domestic affairs. It is true, when a pedantic woman once began to argue on advanced ethics with Rabbi Eleazer, he directed her to pay attention to domestic economy, saying, "Woman's wisdom should be confined to the spindle;"[2] still the Rabbis prescribe the utmost respect for the housewife.[3] They even prohibit speaking to her in a loud voice. "If thy wife is small," says a Talmudic maxim, "bow down and whisper to

---

[1] Mishnah, end of Taanith.
[2] Yoma 66b.
[3] Baba Mezia 59b.

her."[1] We also find that occasionally women took part, with the consent of their husbands or fathers, in philosophical debates.

A heretic once remarked to R. Gamliel, "Your God cannot be strictly honest, else he would not have put Adam to sleep and stolen a rib from him." The Rabbi's daughter thereupon requested permission, which was granted, to make reply. She then requested the scorner to direct her to the seat of Justice. "And wherefore?" inquired the puzzled heretic; "what has happened that requires thy attendance on the Judge?" "Well," said she, "some thieves invaded our premises last night, stole a silver pitcher from us, and left a gold one in its stead." "Would that such misfortunes happened to me daily!" exclaimed the heathen. "If, then, you are of such an opinion," retorted the maiden, "why object to the stealing of the rib? Did Adam not receive in its stead a companion to wait on him and to share with him his joys and his sorrows?"

"I do not mean exactly the rib," rejoined the quibbler; "but I think the manner in which it was taken unworthy of the Deity. He certainly could have accomplished the same while Adam was awake!" Thereupon she took a piece of raw meat, washed, salted, patted and roasted it in his presence, and in conclusion invited him to partake of her preparation; but he declined, declaring that, after witnessing the process of dressing the meat, his appetite was gone. "Ah!" ejaculated the triumphant young

---

[1] Ibid.

woman; "exactly what might have been the case with Adam. Had he seen the process of extracting the rib and forming the woman, he might not have liked to associate with her, as when he beheld her complete, graced with feminine loveliness and beauty."[1]

To the question why woman was not created out of any other part of man's body, the humorous Aggadaists reply: Woman was not formed out of man's head, that she be not too proud and carry her head too high; not out of his ear or eye, that she may not become too curious, desiring to see and hear everything; not out of his mouth, that she may not become too talkative; not out of his heart, that she be not too jealous; finally, not out of his hand or foot, that she may not learn to touch everything or go everywhere. She was formed out of man's rib, which is hidden from view, that her origin might serve her as an emblem of modesty, virtue and moderation.[2]

The Talmudists very forcibly recommend timely marriage,[3] and say that a man without a wife is without happiness, without joy, and without rest;[4] while R. Eleazar says: "A man without a wife is no man."[5]

Equally absurd is the charge that the Rabbis despised manual labor. We have already seen how

---

[1] Sanhedrin 39a.
[2] Yalkut. § 24.
[3] Aboth V. § 24.
[4] Yalkut. Ib.. § 23.
[5] Ibid.; Yebamoth 63a.

many of the Talmudic fathers themselves, while their eagerness for the study of the law was quenchless, earned their subsistence by some handicraft. There is therefore no need for us to enter on a lengthy dissertation on this question; but we will simply quote a few maxims of the Talmudists on this head. R. Judah ben Ilai says: "Labor honors the laborer."[1] He even goes farther than this, and says: "Whosoever doth not teach his son a trade, is as culpable as if he had accustomed him to robbery."[2] R. Gamliel III, says: "It is proper to combine the study of the law with a worldly pursuit; for busying ourselves with both causes us to forget sin. All study of the law, which is not combined with labor, will at length come to an end, and be the cause of sin."[3] "Love work and despise titles," was a favorite maxim of Shemaiah.[4] Moreover, the Rabbis recommend, in case of necessity, to engage in the lowest kind of drudgery, and avoid depending on public support. "Excoriate the dead animal on the public street," says Abba Arekha, "and take thy earnings, and never say, I am a priest, I am a great man, and such work is not becoming a gentleman."[5]

The ethical teachings of the Rabbis, their adages, apothegms, maxims, axioms, pervade almost every page of the Talmud, and a large number of the earlier ones are recorded in the *Pirke Aboth* (chapters, frag-

---

[1] Nedarim 49b.
[2] Kiddiushin 29a; Ibid Tosefta I, § 11; Mekhilta Bo, § 18.
[3] Aboth II, § 2; Cf. Mekhilta Wayassa, § 2.
[4] Ibid I, § 10.
[5] Pesahim 113a; Baba Bathra 110a.

ments, commonly called Ethics of the Fathers) and Aboth de R. Nathan.[1]

We deem it not out of place to transcribe some of them.

In the name of the Great Synod the following three great principles are preserved: Be cautious in passing sentence,[2] train many disciples, and make a hedge for the law.[3]

Simon the Just, the last of the Great Synod, taught:

---

[1] "As Grecian philosophy began with single sentences and proverbs of the so-called Seven Sages, so must we regard the profound maxims and ascetic doctrines of the first teachers, which are contained in the 'Ethics of our Fathers' and the 'Aboth of R. Nathan,' as the beginning and origin of the philosophical studies among the Jews."—Guide for rational Inquiries into the Biblical Writings, page 63.

[2] Cf. supra n. 255.

[3] Aboth I, § 1. Cf. supra n. 34.—This means to establish guard-laws, *sepes legis*. Although the Talmud burdened the Jewish religion with an infinite number of ceremonial observances, in the execution of which the Rabbis were extremely punctilious, still they admit that ceremonial worship is important only inasmuch as it serves to inspire sentiments and feelings raising the soul to God. Illustrations are quoted in the following Mishnah: Quoting the Scriptural passage (Exodus XVII, 11), "When Moses held up his hand Israel prevailed," the question is raised, Why? did the hands of Moses carry on the battle? Whereupon the Rabbis answer: Not the lifting up of hands by Moses gained the victory over Amalek, and not the brazen serpent raised on a pole in the wilderness (see Numbers XXI, 9) healed the Israelites from the serpent-stings; but by these ceremonies the observers were induced to raise their eyes and hearts to their Heavenly Father.—Rosh Hashanah 29ᵃ.

The world is founded upon three great principles, to wit: Law, Worship and Benevolence.[1]

Antigonus of Sokho taught: Be not like those servants who wait on their master with the expectation of receiving reward; but be like those who serve their master without anticipating pay, and then will true fear of God be in you.[2]

Jose ben Joeser taught: Let thy house be a rendezvous for the wise men, rest at their feet, and drink in eagerly their words.[3]

Joshua ben Perahiah said: Engage for thyself a teacher and procure classmates, and judge all mankind favorably.[4]

Nittai, the Arbellite, said: Keep away from an evil neighbor, and never associate with a wicked person, nor forget that there may come punishment for sin.[5]

Judah ben Tabbai was wont to say: When called upon to decide in a law-suit, do not turn advocate; while the contending parties are on trial, consider

---

[1] Ib., § 2.—Elsewhere the Rabbis say, Benevolence having a wider scope, is more meritorious than charity, in these three respects: charity calls merely for an outlay of money, benevolence requires both wealth and body; charity is bestowed only on the needy poor, benevolence must be exercised towards the rich as well as the poor; charity can be given only the living, benevolence can be bestowed also upon the dead.—Succah 49b.

[2] Ibid § 3.
[3] Ibid § 4.
[4] Ibid § 6.
[5] Ibid § 7.

both wrong; when they are gone, and submitted to the sentence, look upon both as innocent.[1]

Abtalion endeavored to inculcate this principle: Ye learned men, be careful how you express your ideas, that your disciples may not misunderstand you, and thus be led astray.[2]

Hillel was the author of these maxims: He who is ambitious of magnifying his name, destroys it.[3] If I do not act for myself, who shall do it for me? If I think only of myself, what do I amount to? If I act not now, when may I?[4]

Shammai said: Make the study of the law thy chief occupation; say little and do much; and receive every man with a friendly countenance.[5]

R. Gamliel I taught: Engage a preceptor, free

---

[1] Ibid § 8.

[2] Ibid § 11.

[3] Ibid § 13.—Elsewhere we are taught: Him who humbleth himself, will God extol; but him who exalteth himself, will the Holy One humble. Greatness flees from him who hurries after it, but follows him who runs from it.—Erubin 13b; cf. Berakhoth 44a; Nedarim 55a.

[4] Ibid § 14.

[5] R. Meir expressed the same sentiments in different words. He said: Busy thyself less with worldly affairs than with the study of the law, and be humble before all men. (Ibid IV, § 12.) R. Simon ben Johai thought otherwise. The punctual observance of the law, argues he, was possible only for those who were fed on manna or the tithes. How should any one be able to study the law day and night, if he is troubled with the cares of food and raiment?—Mekhilta Wayassa, § 2.

[6] Ibid § 15.

thyself from all doubt, and do not express too many opinions.[1]

His son Simon expressed these sentiments: All my lifetime have I spent among the learned, and have discovered naught more beneficial than silence. Not the preaching is the object, but the practice. He who speaks much, causes sin.[2]

R. Simon ben Gamliel, of Jabne, was wont to say: The welfare of humanity is maintained by virtue of the application of the following three cardinal principles: Truth, Justice and Peace.[3]

R. Judah I laid down this plan for man's guidance through life: He should always choose for himself a

---

[1] Ibid § 16.

[2] Ibid § 17.—The following anecdotes, preserved in the Aggadah, we deem too good to be omitted from this connection. R. Gamliel, the father of the author of these sentiments, once ordered his steward, Tabi, to procure something excellent from the market for a feast he was about to give. Tabi departed, and soon returned with a tongue. On another occasion R. Gamliel ordered him to bring something of inferior quality. The servant obeyed, but soon returned again with a tongue. Surprised at this procedure, the Rabbi inquired, How is this? When once I ordered the best, thou gavest me tongue; and now, when I want something inferior, thou again providest me with tongue! Thereupon Tabi replied: From this originates all good, and from the same all evil springs. When the tongue is good, there is nothing better than it; when the tongue is bad, then there is nothing worse!—When once Rabbi Judah I invited his disciples to a repast, he spread before them tough and tender tongues. They, of course, chose the tender ones, when their host remarked: May your tongues be so soft and smooth while arguing with each other!—Yalkut, Psalms, § 767.

[3] Ibid § 18.

path which may be an ornament to him who walks therein, and which may procure for him the reverence of mankind. He should be as careful of the observance of a light precept as of an important one, for no one knows the reward for the execution of the commandments. He should balance the (temporal) loss sustained by obedience to a precept with its (spiritual) recompense, and the (material) profit accruing from a transgression with the (spiritual) injury it occasions. He should constantly reflect of these three things, and he will not lapse into the power of sin; he should always be mindful of what is above him: a seeing eye, a hearing ear, and that all his actions are written down in a book.[1]

Of his son, R. Gamliel III, the following apothegms are preserved: All who are engaged in the services of the congregation ought to act from pure motives (for Heaven's sake), then will the merits of their pious ancestors support them, and their righteousness will stand unto eternity. Be cautious in your intercourse with the powers that be (Romans), as they favor none but when it suits their own interest; they show themselves as friends, while they can derive some advantage, but do not aid a man in time of his need. Do God's will, as if it were thine own, that He may accomplish thy will, as if it were His. Sacrifice thy will for the sake of His, that He may sacrifice the will of others for the sake of thine.[2]

---

[1] Ibid II, § 1.
[2] Ibid §§ 2-4.

R. Eliezer said: Let the honor of thy fellow-man be as dear to thee as thine own: do not fall easily into passion; repent one day before thy death;[1] and warm thyself by the fire of the sages.[2]

As the New Testament was written during the progress of the Talmud, and as some of the earliest Christian writers were reared under rabbinical influence, we should deem our sketch incomplete if we refrained from analyzing some doctrinal portions of the former in their relationship to the latter.[3] We propose to quote passages from Saint Matthew, and, following the order of the Talmud, place next to them their equivalents from Rabbinic sources. And thus we begin:

"I say unto you, that if two of you shall agree on earth as touching anything that they shall ask, it shall be done for them of my Father which is in

---

[1] When asked by his disciples how any man could forsee the exact day of his death, and thus avail himself of this advice, to prepare himself one day before to meet death, the author of these maxims replied: Because no one is certain that the morrow will see him alive, he must consider every day as his last, and repent daily (Sabbath 153ª).

[2] Ibid § 15.

[3] The learned author of "Judaism, its Doctrines and Duties" (p. 6,) says: "There are three different Talmuds, in the opinion of those who believe in the Bible, viz: the Talmud of the Hebrews, comprising the whole of the ancient rabbinical literature; the Talmud of the Christians, containing the New Testament and its commentaries; and the Talmud of the Mohammedans, consisting of the Koran and its commentaries. Either of these Talmuds was intended to expound the Bible from peculiar stand-points, influenced by various conceptions and convictions,'

heaven. *For where two or three are gathered together in my name, there am I in the midst of them"*—xviii, 19-20.

R. Isaac raises the question, Whence do we infer that the Holy One, blessed be He, is present at the house of prayer? From the passage in Psalms (lxxxii, 1): "God standeth in the congregation of the godly."[1] Whence do we learn that when ten congregate together in prayer, the *Shechina* (Theocracy) abideth with them? From the same verse (*Edah* representing ten). Whence do we know that the same is the case with three persons? From the Psalmist's saying (*Ibid.*): "God judgeth in the midst of the judges."[2] Whence do we know that, when only two persons are engaged in the study of the law, the Shechina is with them? From the verse (Malachi iii, 16): "Then they that feared the Lord spoke often *one to another*, and the Lord hearkened and heard it." And whence do we learn that even if one occupies himself with the law, the Shechina watches over him? From the passage (Exodus xx, 24): "In all places where I record my name will I come unto thee, and I will bless thee."[3]

"I say unto you, love your enemies, bless them that curse you, do good to them that hate you, and

---

[1] We cannot always quote Scripture from the "Authorized Version;" it very often misrepresents the original. Right here we have an instance: The original reads, "Adath El," meaning *congregation of God*.

[2] The Hebrew in this case is *Elohim*, and means, as we translate it, judges. See Exodus XXI, 6, where this term is so rendered.—Three persons constituted a *Beth-Din*, court of justice (Cf. supra n. 190).

[3] Berakhoth 6ᵃ; Aboth III, § 7.

pray for them that despitefully use you and persecute you" (v. 44).

In the Talmud we read of a Rabbi who was greatly vexed by a neighbor of his, and was about to invoke the curse of heaven upon his tormentor, but he concluded that it was not meet for the righteous to call down punishment.[1] R. Meir was once provoked at a foul-mouthed neighbor, who slandered him repeatedly. He was about to curse, but his noble spouse reproved him by pointing out that David had prayed (Psalm civ, 35): "May *sin* cease from off the earth," but had not asked for the extermination of the sinful. Moreover, she said, "look at the conclusion of David's prayer. He says: 'The wicked will be no more,' as soon as sin will cease from the world. Rather pray that thy persecutors should repent."[2] Again: Those who are insulted, and revile not in return, bear invectives in silence, are persecuted and retaliate not, are meant by the Scriptural expression (Judges v. 31): "Those that love Him will be as the rising sun in his might."[3]

"Blessed are the merciful, for they shall obtain mercy" (v. 7).

R. Gamliel says: "Whosoever is merciful to his fellow creature, to him Heaven is merciful."[4]

---

[1] Berakhoth 6a.
[2] Ibid 10a. Cf. supra p. 220.
[3] Sabbath 88b; Joma 23a; Gittin 36a.
[4] Sabbath 151b. Compare also Bezah 33b, where the version is entirely different, although it amounts almost to the same in meaning.

"All things whatsoever ye would that men should do to you, do ye even so to them: for this is the law and the prophets" (vii, 12).

R. Akiba taught: "Love thy neighbor as thyself" is the foundation of the whole law.[1] Hillel I said; Whatever is hateful unto thyself, do not unto thy fellowman. This is the essence of the law; the rest is but its commentary.[2]

"Blessed are the peace-makers, for they shall be called the children of God" (v. 9).

Hillel taught: Be a disciple of Aaron, loving peace and pursuing it.[3] R. Simon ben Gamliel said: The welfare of the world is maintained by virtue of the application of the following three cardinal principles: Truth, Justice and *Peace*.[4] He who maketh peace between man and man, enjoys the fruits of his works in this world, while the principal reward he will receive in the hereafter.[5]

"What is a man profited if he shall gain the whole world and lose his own soul, or what shall a man give in exchange for his soul?" (xvi, 26.)

R. Judah I taught that man should balance the material loss sustained by the performance of a precept, with the spiritual recompense; and the gain accruing from a transgression, with the spiritual injury it occasions.[6]

---

[1] Yer. Nedarim 9.
[2] Sabbath 31ª; Aboth de R. Nathan XV. Vide supra, p. 202, where the occasion on which this was said is recorded.
[3] Aboth I. § 12
[4] Ibid § 18.
[5] Peah I.
[6] Aboth II. § 1.

"Render unto Cæsar the things which are Cæsar's, and unto God the things which are God's" (xxii, 21).

R. Eliezer said: Render unto God of the things which are his own: thou and all that thou callest thine are his.[1]

"Judge not, that ye be not judged" (vi, 1).

In the name of the Great Synod the principle is preserved: Be cautious in passing sentence.[2] R. Joshua constantly endeavored to teach his disciples to judge all mankind favorably.[3] Hillel taught: Judge not thy neighbor until thou art placed in his circumstances.[4] Further we read: Man is measured with the same measure he uses for others.[5]

"Ye are the light of the world" (v. 14).

The Talmudists very often styled their savants Lights. R. Meir was so called because he *enlightened* the mind's eyes of the wise men.[6] R. Nehorai was so styled for the same reason.[7] The same epithet was also applied to R. Johanan ben Zakkai, the preserver of the Oral law at the downfall of Judea.[8]

"Take heed that ye do not your alms before men to be seen of them" (vi, 1).

R. Janai saw a benefactor dispensing alms, and he admonished him, saying: "It were better for

---

[1] Aboth III, § 8.
[2] Ibid 1, § 1.
[3] Ibid § 6.
[4] Ibid II, § 5.
[5] Sanhedrin 100a.
[6] Cf. supra, p. 217.
[7] Erubin 13b.
[8] Aboth de R. Nathan, XXIV.

thee to give nothing than to do so publicly and make the poor blush.'"[1]

"Behold the fowls of the air, for they sow not, neither do they reap, nor gather into barns; yet your heavenly father feedeth them" (vi, 26-28).

Abba Arekha says: The Holy One, blessed be He, observes and sustains all his creatures, from the horn of the rhinoceros to the ova of the minutest insect.[2] Hast thou ever seen the fowl of the forest or the beast of the field laboring for its sustenance? God feedeth them without their labor.[3]

"Be ye not called Rabbi" (xxiii, 8).

Shemaiah said: Love work and despise titles.[4] Hillel foretold destruction to him that made use, for his personal aggrandizement, of the "crown of the

---

[1] Haggiga 5ª.—The Rabbis were very scrupulous in this respect, as the following anecdote, one out of the many, will show. Mar Ukbah had a poor neighbor, whom he stealthily supported by throwing into his house, through an aperture in the door, four sous every day. The recipient of this bounty tried to detect his benefactor, but in vain. As soon as the money was deposited, the Rabbi sped away. Once, however, the Rabbi, accompanied by his wife, deposited the alms at the usual hour, when suddenly the door opened and the poor man appeared on the scene. The couple hurried away, and noticing that their inquisitive pursuer was gaining on them, they threw themselves into an oven, the only shelter they could find, to escape discovery and avoid making the needy one blush, for their maxim was, Man should rather throw himself into the fire than humiliate his fellow-creature.—Ketuboth 67ᵇ.

[2] Sabbath 107ᵇ; Abodah Zara 3ᵇ

[3] Kiddushin 82.

[4] Aboth I. §9.

law," and similarly R. Zadok.[1] Be not ambitious, and do not covet honors, was a standing maxim with the Talmudists.[2]

We might thus go on *ad infinitum* quoting New Testament doctrines and their Talmudic parallels; but time and space bid us desist, and take leave from our readers.

---

[1] Ibid VI. § 7.
[2] Ibid VI, § 5.

INDEX.

Bold faced figures denote the Sections; plain ones, the Notes; and those enclosed in [ ], the pages of the Appendix.

Ab-Beth-Din..**55**
Abduction, cf. Kidnapping.
Abridgment of parental power 106
               slavery 414
Abtalion ....[193, 198, 244]
Accessories, in general..274
              homicide **24**, 128, 297
Accidental homicide..**35**
              by, or of high priest 406
              in city of refuge..............................**135**
Accuser, cf. Prosecutors.
              a single, how treated 259
Action required to constitute crime. **12**, 36, 37, 144
              exceptions to this rule.................36, 62
Adolescence...**49**
Adultery..**29**, 97
              by a priest's daughter......................**27**
Affinity, cf. Relationship.
Age of liability to capital punishment..........**50**, 182-188
Agency in crime..155
Akiba, R...**6**, 391, [211-215]
Amercement, cf. Damages...402
Antigonus...[192, 243]
Appeals, court of..198, **62**
              how carried 226
Apostasy, communal...................................**28**, **32**, 106
              individual, cf. Idolatry.
Argument must be offered for defendant............**101**, 330

Arrest of accused 79, 84, **40, 71**
Astronomy cultivated by the Rabbis .... 205, [209, 237]

Babylonian Talmud .... [236]
Banishment, cf. Exile.
Bannaa, R., amends a Roman legal maxim 428
Being, what constitutes a legal **38,** 136–143
Benefit of clergy **45**
Beruria .... [218–220]
Bestiality **26,** 87
Beth-Din (court) 190
BETWEEN LIFE AND DEATH **116-120,** 363
Blasphemy **26,** 88, **128,** 395
      when punishable 91
Blindness disqualifies the witness 77
Bribing a judge **67**
      what is viewed as such 236
Bruising a parent **29,** 98
Burglary **19, 34,** 113
Burial of convicts **131,** 398
      refugees 408
Burning, mode of execution by **124,** 383–385
      offences punished with **27**

CAPITAL CRIMES **26-29**
      classification of 19, **30,** 101
      number of, by Rabbinic law **7,** 19, **30,** 101
        in England **3,** 9
        Greece **2**
    punishments **25**
      aggravated by other nations, 372, 383, 391, 419
      alleviated by the Jews 363, **120,** 382
      inadequacy of 18
      modes of, by Rabbinic law **123-126**
        in England 87, 390, 395
        Greece and Rome, 86, 87, 91, 383, 391
        other countries 91, 383, 387, 391
      not accompanied by other punishments **18**

INDEX. 257

Capital punishments.—*Continued.*
    opposed by some Rabbis............**6, 9,** 68
    right to inflict, taken from the Jews..........33. 224
CAUTIONING WITNESSES..................**78-79**
Children, status of, not affected by parental crimes.....**133,** 401
    suffer for parental crimes in other countries...401–403
Circumstantial evidence..................**82,** 287
City of refuge..................76, **134,** 407
Collectors of imposts..................**77,** 271, **141**
Collision with irresponsible parties..................46
Commutation for injuries, cf. Damages..................**8,** 23
    in homicide, not permitted..................95, 405
    practised by other nations, 95, 123, 405
    in England..................95
Competent tribunal..................**69**
    witnesses..................**76,** 260
Conditions, cf. Provisos.
Confession before execution..................**120,** 371
    in capital cases, not admissible..................**93,** 311
    finable cases, exempts from fine..................76
Confiscation, not in vogue among the Jews..................**133**
    practised among other nations..................402–403
Confutation of witnesses..................**31, 95,** 317
    effect of, on the case..................**97**
    witnesses.....**31, 97,** 319, 323, 324
CONSUMMATION, THE..................**122-127** and notes.
Convict, escaped..................**115,** 359
    incompetent witness..................**77**
    on the way to execution..................**118-120**
    rehabilitation of..................**140-141**
    when he cannot be identified..................**127,** 389
Corporal punishment, cf. Flagellation.
    not accompanied by fine..................62
Correcting testimony..................**91,** 307
Counsel, excluded from Jewish courts..................327
Counting the votes..................**106**
Court, cf. Synhedrion.
    of Three..................**52,** 192, 226

17

INDEX.

Crimes **7**, 9, **30**, 101
    and penalties **20-29**
    committed under duress **14**, 47, 48
Cross-examination **91**, 305
Cruel laws are evaded **2**, 6
    do not prevent crime **5**
Cruelty of ancient laws accounted for **2**
Culpable homicide **36**
    penalty of **37**
Cursing a parent **26**, 91

Damages 148, 402
Deaf and dumb persons, incompetent witnesses ... **77**, 266
    not indictable **47**
Decapitation, crimes punished with **28**
    execution by **125**
DEFENDANT, THE .... **92-94** and notes.
    arrest of 79, **40, 71**
    confession by, cf. Confession.
    deliberations must open with argument for.. **101**
    is not considered guilty before conviction.. **71, 93**
    may argue his own case **93**
    not put under oath 312
    witnesses for **94**
Degree of guilt, how determined **16**, 49, **17**, 60, **18**
DELIBERATIONS, THE .... **100-104** and notes.
Demented persons, cf. Idiot.
Disabilities of judges, cf. Judges.
    witnesses, cf. Witnesses.
Diseased criminal **38**, 143
    victim **38**, 141
DISPROVAL AND CONFUTATION .... **31, 95-99** and notes.
    effect of **96, 98**, 320
Division on verdict 348
Divulging judicial proceedings **112**, 356
Drunkenness excuses crime, when **48**
Dumbness excuses crime, when **47**
    incapacitates the witness **77**, 266

INDEX.

Duress excuses crime.............................**14,** 47, **46**
    when it does not excuse...............**15,** 47, 48
Duty to bear witness................104, 260, **79,** 281

Eleazar ben Azaria.....................................**6**
    Jose ha-Gelili.............................[196, 210]
Eliezer, R..[209]
Escaped convict, cf. Convict.
Ethical maxims....................................[242-247]
Evidence, cf. Witnesses..............**82** sq. and notes.
    circumstantial....................................**82,** 287
    must be parol....................................**83,** 288
        cover the whole case...................**83,** 291
    presumptive......................................287
EXAMINATION.......................**80-91** and notes.
    preliminary......................................**40**
Excision...**21,** 71
Excusable homicide...................................**35**
Execution by burning.............................**124,** 385
    decapitation....................................**125**
    stoning.....................................**123,** 382
    strangling..................................**126,** 387
    is forbidden on Sabbath or festival..............**74**
    place of.............................**117,** 364, 365
    shall closely follow the verdict......18, 254, **116,** 363
EXECUTIONERS, THE...............................**121,** 376
Exile...........................**23,** 76, **134-135** and notes.
    accidental homicide committed in................**135**
    ends with high priest's death.........**134,** 405, 406
    no commutation allowed.......................95, 405
    roads leading to...................................407
Exposing executed criminals not allowed.........**131,** 391
    practised elsewhere........392, 396
Ezra and tradition..................................[192]
    institutes regular court days...................**59,** 217

False prophecy.......................................**29**
    witness, cf. Disproval.
        punishable without being forewarned.......**19**

Farmers of imposts, incompetent witnesses............ **77**, 271
                 rehabilitation of............................**141**
Father and son, verdict by.............................**106**, 341
                 killing son...**35**
                 son abusing his....................**26**, 91, **29**, 98
Fees to judges....................................**66**, 234
                 witnesses..274
Felo de se......................................**44**, 160–163
Felonious homicide, cf. Murder.
Fine not imposed together with flagellation................62, 63
                 remitted on voluntary confession............76
Flagellation, offenses punished with........**21**, 74, **24**, 83
                 punishment by..........**138-139**, 418, 421, 422
Forewarning would-be offenders............**16-19**, 55, 60, 61, 68
Fortuitous homicide................................**35**
Frightening to death...............................144

Gamblers are incompetent witnesses...............**77**, 269
                 rehabilitation of...........................**141**
Gemara.......................................13, [229]
Gibbet......................................393, 394
Golah (exile)....................................76
Gospel teachings and the Talmud................[247–253]
Great Synhedrion, cf. Synhedrion.

Hakham (sage).............................**55**, 200
Hanging blasphemers and idolators...........**128-130**
                 women are exempt from.......................395
Hearsay evidence, cf. Evidence..................**78**
High priest as a witness..........................261
                 committing accidental homicide..............406
                 his death frees exiles................**134**, 406
                 subject to Great Synhedrion............**45**, **54**
Hillel................................199, [193–203, 244]
HOMICIDE..............................**33-37** and notes.
                 at victim's request....................**42**, 155
                 committed by several persons......**36**, **43**, 159, 297
                 culpable..........................**36**, 324, 326–329

Homicide.—*Continued.*
       excusable: accidental............**35** and notes, 124
                  fortuitous ....**35** and notes, 124
       felonious, cf. Murder.
       justifiable............**34**, 115
       while engaged in idle sports............**42**, 156
HONORARIUM............**65-67** and notes.
Horæ judiciæ............**60**, 218, **72**
Hunger, killing by............144

Identity of criminal.............**86**, 297, **127**, 389
       victim............**86**, 297
Idiot, incompetent witness............**77**, 266
       not indictable............**46**
       who is considered an............**48**
Idolatry.............43, 48, **26**, 89, **128**
       instigating............37, **19**, **26**, 326, 333, 358
Ignorance of fact............68
              law............55, 68, **36**
Illiteracy disqualifies the witness............**77**
— Ill-treatment of parents............**26**, 91, **29**, 98
Immodesty disqualifies the witness............**77**, 272
Immolating children............**26**
Imprisonment............**24**, 79, 82
Impubescence............**49**, 179
Incest............**26-27**, 287, 378
       duress does not excuse............**15**
Incompetent testimony............43, **82**, 287, 291, **86**, 303
       witnesses, cf. Witnesses.
— Incorrigibles are imprisoned............**24**
Indictable persons, cf. Persons.
Infancy.............**49-50** and notes.
       disqualifies the witness............**77**, 264, 385
Injuries, cf. Damages.
       inflicted by convict............402
                  prisoner............**71**
       on convict............**36**, 126
            prisoner............**71**

Inquest..**40**
Instigating apostasy, cf. Idolatry.
        murder...**24**, 82
Instrument of death **39, 41**, 151, 152
Insubordination 74
Interpreter, not allowed in Jewish courts...........204, cf. 288
Ishmael, R.....................................[196, 210, 225]

Jerusalem Talmud...[235]
Johanan, R.....................................[230, 235]
        ben Zakkai, R..............................[203-209]
Jose ben Halafta, R...[220]
Joshua ben Hanania, R.....................................[209-210]
Judah I, R......................................[222-229, 246]
        ben Baba, R...........................225, [217]
Judge, candidature for office of........................**64**
        doubting evidence..........................306
        honorarium of..........................**66**, 231
        if not elected fairly.........................212
        must be guarded in examining witnesses.................**94**
            fast the day of passing death-sentence....37, **113**, 357
            give reason for his vote...............**104**
        promotion of..........................**64**, 229
        qualifications...............**57**, 208, 210, **58**, 215
        receiving presents..........................**67**, 236
Judgment, cf. Verdict.
        appeal from, cf. Appeals.
        if paid for..........................234
        implies sentence,..........................365
        reversal of..........................**114-115**, 358
Jurisdiction of Court of Three............................**52**
        Great Synhedrion **54**, 197, 198
        Lesser Synhedrion **53**, 195

Kidnapping.............................**29**, 99, 291
Killing embryo in mother's body.................136, 355
        to prevent crime, when culpable....................**36**
            justifiable..............**34**, 112, 115

King, excluded from Synhedrion......210, 260
  not exempt from duty to testify......260
  subject to Great Synhedrion......**45,** 167, **54**

Laws, consequences of cruel......**2,** 6
  cruelty of......**2, 3,** 6-9
  doubtful right of cruel......**5**
  founded on necessity......**1,** 1-3
  framers of early penal......**2,** 4
  humanity of..**4,** 10, 12, **8, 9, 16,** 100, 115, 161, 345, 351
    113, 357, **116,** 363, 365, **118, 119,** 370
    120, 373, 382, 421
  Talmudic, based on Mosaic system......33, 100, 340
    the laws of Nature......47, 115, 288
Lex talionis, inadequacy of the......23
  practised by other nations......**8**
  substituted by fines......**8,** 23
Limitation, statute of......[197]
  in criminal proceedings......300

Magics......**26, 32,** 107, 108
Magistrate......233, 236
Major, majority......**49-50**
Majority, not necessary for disproving testimony......324
  required for acquittal......**105,** 338
  conviction......**105,** 338
Mala in se,—prohibita......115
Maladministration......**29,** 226, 255, 285, 355
Malice......**16,** 57, **42**
Maniac, cf. Idiot.
Master killing slave, when excusable......138
MAXIMS AND RULES......**142,** 428-458
  ethical......[242-247]
Meetings of courts, cf. Sessions.
Meir, R......[216-222]
Mekhilta......[214, 228]
Messengers of court, cf. Servitors......**56**
Minor, cf. Infancy.
  has no discretion......183

MINOR PUNISHMENTS. ....**134-139** and notes.
                   exile...... ....**134-135,** 405–409
                   flagellation.. ....**138-139,** 418, 421, 422
                   imprisonment........ ....**24,** 79, 82
                   penal servitude......**136-137,** 412, 414–416
MISDEMEANORS, CRIMES AND PENALTIES,
                                   20-24 and notes.
Mishnah...... ....13, [214, 226, 227]
         compilations.. ....[193, 214, 220, 221, 225, 228]
         history of the...... ....[191–229]
Missile producing death........ ....**39, 41**
         when lost, how substituted...... .... .151
Mistaken verdict, when reversible...... ....**114,** 358
Modes of death penalties, cf. Capital.
Monomaniac, cf. Idiot.
MURDER...... ....**38-44** and notes.
         at request of victim........... ....**42,** 155
         malice required to constitute...... ....152, **42**
         must be committed by an individual.. ....**43**
         penalty of...... ....**28**
         self... ....**44,** 160–164
         what constitutes **38-39,** 136–143
         when punishable as such **38**
Murderer, by whom brought to justice........ 95
         diseased....... ....**38,** 143
         not permitted to escape punishment 159, 359, 377
         of diseased person...... ....**38,** 140

Nasi (Prince)...... ....**55**
Nathan, R ....[216, 221, 222]
Nature of capital crimes.. 101
Necessity, cf. Duress.
Necromancy, cf. Magics........... ....**26**
Nittai, the Arbelite ....[192, 243]
Nonage, cf. Infancy...... ....**49**
Number of capital crimes........... ....**7,** 19, **25,** 101
         crimes punishable with burning **27**
                                 decapitation...... ....**28**

Number of crimes punishable with—*Continued.*
                      stoning. **26**
                      strangling **29**
      misdemeanors not punishable................**12,** 37, 39
           punishable with exile..................**23**
                    flagellation......21, 74
                    imprisonment....**24**
                    penal servitude...**22**

Oath, not required of defendant.........................312
                witnesses.........................**78,** 276
      punishment for uttering vain......................36
Object of punishment..................3, 184, 202, 363
Offenses, aggravated, how punished..........**17,** 60, 61, **24,** 378
Official accuser..............................**70**
       executioner........................**121,** 374
Ordination of Rabbis..................**58,** 215, 225
ORGANIZATION AND JURISDICTION.......**51-56** and notes.
Outlawry, unknown to Jewish law....................283

Palistinean courts..............................360
           Talmud.........................[235]
Pardoning power..............................424
Parent, cf. Father.
Pederasty..............................**26,** 87
Penal laws, cf. Laws.
      servitude...........................**22,** 75
           how imposed..................**136,** 412, 413
           treatment during................**137,** 415, 416
Perjury, cf. False.
PERSONS INDICTABLE..................**45-50** and notes.
       incompetent as judges....................210
           witnesses.........................**77**
       not indictable.........................**46**
Physician killing patient..........................**35**
Place of execution..........................**117,** 365
      holding court.................**61-62,** 224-225
      where crime is located.................**88,** 302

Pleading for defendant... **101**, 330, **103**
    not for instigator... 333
Positive commands, number of... **11**
    transgression of... **12**
POSTHUMOUS IGNOMINIES... **128-133** and notes.
    burying in felons' graves... **131**
    hanging... **128**
    not mourning... **132**
Presumptive evidence, cf. Evidence.
Preventing crime by homicide... **34**, 112
Priest removable from altar to scaffold... 166
Principals alone are punishable... 132, **43**, **86**
Probationers... **63**, **64**
    participate in deliberations... **102**, 331, **107**, 343, 109
    promotion of... **64**, 229
— Prodigal son... **26**, **32**, 106 —
Prohibitive laws, number of... **11**
    violations of... **12**, 37
Prosecutor... **70**
PROVISOS... **13-19** and notes.
    respecting criminality... **13**, **14**, **16**, **27**, **38**
    punishment... 43, 48, **17**, 60, **18**, 68, **23**, 91
    31, 106, **35**, **39**, 319, **99**
Puberty... **49**, 264
Punishment, the less is discharged in the greater... 63
Punishments, cf. Capital, Minor.

QUALIFICATIONS of judges... **57-58** and notes.
    witnesses... **76**, 260
Questions to be answered by witnesses... **84-85**
    regarding the manner, *how*... **89**, 303
    person, *who* and *whom*... **86**, 297
    place, *where*... **88**, 301, 302
    time, *when*... **87**, 301
    test... **90**, 304, 305

Rabbis, ordination of... 215
Rabh... [230-233]

Rebellious Elder, cf. Maladministration.
Recanting testimony. 239, **91,** 307
Refuge, city of, cf. Exile.
Refugee, accommodations of..407
    dying on his way to city of refuge..................408
    leaving protected precincts.......................409
    protected against molestation..............**135**
REHABILITATION.......................**140-141**
Relation between actions and laws................33, [195]
Relationship among judges.............................210, **69**
    witnesses..................................**77,** 273
    between judges and clients.....................**69**
    witnesses and clients or judges.......273
Relatives of executed criminals..................370. **132**
Resisting execution...376
Retaliation, cf. *Lex talionis*.
REVERSAL OF JUDGMENT............**114-115** and notes.
Rigor, judicial......................................**9, 37**
Roads to exile, cf. Exile.
Rosh, (chief)..**55**

Sabbath, cf. Violation.
Sanctuary, cf. Exile.
Scale of crimes and punishments...............**20**
Secretaries.........................**56,** 201, **65, 104,** 345
Seder Olam (a Rabbinic history)................[220]
Self accusation...................................76. 268. **93,** 311
    defense......................................47, **34,** 113
    destruction, cf. Murder.
    exculpation..................................**93, 119**
Sepes legis..34, 98, **143**
Servitor...**65**
    causing death of convict......................**35**
    functions of....................................202, **138**
    qualifications of..................................418
    when his parent is the convict...............418
Servitude, cf. Penal.
SESSIONS AND RECRUITMENTS............**59-64** and notes.

INDEX.

Shammai .... [193, 201]
Shemaia and Abtalion .... [193, 198]
Simon ben Gamliel, R. .... [216]
   Shettah .... **32,** 108, 239, 287, [193]
   the Just .... [192, 228, 242]
Simultaneous verdict of guilty acquits **101,** 330
Slander 36, 62
Slave, master killing 138
   not competent as witness **77,** 263
Slavery, cf. Penal.
Soferim (scribes) .... [192]
Stoning, crimes punished with **26**
   execution by **123**
Strangling, crimes punished with **29**
   execution by **126**
Stripes, cf. Flagellation.
Suicide, cf. Murder.
Summary conviction 293
   punishment 246
Suspects are incompetent witnesses **77**
   rehabilitation of **141**
Synhedrion, the Great, antiquity of 196
     constitution of **54**
     jurisdiction of **54,** 197, 198
     location of **62,** 224, 225
     organization of **55-56**
     promotion into **64**
     qualifications .... **57-58** and notes, **64**
     quorum of 222
     seats of **63**
     sessions of **62**
   the Lesser, constitution of **53**
     jurisdiction of **53,** 195
     location of **61**
     organization of **55-56**
     qualifications of **57-58**
     recruitment **64**
     supplemented when necessary,
        109-110 and notes.

Talmud, the. .... 13, 33, [206, 236]
        based on Mosaic code. 33, 100, 340
        history of .... [189–236]
Teacher and pupil in one court. 341
        verdict by **106**
        killing pupil. 35
Test-questions. 90, 304, 305
Testimony not subject to confutation. 143, 301
        part of which is invalidated. 318
Theft **22**, 75
TIME OF TRIAL .... **72–74** and notes.
        when crime is laid **87**, 301
        execution takes place. 250, 357, **116**
Tortures, frequent among other nations. 263
        never applied by the Jews. 310
Tradition, cf. Talmud.
        sources of. .... [192, 194]
Tribunal, a murderous. **6**
Tryphon, R. .... **6**, [210, 212]
Two capital cases not tried on one day 73, 252
        punishments not imposed for one offense. **18**, 62, 63
        witnesses always necessary **13, 75,** 259

Unanimous conviction acquits. **101**, 330
Usurers, incompetent witnesses. 77
        rehabilitation of. **141**

VERDICT, THE. .... **105–113** and notes.
        by father and son, or teacher and pupil **106**, 341, 342
        of acquittal may be rendered any time. **100**
                not be reversed **114**, 358
        conviction, deferred till next day **100**, 326, **108**
                may be reversed. **114**, 358
                simultaneously rendered. **101**, 330
Violation of positive commands. **12**, 39
        prohibitive ordinances **12**, 37
        the Sabbath 9, 68, **26**
Votes, particulars in counting the **106**, 340–342

Warning would-be criminals.......................................**16**, 68
    crimes not conditioned by.........................**19**, 68
    its effect on verdict......................**17-18**, 60-63, 68
Whipping...74
Witchcraft...**26**, 90, **32**, 107
Witness, cf. Evidence.
    competent..**76**
    confutation of...**31, 95**
    correcting evidence................................**91**, 307
    disproval of..**31, 95**
    duty to bear.........................104, 260, **79**, 281
    for defendant...**94**
    high priest as a..261
    incompetent..**77**
    may not act as judge............................144, 293
        argue the case....................**103**, 332
    not required to swear..........................**78**, 276
    penalty of, confuted...........**31, 97, 98**, 323, **130**
        when not imposed............**97**, 319, 323
    questions to be answered by, cf. Questions.
Witnesses are the only legal executioners................**121**
              prosecutors........................**70**
    cautioning..**78-79**
    contradicting each other......................305, **98**
    may testify to what they saw only..........**78, 82**
    not less than two, always required....**13, 75**, 259
Woman, immunities of.........................373, 395, **136**
    incompetent as a witness............................**77**
    not reprieved when pregnant......................355
    position of, in Talmudic lore..................[237-240]
Written testimony is not valid....................................388

Zaken Mamre (rebellious elder), cf. Maladministration........**29**

www.ingramcontent.com/pod-product-compliance
Lightning Source LLC
Chambersburg PA
CBHW032000230426
43672CB00010B/2221